If You Lived Here, I'd Know Your Name

News from
Small-Town
Alaska

HEATHER LENDE

Author of *Take Good Care of the Garden and the Dogs* and *Find the Good*

Praise for *If You Lived Here, I'd Know Your Name*

"Delightful. . . . The writing is simple yet graceful. . . . A pleasure to read."
—*USA Today*

"Lende offers touching stories about neighbors with whom she shares wedding celebrations, potluck dinners, tears for missing fishermen— all the joys and sorrows of family life in a remote town." —*People* magazine

"[A] beautiful, funny, compassionate story. . . . When, now and again, your reading is interrupted by tears, they will be the sweet sort."
—Michael Perry, author of *Population: 485*

"Part Annie Dillard, part Anne Lamott, essayist and NPR commentator Heather Lende introduces readers to life in the town of Haines, Alaska . . . subtly reminding readers to embrace each day, each opportunity, each life that touches our own and to note the beauty of it all."
—*Los Angeles Times*

"Dense and powerful. . . . Tiny jewels that, gathered together, create a stunning effect of pure, dazzling light." —*The Grand Rapids Press*

"This is something tender and brave— using death as an introduction to lives and loves and fabric of community in a northern town. Heather Lende provides powerful witness."
—Seth Kantner, author of *Ordinary Wolves*

"Heartfelt, homespun essays about life." —*Seattle Post-Intelligencer*

"Lende's quiet voice resonates long after the book is finished."

—*Booklist*

"A true tale of ordinary people who do extraordinary things with (and to) one another in one of the most beautiful backwaters on Earth."

—Tom Bodett

"Full of joy and insight, humor and sobering truth."

—*Salem (OR) Statesman Journal*

"Written with ease and empathy, this is both about maintaining a household in Alaska and about being at home in the world."

—*Kirkus Reviews*

"Absorbing and reflective."   —*Library Journal*

"Lende presents a remarkable sense of place."

—*The Oklahoma City Oklahoman*

"Heather Lende is the perfect frontier guide—clear-eyed and big-hearted, tackling family and community and life and death with humor and hope."   —Stewart O'Nan, author of *Wish You Were Here*

If You Lived Here, I'd Know Your Name

News from Small-Town Alaska

HEATHER LENDE

ALGONQUIN BOOKS OF CHAPEL HILL
2006

Published by
ALGONQUIN BOOKS OF CHAPEL HILL
Post Office Box 2225
Chapel Hill, North Carolina 27515-2225

a division of
Workman Publishing
708 Broadway
New York, New York 10003

Library of Congress Cataloging-in-Publication Data
Lende, Heather, 1959–
     If you lived here, I'd know your name : news from small-town Alaska /
Heather Lende.
        p. cm.
     ISBN-13: 978-1-56512-316-8 (HC)
     1. Haines (Alaska)—Social life and customs.   2. City and town life—Alaska—
Haines.   3. Outdoor life—Alaska—Haines.   4. Frontier and pioneer life—Alaska—
Haines.   5. Lende, Heather, 1959–   6. Lende, Heather, 1959– —Family.   7. Lende,
Heather, 1959– —Friends and associates.   8. Haines (Alaska)—Biography.   I. Title.
F914.H34L46 2005
979.8'2— dc22   2004066036

     ISBN-13: 978-1-56512-524-7 (PB)

20 19 18 17 16 15 14 13 12

For Chip

We bring our years to an end, as it were a tale that is told.

— from Psalm 90

CONTENTS

Acknowledgments

My heartfelt thanks to the people of Haines for giving me so many stories to tell, especially Doris Ward, who began the "Duly Noted" column I inherited, and to these friends, neighbors, and editors both near and far: Bonnie Hedrick, Tom Morphet, and Steve Williams at the *Chilkat Valley News;* Lee Heinmiller at Alaska Indian Arts; Liz Heywood from the Babbling Book store; James Alborough and Sarah Posey of Bear Star Communications; George Bryson, Kathleen McCoy, and Mark Dent at the *Anchorage Daily News;* Audrey Wynn and Greg Allen at National Public Radio; Tom Reagan, Sara Terry, and Duncan Moon from the *Christian Science Monitor* and the former Monitor Radio; and everyone at Algonquin, especially Amy Gash. Amy heard me on the radio, called to ask if I thought I could write a book, and then helped me do it with wit, wisdom, and grace. Thanks also to my family for giving me the confidence and time to write—from my in-laws, Joanne and Phil Lende, and my parents, Bob and Sally Vuillet, to my children, Eliza, Sarah, Christian, Joanna Jeanne, and Stojanka, and a friend who is like family, Linnus Danner. Above all, thanks to my husband, Chip.

Over the past four years, five people in Haines have asked when this book would be done every time they've seen me—which was almost daily: postmaster Wayne Selmer, artist Jenny Lyn Smith, librarian Ellen Borders, and my neighbors Don and Betty Holgate. Here it is. I sure hope it's worth your wait.

INTRODUCTION

We Are What We Want to Be, Mostly

I HAVE LIVED in Haines, Alaska, all of my adult life but there are still times, especially winter evenings when the setting sun washes over the white mountaintops, the sky turns a deep blue, and the water is whipped into whitecaps by the north wind, that I can't believe my good fortune. It's so wild and beautiful that all I can do is walk outside my house and stare. Looking south, I can see the red cannery at Letnikof Cove on one side of the inlet and Davidson Glacier on the other. Out front, Pyramid Island breaks the surface where the Chilkat River meets the sea. Behind it, steep mountains rise right up from the beach. On this fading winter evening, standing in the snow in my yard, I think I hear a wolf howl up the Chilkat River Valley and hold my breath, hoping to hear it again. But I don't. Maybe it was just the wind. I turn around and look back at my house—our youngest children moving in front of lighted windows, the teenagers doing homework at the table, my husband, Chip, reading by the woodstove—and my heart swells in my chest like a balloon.

It took us a year to build our shingled home on the beach down Mud Bay Road, a mile and a half from Main Street. From my bedroom window, I've watched bears wading in the channels along the shore in the summer. When I walk the dogs to the cove in the fall, the icy tidal flats are covered with bald eagles. The oily, smeltlike fish called eulachon return to the river in the spring, and the sea lions chasing them are so loud that they wake me up from a sound sleep. I see the light on across the road and, even though it's two in the morning, call my neighbor Linnus. The sea lions woke her up, too. She and her husband, Steve, walked to the beach in their pajamas. The sea lions were having a wild party down there, Linnus says.

JOHN MUIR CAME to Haines in 1879 with a friend, who established a Presbyterian mission where the city of Haines now sits. Muir, one of the first non-Natives to explore this region, afterward advised young people not to come to our part of Alaska. He warned that they'd have to either stay or know that every other place they'd see for the rest of their lives would be a disappointment.

But just because it's beautiful doesn't make Haines an easy place to live. It is isolated, cloudy, and cold. Everything from land to groceries is expensive, and there's little work to help with the high cost of living. There are twenty-four hundred residents in the Chilkat Valley, although I don't think they've ever all been home at once, and probably a third leave in the winter. There's no hospital and the high school has just ninety-three students. There is no shopping mall, no McDonald's, no movie theater—heck, we don't even have a stoplight. Tony Tengs, a friend of mine who grew up here, says there's nothing wrong with Haines "a couple thousand people couldn't cure." Still, half of the residents don't want any changes at all. We have terrible community fights every time there's a local election or public hearing. We usually split the vote on everything, fifty-fifty. I won't sign any more petitions, no matter what they're for.

On a map of Alaska, Haines is up near Skagway, at the northern tip of the Inside Passage, an archipelago that stretches five hundred miles from the southern end of Prince of Wales Island, near Ketchikan, to the head of Lynn Canal, the largest fjord in North

America. We call this region Southeast, in the same way some eastern states are called New England. Most of it is very wet, and all of it is covered with big trees. To get anywhere from here you have to drive hundreds of wilderness miles. In the winter the Chilkat Pass into Canada is often closed because of heavy snow. Anchorage is eight hundred miles away. Whitehorse, the capital of the Yukon Territory, is about two hundred and sixty miles. It's possible to keep going past Whitehorse and drive all the way to Seattle, but few of us do. Instead, we take the ferry or fly ninety miles to Juneau, the state capital—a small town by most standards, with thirty thousand people—and catch a plane south. Every time I get on a jet to or from Juneau, I know people. The planes are different from the ones that cross the Lower Forty-eight. They're noisier, because everyone is talking to everyone else.

My sister-in-law came to Haines for Christmas, some years ago, from her home in Virginia. She took a plane from Dulles to Seattle, and then had to wait in Seattle two days for snow to clear in Juneau so the Alaska Airlines jet could land. On the way up it stopped in Ketchikan and Sitka. Each time they screeched to a halt on those short island runways, she braced herself against the seat in front of her. Local passengers cheered when the plane stopped. In Juneau she learned she couldn't fly up to Haines because of snow and fog, and was advised to take the ferry instead. After four hours of cruising by waterfalls, glaciers, and forested coastline she docked in Haines just as the day's six hours of light were being replaced by inky darkness. The first thing she said after walking up the boat ramp to greet us was "People have a lot of nerve living here. Maybe you shouldn't."

Well, it's too late for that. John Muir was right. Chip and I both grew up on the East Coast, met in college, and drove to Alaska when we graduated. This is our home now, and I have a feeling it always will be. In many ways Haines is a place out of time. Chip and I don't lock our doors, or even take the keys out the car. Ever. We don't expect to read the daily papers from Juneau and Anchorage on the day they are printed; they rarely get here on time. In the winter, when snow or rain or lack of daylight limits flights to and from Juneau, they sometimes don't arrive at all. We haven't had TV at our house for months because a new water tower blocked the transmitter for the one free channel we could get from Anchorage. I have never seen *Survivor*.

I get my wider world news from the public radio station, which plays NPR early in the morning and country music and rock and roll all afternoon. I have the radio on all the time. The eclectic mix is the soundtrack to my life. Everyone reads the *Chilkat Valley News,* our weekly paper, all eight or twelve or sixteen pages of it (depending on the season, the ads, and the letters to the editor), from headlines to the unclassifieds. When someone is selling a house or boat and only the phone number is listed, we find out who it is by running a finger down the few pages that the Haines listings take up in the southeast Alaska phone book. The two reporters joke that most readers are checking for mistakes, since they already know the news. I took over the paper's "Duly Noted" social column from its creator, Doris Ward. When her husband died, Doris needed a break from recording who went on vacation or who bid on what at the fund-raising auction for the Alaska Bald Eagle Festival. It wasn't much of a leap to go from reporting on the living to chronicling the dead, so I began writing the obituaries, too.

Death is a big part of life in Haines. As they do everywhere, people get cancer and have heart attacks. Teens die in car wrecks on the Haines Highway. One middle-aged man even succumbed to a weird flesh-eating bacterium. But there are many accidental deaths, too. This is a dangerous place. One man died falling off a cliff while goat hunting. Another was lost diving for sea cucumbers. Skiffs capsize in icy water, planes disappear in the mountains. Sometimes people vanish without a trace.

The house next door to ours is empty now. The neighbors crashed their plane on Douglas Island last summer. They died instantly, along with two passengers: their best friend's newly wed son and daughter-in-law. They were the second owners of the house. The couple who built it came here from New Zealand after buying a local air taxi service. The wife flew me back and forth to Juneau for my prenatal appointments. She had gray hair and five children. She died when her plane hit a mountain on a flight over the ice field between Glacier Bay and Haines. No wonder I'm afraid to fly.

In Haines, funerals are community affairs. I've been to memorial services in churches, gardens, the Elks Club, the Alaska Native Brotherhood Hall, and the American Legion. At Paul Potter's funeral, held in the high school gym, the pastor invited everyone to come up in front of the coffin and sink a basket for Jesus. Paul was a popular youth basketball coach who had recently joined the Haines Cornerstone Foursquare Gospel Church. Even people who don't normally attend church turn to God for comfort when someone dies. Being with men, women, and children who have lost the person they loved most in all the world only days before yet still open the door and invite me in, ask if I want honey in my tea, and then thank me for helping them when I leave is all the proof I need that God is good.

In most places, families write their own obituaries for local papers — or they send in an even shorter death announcement to larger newspapers. They pretty much say what they want. When my grandmother died back East, my parents gave the *New York Times* her incorrect age, by mistake, but the *Times* printed it just as they wrote it. Only celebrities or prominent citizens get the kind of treatment I give everyone who dies in Haines.

I spend as much time as I can researching a life but, with a weekly deadline, invariably I'm talking with friends and family heartbreakingly close to the death. Often within a day or two. Mostly I just listen. The details I need for the obituary are usually given right away, but the visit lasts much longer. By the time I'm ready to write, I know a lot about the person, and their friends and family. Much more than we'll ever print in the paper.

HAINES IS THE kind of town where if you live here long enough you recognize everybody and everybody recognizes you. High school basketball games are the biggest thing happening on most winter weekends, and on Sunday morning the church parking lots are full. So is the driveway at the Buddhist-style meditation hut. Picking up the mail at the post office (we all do; there is no home delivery) is a chance to socialize. If I arrive at the post office in a bad mood, I usually leave in a good one after chatting with everyone in line. Haines is so full of local color that if they ever made a movie about us, no one would believe it. There's an artist who lives with his wife, a weaver, in a fanciful cabin overlooking Rainbow Glacier. He keeps a dead temple pit viper in a big jar filled with vodka and takes sips of the "snake juice" every now and then to ward off illness. He'll offer you some if you stop by. The controversial new Presbyterian pastor's arms are covered with tattoos. The sewer plant manager rides a Harley-Davidson and has a ZZ Top beard. Recent mayors have included an artist, a heavy equipment operator, a Tlingit Indian woman, a Scotsman with a burr in his voice, and a white-haired former Vermonter. One school principal was a Roy Orbison impersonator; he dressed all in black and sang "Pretty Woman" at fund-raisers. Dave Pahl has collected so many hammers the Smithsonian sent him their old life-sized manikins to help him display them in action — right in his house, which doubles as the Haines Hammer Museum. I haven't even mentioned the Mormon spelunkers, the one-legged lady gold miner, or my friend Tim, a salmon fisherman and carpenter who spent eleven years building a classic thirty-six-foot reproduction Herreshoff ketch, doing all the work himself, from sewing the sails to melting lead from old car batteries for the keel. When it was done, he asked me to teach him how to sail.

John Schnabel, an old-timer who owns the Big Nugget Gold Mine in the historic Porcupine mining district, is the reason we were able to stay in Haines when the sawmill Chip worked at closed. John offered to sell us a building supply business he also happened to own. Twenty years and five children later, Chip still runs the same lumberyard and hardware store at the bottom of the hill, just across the road from the new cruise-ship dock. There are a lot more tourists than loggers in Haines now.

We have a weekend cabin off an old logging road eight miles south of town. You can get to it in a four-wheel-drive truck that you don't mind scratching with tree branches, or you can walk. That's in the summer. In the winter you have to snowshoe, ski, or snowmobile in. Our cabin is built on the former homestead of a writer and Danish seaman, Hjalmar Rutzebeck. The pond it sits on is called, optimistically, Rutzebeck Lake. It's mostly muskeg and about eight feet deep in the deep end. If you're brave, you can wade in the muck all the way across it. The shallow water gets warm enough on sunny days for skinny-dipping. Rutzebeck, who came to Haines in the 1920s after jumping ship somewhere on the West Coast, wrote two fat novels about his life here. He shot ducks on the pond and didn't have a dog, so he dove in and picked them up in his own mouth. He killed a man and was sent to jail in Juneau, but he escaped and walked the hundred-plus miles home over the ice fields, around Skagway, and back down the peninsula. He hadn't shot the fellow in cold blood. He'd been hired as a watchman for a cannery because people were stealing supplies from the warehouse.

Before he went to sleep one night, he rigged a string to the trigger of a loaded shotgun behind a door with a sign that said IF YOU OPEN THIS YOU WILL BE KILLED. A would-be thief ignored the warning and was shot dead.

When asked to sum up his philosophy of life, Rutzebeck wrote something that holds true for most people in Haines today: "We are what we want to be, mostly."

Most folks in Haines know I write obituaries, so while I've spent a lot of time sitting at kitchen tables thumbing through old photo albums, I've also had people stop me on the road while I'm out running to tell me something about their friend who recently died. They talk with me about dead people over coffee at Mountain Market, at the back booth in the Bamboo Room Restaurant, in the aisle at the grocery store, and when they are looking for garden tools at the lumberyard. I've stood on the sidewalk in front of the bank while a father told me he felt the presence of his dead son, and I quietly left the Pioneer Bar during a wake when two grown sons fought about cremating their father's remains. One Tlingit elder helped me write her obituary *after* she'd been buried—I learned everything I needed to know about her, and much more about the first people to live in the Chilkat Valley, from watching a series of interviews Anne Keener had given on videotape at the museum a few years before she passed away. When an older man was dying at home, his neighbors let me know they didn't expect him to last through the weekend. Just so I'd be ready. Recently, one new widow even called the newspaper office and asked when I was coming over. I didn't mind at all.

Because I love what I do. Being an obituary writer means I think a lot about loss, but more about love. Writing the obituaries of so many people I've known makes me acutely aware of death, but in a good way, the way Emily Dickinson meant when she wrote, "That it will never come again / Is what makes life so sweet." My job helps me appreciate cookouts on clear summer evenings down on the beach, where friends lounge on driftwood seats and we eat salmon and salads by the fire while our children play a game of baseball that lasts until the sun finally sets behind the mountains, close to eleven o'clock. And it helps me savor the quieter view from the top of Mount Ripinsky on New Year's morning when Chip and I and our neighbor Steve snowshoe up at sunrise.

Most of all, though, writing about the dead helps me celebrate the living—my neighbors, friends, husband, and five children—and this place, which some would say is on the edge of nowhere, but for me is the center of everywhere.

DULY NOTED

An article in the *New York Times* travel section recently called Haines "the real *Northern Exposure*." Tourism director Michelle Glass said that while the television show may not be how we see ourselves, the comparison can't hurt. "We couldn't buy this kind of publicity," she said. The article also mentioned that women in Haines have a fashion sense twenty years behind the rest of the country. When asked what she thought about that, Michelle pondered for a minute, then said, "No comment."

Tammy Hotch took matters into her own hands Friday in Ketchikan where she assisted in the birth of her son Casey Logan. "She reached down and pulled him out herself," said Tammy's mother, Linda Terracciano, who watched Casey's birth at Ketchikan General Hospital's new birthing facility. Casey joins brothers Steve and Alex and dad Stan Hotch.

Tlingit Barbie is here. The iconic female doll now comes in a Northwest Native American version, complete with a Chilkat blanket, headdress, and other regalia. The Mattel Corporation sent a shipment of dolls to the Chilkat Valley Historical Society last week. Joan Snyder said the group asked for three but were given eight, so the extras will be raffled off.

The bad news was that Judy Clark was stuck in Haines three days longer than she'd planned following the eightieth-birthday celebration for her mother, Betty Heinmiller. Planes were grounded because of snow and rain, and there were no ferries scheduled until later in the week. The good news is that she was able to stay and celebrate brother Lee's birthday as well. "We half-expected it," Lee said. "It is winter, after all."

Brian and Laura Johnson are trying a unique approach to selling the Bear Creek Camp youth hostel in Haines. They are sponsoring a nationwide essay contest, offering the 2.5-acre Small Tracts Road facility to the winner. Entrants must submit a four-hundred-word essay describing how owning the rural Alaskan camp would change their life.

If Things Hadn't Gone Right

IT WAS JUST us and the small Haines clinic staff eighteen years ago when I had our second daughter, Sarah. Dr. Jones had the day off, so Dr. Feldman was in charge. Some people called him the "hippie doctor." He lived on his boat and had a beard. He'd also graduated from Johns Hopkins Medical School. I liked him. The worst blizzard in a decade raged outside. Inside, I was pushing. I had started at one in the afternoon. Two hours later, I was still at it. I pushed and breathed and pushed and breathed and pushed some more. Then I gave up. "I can't do this," I said. Chip got pale. Mary, the nurse, who had been a friend just moments earlier, snapped, "Of course you can." Dr. Feldman was even firmer. He said that the only way this baby was coming out today or, for that matter, any day, was if I made it happen. He was deadly serious.

It was snowing so hard that looking out the window I could barely see beyond the curtains to the log visitor center across the alley. There were no regular planes flying and no ferry. A Coast Guard helicopter flight to the nearest hospital, in Juneau, would risk the lives of the crew. And there might not be time anyway. There was no operating room in the clinic. Dr. Feldman said all these things to me as I tried not to cry. Dr. Jones, who owned the clinic, was coming in the door to help when Mary leaned over and whispered, "Come on, Heather, you can do this." On the next contraction, I pushed as hard as I could, and out she came with a shout—a healthy baby girl with a head as round as a baseball.

The mood instantly changed. There were smiles all around. We took turns holding the baby and taking pictures. When they heard the news across the street at the Fogcutter Bar, they brought us all sandwiches and cold drinks. Cranberry juice with ice cubes never tasted so good. By six o'clock, we were back home with Sarah's older sister and my mother. Mom had arrived from New York a few days earlier on a ferry coated with ice. The usual four-and-a-half-hour trip had taken nearly eight as northern gales kept the boat from moving at full speed. Mom was one of the few passengers who didn't get sick. She also didn't know it was dangerous at all. She'd never been on the ferry before and assumed it was always like that. She was much more concerned about me having a baby with no hospital nearby.

When we walked in with Sarah, Mom thought I should go right to bed. She was even less happy when I got to the kitchen before she did the next morning. Our friends Steve and Joanne were co-hosting a radio show on KHNS, and they talked on air about the new Lende baby, telling listeners that her name was Sarah (after my mother) and her weight was eight pounds, two ounces. As for the state of the mother's health: "I saw Heather shoveling the driveway today on my way to work," Steve said.

I thought my mother would kill me. "He's kidding, Mom," I told her. "It's a joke." She was not amused. She decided to go out for her morning walk but found she couldn't get out the door. The snow had drifted up to the second-floor windows. The dog had to burrow down to scratch the top of the door. It would take Chip most of the morning to dig us out. Dr. Jones snowshoed down the hill from his house to make sure we were well. By then, I felt great—like Wonder Woman, like a pioneer. This was better than *Little House on the Prairie*.

The high cost of malpractice insurance was one of the reasons the clinic quit deliveries in Haines in 1987. Dr. Jones retired shortly afterward. With 620 births in twenty-five years, he'd never lost a mother but hadn't been able to save a "few" infants, he recollects now. Even so, he says, his clinic had "a very, very good record. I'd put it up against anyone's in any place." They did it all without an operating room, fetal monitors, or anesthesia. Dr. Jones had a gift for anticipating who would need help. If he thought there was any reason you might not be able to have a baby in Haines, he made sure you went to Juneau, Whitehorse, or even home to Mother. He informed you of the risks of not being able to fly or drive out in bad weather and of being in labor on a plane or a slow ferry to Juneau. He had great confidence in the Coast Guard helicopter pilots but little cause to call them, even when things didn't go exactly as planned.

Once, a young woman was in labor—a girl, really; she was still in her teens—when Dr. Jones discovered that something was not right. The baby was coming out feetfirst instead of headfirst. When children are delivered this way, their lungs inflate as soon as they are out of the womb. But with the head still inside, they can't breathe. If they aren't pushed out right away, if there is any delay, they suffocate. The only way to make sure that a baby in this position survives is to perform a cesarean section. Dr. Jones had to get his patient to the hospital in Juneau, quickly. Luckily, it was clear and cold, a good day to fly. Dr. Jones called a flying service and chartered a plane.

Pilot, doctor, and laboring mother-to-be flew as far as the Eldred Rock lighthouse—it's on an island in Lynn Canal about thirty miles south of Haines—before the baby started to come. Somehow, in the back of a rattling, drafty plane as big as a taxicab and half as comfortable, Dr. Jones pulled that baby out in time. Then he tucked it safely inside his coat to keep it warm, double-checked to make sure both mother and child were well, and told the pilot to turn around and head back home to Haines.

Outside actuaries didn't see childbirth in Haines the same way Dr. Jones did. They saw the potential for disaster and advised insurance companies to make sure that they asked Dr. Jones to pay for it. Alaska Native insurers concluded that it would be best not to take the risk, and all their clients were advised to give birth in the Native hospital in Sitka. Other Haines families couldn't afford what Dr. Jones would have had to charge to break even. That was the end of that.

THESE DAYS, WHILE Dr. Jones no longer practices, the once young Dr. Feldman is my neighbor. He has two children of his own now and a private office in his house. On Sarah's eighteenth birthday, I stopped to talk with him on the way back from my morning run. The weather was better than it had been when she was born, but we'd gotten a few inches of snow overnight. Dr. Feldman was out shoveling his front steps. I reminded him that it had been eighteen years to the day since he'd delivered Sarah. "Remember the blizzard?" I asked.

He said he'd never forget it. Then I asked him, a little wistfully, if he thought babies would ever be born in Haines again. His answer startled me. Sarah's birth, he said, was "the perfect example" of why he'd quit obstetrics. "If things hadn't gone right . . ." he began. Then, seeing the look on my face, he changed his tack. "Healthy women who are well prepared can and do have catastrophes. It really isn't safe," he said. "I loved delivering babies. Those were wonderful, almost home births, but I hated being so apprehensive, doing acrobatics without a net."

This week safety was very much on my mind. I had four obituaries to write: An old man had died of cancer at home and three people closer to my age had been killed when their skiff had capsized in rough water between Haines and Skagway. Gathering information for the obituaries of the drowning victims was painful and sad. At the Pioneer Bar, where the woman who died had worked, I learned she had been afraid of the sea. "I just can't imagine how terrified she was when the skiff turned over in that cold, cold water," Christy Fowler, the bar owner, said.

The skiff captain, Dan Burnham, had regularly taken his little boat between Skagway and Haines—about fifteen miles—and had never had any trouble. Dan was a lifelong Skagway resident who had recently moved here. "I'm sure he thought it was perfectly safe or he wouldn't have done it," one of his friends told me. While I was at the house of the third victim, a retired logger, his grown sons got into a big fight about where their father wanted to be buried. When someone you love dies senselessly, the line between grief and anger gets really blurry.

As I was researching the obituaries for the drowned trio, Jim Hatch lay dying of cancer with a church choir at his bedside. "They sang him into heaven," his widow told me when he finally passed away late that day. Even though his family assured him that it was all right if he said good-bye, that he was so sick they would understand, and that it was time for him to go—Jim stayed. He hung on so long that the choir started repeating songs. "He liked the music so much he didn't want to leave," said one of the singers. Which put me right up against the paper's deadline.

After turning in Jim's obituary late that night, I lay in bed, not sleeping. Three bad deaths and one good one, but the endings were all the same. "What's the point?" I said loudly—twice—to wake up Chip. When he turned toward me, I told him that if the biblical "three score and ten" life span was correct, we were past the halfway mark. "Shouldn't we stop for a minute and reevaluate here?" I asked. "I mean, why get up and go to work if we're just dying anyway?"

Chip yawned. "Because that's what people do," he said. Then he put his arms around me and fell back asleep before I could argue. I listened to his heartbeat and thanked God I'd married such a steady, good man.

THE SOUTHEAST ALASKA Regional Health Consortium has transformed our former clinic into a million-dollar state-of-the-art rural health center, with three doctors, a dentist, nurses, counselors, and physician's assistants. When my son, Christian, broke his hand a few months ago, we got to look around. The X-rays came up on a computer, instead of a plastic sheet developed in the closet, like in the old days. Now they are e-mailed to a bone doctor in Seattle for advice. The little brown paneled room where I was in labor with Sarah is long gone.

The new clinic is beautiful, but I miss the old one. Not the building, but what happened in it. I'm sad we can't begin the circle of life in Haines anymore. My friend Nancy, who had all her four children in Haines, says that even with the new clinic, without a hospital nearby we still have to "accept medical risks just living here."

It is precisely because Dr. Feldman understands those risks that I took Christian to his new office next door to our house when he complained of terrible stomach pains. I knew Dr. Feldman would know what to do. Dr. Jones had taught him well. My great-grandmother had died when her appendix ruptured. My grandmother lived with us when I was growing up, so I heard the sad story every time anyone had a stomachache. The day we visited Dr. Feldman, the weather was bad: raining hard sideways on the shore and snowing on the mountains. No planes were flying to Juneau, and the ferry had left a couple of hours ago. The only way out was the road to Canada.

Dr. Feldman prodded, and Christian jumped in pain. An old

dog pushed open the door between the living room and the office and walked in, but the good doctor didn't notice. He scratched his beard and looked out the window. He thought for a long, silent minute and said, "I'm pretty sure it's appendicitis. If he was my kid, I'd be on the way to Whitehorse." He guessed we had twenty-four hours from those first bad pains—which meant we had about ten hours—until it might rupture. "And you don't want that to happen in Haines," he said. He called the Alaska-Canada border. The officer said it was snowing and the road was closing for the night. We had to leave right then or we wouldn't get through.

In the summer, on a nice day, you can drive to Whitehorse in four hours, or so I've heard. It takes twice that long in a car full of children who never pee in the bushes at the same pit stop. Eliza and Sarah were old enough to be in charge while we were gone, so we didn't have to take the whole gang. But we were in the middle of a winter storm, and our new snow tires hadn't arrived. The old ones were fine for around town, but we couldn't afford to skid off the road right now. We borrowed our neighbors Steve and Linnus's sturdy truck and, in a flurry of purposefully calm activity, they helped us grab essentials before we kissed the girls good-bye. Following an old Haines rule, we dressed for the weather, not the vehicle. Just in case. It was snowing hard when the officer waved us through Canadian customs. From there, we headed over the Chilkat Pass through 120 uninhabited miles, to Haines Junction, Yukon Territory—population six hundred.

At the top of the pass falling and blowing snow brought us to a complete stop. We couldn't see the road. I hoped we wouldn't have to turn back—what would we do then? But the headlights caught the reflective tape on the tops of the eight-foot-tall snow-plow guide poles, spaced about every fifty feet on either side of the road. Chip shifted into a lower gear and we skidded from pole to pole, hoping the road was still underneath us somewhere.

We navigated like that for two and a half hours, without seeing another vehicle, in the thick snowy silence, on high alert, moving full speed ahead, or at least as fast as we possibly could in the storm. Having a sick child helps make warriors out of ordinary parents. When we got near Haines Junction, the skies cleared and a full moon rose over Dezadeash Lake and the broad white hills of the Yukon. It was beautiful. I put in a CD and Muddy Waters sang the blues. That's when Chip, who was driving, exhaled and said, "This is surreal."

The bumps on the last leg, an old roller coaster of a road through the empty countryside, hurt Christian. I helped him breathe through the pain the way I had been taught in childbirth class. Five and a half hours after we'd left home we walked into the sixty-bed Whitehorse General Hospital.

No one asked us for any ID or if we had insurance. They didn't even know our names until the nurse examining Christian in the emergency room asked us. She said Dr. Feldman had been right, and she called a surgeon (there are two). A nurse with a German accent said, "I've come to take your blood," just like Dracula. We smiled. Christian winced. It hurt to laugh. We helped him into a hospital gown and didn't look when they stuck the needle in for his IV. When the doctor arrived and learned we were Americans, he had us sign a paper saying we wouldn't sue him. Then we trotted alongside the gurney with coats flapping, still in our boots, and kissed Christian before he went through the swinging doors and was gone. That's when I walked around the corner, where Chip couldn't see me, and cried. For just a minute.

An hour later Christian was wheeled by on the way to a recovery room. The doctor said he was fine. He had removed the inflamed appendix just in time. Three days later, we were headed back south in snowy sunshine, veterans of a successful campaign with only good stories to tell. Christian gets carsick, so we had all the windows down and our hats on. The windchill must have been minus thirty. I said we'd all get frostbite, and we all laughed. I wondered out loud if it was crazy—or just plain irresponsible—to raise a family so far from a hospital. Chip didn't think so. He said, "This proves we can get anywhere—when we need to."

ON A COLD, windy afternoon, not long after the appendix adventure, my youngest daughter, J.J., and I took a walk on the beach. The calendar said April, but it felt more like February. After pulling hats over our ears, zipping jackets, and tugging on rubber boots, we opted to walk into the wind first, so the way home would be warmer. Living in the northern end of the Lynn Canal makes you appreciate what a blessing the old Irish prayer "May the wind be always at your back" really is.

We held hands and leaned into the southerly gale, occasionally throwing driftwood sticks for her little terrier, Phoebe, and my big Lab, Carl. The wind carried them so swiftly, and so far off course, that by the time Carl got halfway down the beach, he'd turn back, confused, forgetting what he was chasing.

J.J. took this rare one-on-one time as an opportunity to tell me about her third-grade writing project. "It's a story about a girl with a perfect life, who lives in a perfect house. Until she gets kidnapped by aliens," she said. I think every mother wants her child to have a perfect life. I don't know if other parents worry as much as I do that it may end prematurely. I can't help it.

In the cold, bright light of day with my little daughter's hand in mine, I tried to forget about what might happen if sick children don't get to hospitals on time. I didn't want to wonder why I had a healthy baby in a blizzard and Christy's friend drowned on a routine boat ride. I didn't want to think about what happens if a baby coming out feetfirst gets stuck or why old men dying from cancer just want to hear one more song before they go. Instead, on that blustery spring day I concentrated on something happy and very much alive—J.J.

As we climbed over slimy boulders, I asked about the details of the story she was writing. "You said your main character has the perfect life, in a perfect house. How is it like ours and how's it different?"

"Well, her life is pretty much like mine," J.J. said. "And she has a house a lot like ours." I felt better already. "Only nicer."

Only nicer?

I looked back down the beach at our home tucked into the spruce trees. I think it's a perfect house, in the nicest town, in the prettiest place on earth. But J.J. said she wants a house more like the one farther down the road, the grandest private residence in Haines. She had good taste, anyway. "What do you like most about it?" I asked, curious which fancy details caught her young eyes.

"The bowls with Jolly Ranchers in them," she said. "I think we should have little dishes of candy everywhere at our house, too." I remind her that we do, at Christmastime. Then J.J. asked if Santa Claus is real.

Is life good? Will summer ever warm this beach? Should we believe in magic? "Sure, Santa Claus is real," I said, "and the best stories have happy endings."

DULY NOTED

During a city council discussion on the new zoning plan last week, councillor Norm Smith asked, "What about the cemetery, is that going to be zoned as park, or a greenbelt, or as commercial area or what?" Mayor Don Otis replied, "Norm, we are going to call that multifamily residential."

"It is great to be back," said Kate Rineer. Kate and Stan Boor have returned to their Highland Estate's home after a winter working in Salt Lake City. "The city is such a rat race," Kate said. "I know Haines has its little problems, but it's really such a nice place."

Warm weather has melted the snow and ice so rapidly that the Chilkat River has swelled to just a foot below flood stage. Tall cottonwood trees have toppled over the bank at 14 Mile, and River Adventures guide Ken Gross said moose calves are drowning in the swift current. Fisherman Gregg Bigsby reported that the mud from the rivers has colored Lynn Canal brown all the way to Sherman Point. "I've never seen anything like that before," he said.

Lisa Schwartz said she and Gordon Whitermore are canceling their subscription to *Shack Life* magazine. The couple moved into their new home at 18 Mile after living in a less substantial dwelling for a period of time she refuses to disclose. It took four years for them to complete the new house. Lisa said their new digs are fine. "This is a real home; my heart goes out to all those women who have lived in a shack."

LICY WINDS

Nedra's Casket

LAST YEAR SEVEN people were buried out at the Jones Point Cemetery, near the Chilkat River on the edge of town, behind the softball park and the Eagles Nest Trailer Court. That's not enough deaths to support a funeral parlor, and Haines isn't close enough to anywhere with one to move bodies back and forth affordably. Families have to charter a small plane to Juneau if they want cremation or embalming services. There are lots of stories about both bodies and ashes getting lost on flights back from Juneau or even Anchorage, where the state sometimes requires them to be shipped for autopsies.

This winter one urn filled with the ashes of an old-timer who died at the Pioneer Home in Juneau didn't make it back to Haines for the funeral, which was held anyway with a cloth-covered cardboard box standing in for the ashes. Out-of-town family members couldn't wait for the weather to clear. They had to get back to homes and jobs in the Lower Forty-eight.

It's much simpler to stay in Haines if you're dead than to go anywhere else. Haines can be a hard place to live, but it's a good place to die, thanks to a handful of dedicated volunteers, service clubs, and churches.

One woman had the sad experience of burying her father in

Haines, then two months later going through the whole thing all over again with her husband's dad in Pennsylvania. "In the Lower Forty-eight for thousands of dollars strangers will take over and do everything for you, in the mistaken assumption that they are helping," Randa said. "It was so much easier for me to work through the grieving process when I had an active role in the preparations for burial."

That's where Annie Boyce and Paul Swift come in. The husband-and-wife team prepares the dead for viewing and burial. They do this for free, for anyone who asks. Family and friends stop by the makeshift morgue — a garage with a walk-in cooler at City Hall, next door to the jail — to help them, or to just take a last look at a parent, child, or friend.

Paul has bathed and dressed over one hundred bodies in the fifteen years since he inherited the job from a Presbyterian pastor. Annie started helping a few years ago. "It's good to have a woman, too," Paul says. "The main thing is to keep it dignified and respectful." He doesn't find the work creepy or morbid at all. "I think it's my Christian background," he says. "I feel the soul's departed . . ."

"Even," says Annie, quietly finishing his thought, "with people we've been close to, it's good to be able to help. Yes, it can be difficult and emotionally exhausting. Nevertheless, I believe what we do is a powerful witness."

"JUST BE SURE you have three points of contact," Paul yells. We are a long way from the morgue, on the steep, snow-covered slope of Mount Ripinsky. "That's two poles and one snowshoe, or two snowshoes and one pole," he adds, looking down at me over Annie's head. It is a brilliant Thursday morning in February. The snow is white, the sky is blue, and when Annie called to see if I could get away for a day outdoors I didn't hesitate, even though I'd never gone up this section of the mountain on snowshoes before.

"You'll be fine," Annie said. "You're in shape and you have good equipment." My snowshoeing has been limited to the gentler trail up Mount Riley or the flats along the river. Now we are going very slowly, straight up. Above me, Annie and Paul methodically dig snow steps with the crampons on the toes of their snowshoes. I follow, shoving my boots hard into each one, double-checking them before planting my foot too firmly. Gripping like this, with just my toes, makes my calves hurt. I'm thinking we should be roped to something, or one another, like those photos I've seen of Mount Everest expeditions.

Paul and Annie are experienced mountaineers. They climb this route in December, after work, in the pitch dark with headlamps. They do it in the rain, in the snow, and when you can barely see your feet in the fog. Annie says they hike as much for their heads as for their hearts. It feels good to be outside and alive.

Annie and Paul don't have that *Outside* magazine kind of style. Annie has a faded bandanna around her head to keep the sweat from stinging her eyes. Paul's cap advertises Aspen Paint—most days he works in a hardware store. They both wear faded plaid wool shirts. Paul is sixty-three years old, has a white beard, rosy cheeks, and a hearing aid. We all celebrated Annie's fiftieth birthday a couple of years ago.

I'm no slouch, but the going is hard, slow, and takes all of my strength. My muscles quiver. I'm sweating, breathing hard, and gripping my climbing poles tight. I hope the new ligament in my knee holds. While it works great on the flats, cycling or running, this is a big test. On the other hand, Annie had the same surgery, more recently—and just watch her go. After looking way down, over my shoulder, I resolve not to do it again. We're a thousand feet up. I jam my boot into the step made by Paul and packed down by Annie, and the snow gives way—not completely, but enough for me to hear the blood rushing through my veins.

It's Paul's regular day off, but Annie has taken a leave day from her job as high school secretary. It's been a long, dark winter. The last time we had sunny skies, warm temperatures, fresh white snow, and no wind was a year ago. There was a little debate at the trailhead if this route was too difficult for me, but I assured them I could do it.

Now I'm not so sure. I slip a little and my forehead touches the snowy wall. Maybe I should just crawl up it. Leaning into the hill makes me lose any purchase I have, and I slowly slip down.

"The runoff isn't too bad," notes Paul, the leader with eyes in the back of his head. "If you feel yourself going, dig the poles in or grab the snow with your hands." Annie tells me to go with the fall, maybe even roll a little if I can't stop.

"Stay loose," she calls down. "Just stay loose if you're going."

My body is tall and angular, more Tin Man than Kathy Rigby. I'm pretty sure I'll break before I bounce. I wonder, for just a moment, if I could get killed doing this and decide, just as fast, that yes, I could. I jam the poles hard into the bank to stop myself from sliding, but they don't catch. It feels like I'm falling forever. I don't see my life flash before my eyes; I don't see a bright light. I don't see anything at all. My eyes are shut. Finally I stop. Turns out I've only skidded about twenty feet.

My partners continue up, unconcerned. Maybe it's because Paul and Annie are the undertakers that they don't have my fear of falling. They know death is inevitable and would rather meet theirs on a mountain than at home in bed.

On a good day, a day like today, Haines is often compared to heaven. But on a bad day, these mountains and the water below them are deadly.

I know that, but I still want to be up here. I keep climbing, not only because I can't back down without falling but because I feel so good all of a sudden. I faced my fears and won. For now anyway. I want to sing—but I don't dare because it takes all my concentration just to hold on to the hill.

At last, we step up onto the ridge, and rest before heading up and over the gentler hiking trail for the trip back down. I try to drink from the water bottle on my fanny pack, but it's frozen. Paul offers me some from the flat old Listerine bottle he keeps tucked into an inside pocket. We break an energy bar and pass it around with some cold orange slices. The only other tracks in the snow belong to a wolverine. Below us, eagles glide over the treetops.

Paul shakes his head in awe of the view. He's seen it a thousand times and it still moves him. Annie sighs and then smiles a big, wide grin. It's a face she never wears down in town. Seeing them now so happy reminds me of a more somber afternoon, back when I didn't know them as well but was just as impressed by their bravery and teamwork.

ANNIE AND PAUL worked quickly. They bathed Nedra and shampooed and dried her wispy white hair before slipping her thin arms and legs into undergarments and sliding over all of it the royal blue dress that once showed off her eyes.

Nedra was my friend Joanne's mother. Joanne had helped Paul and Annie get her dad in his last suit, but she said that with "Mom" it was different. The long illness had reduced Nedra's already small frame to veins and skin, nothing really, and Joanne didn't want to remember her that way.

Taking care of Nedra, especially near the end, wore Joanne out. One afternoon I came home and found her asleep on my couch. Sometimes after Nedra went to sleep, Joanne would go for a drive with her dog and park someplace where he could run around, while she lay on the warm hood of her pickup, watching the northern lights.

Joanne did finally call the hospice people for help, but Nedra was already dead before they arranged for her care. She had bad lungs and died of emphysema. Seneca wrote that asthma is a rehearsal for death. If that's true, then Nedra had about ten dress rehearsals and time enough to prepare for the final curtain. Her last instructions requested an Emblem Club funeral, an Episcopal burial, and Joanne to make her casket.

The casket part came about because when Joanne's dad died, she and Nedra had tried to buy one at the True Value hardware store, the only place in town that sells caskets. The coffin that matched their budget was green fiberglass. Joanne said it looked like a submarine, and she knew her dad wouldn't want to be buried in something with a snap-on lid, like a plastic garbage can. Since Joanne had just finished building her kitchen cabinets, she thought she could make a wooden casket. Nedra was so pleased with Joanne's first one that she ordered another, for herself.

Joanne's sisters, Kathy and Julie, live in California and Nevada now. Kathy flew up as soon as Joanne called to say Nedra was going fast, but she missed saying good-bye to her mother by one flight from Juneau. Julie and her husband were driving up the Alaska Highway in their motor home, and weren't expected to arrive until the day before the funeral. Julie's two daughters and their children drove down from Anchorage as soon as they got the word that Nedra had died.

On Tuesday morning, we sat at Nedra's kitchen table writing her obituary. It was my first one. I'd volunteered to do it because Nedra hadn't liked a new reporter at the paper. He was an investigative type from down south. I also wanted to do something for Joanne. She's the kind of friend who brings her mother and her dog to dinner. The last time we'd carried Nedra into our house in a lawn chair; it was Joanne's fortieth-birthday party.

I listened as the two sisters struggled with the Victorian language of death—"passed away," "gone to her reward," "resting eternally," "met her maker," "entered into the kingdom of God." None of it fit Nedra. She was a direct woman and would have appreciated letting people know right up front how and when she died. We wrote, "After a long illness, Nedra Allen Waterman died from emphysema Saturday evening at her Small Tracts Road home. Her daughter Joanne was by her side. She was seventy-eight years old."

The rest was easier, because Nedra had written most of it down herself. There was her ride on the first steamship into Seward after the Japanese bombed Pearl Harbor, how she met and married Wes Waterman, the years at the gold mine, the babies, leaving Alaska for California and coming back again, the hotel she ran in Anchorage, and the volunteer work she did in Haines for the Emblem Club. Nedra had even included the date and place of her high school graduation, and the middle names of her parents. All seventy-eight years in two letter-sized, handwritten pages.

When the obituary was finished, Kathy turned her attention to Joanne and the casket. "It's now ten A.M. on Tuesday and the funeral is six P.M. on Thursday," she announced, taking a long pull on her cigarette. She was still in her pink bathrobe. "Mom better be buried in something sturdier than an old bedspread." She didn't say it in a mean way, and succeeded in making Joanne laugh for the first time all morning. Joanne has a great laugh, a deep-throated belly chuckle that makes anyone who hears it smile.

The casket had to be finished in time to put Nedra into the dress she wanted to be buried in, the one she wore to her fiftieth high school reunion.

Karl Johnson walked over from next door to see if Joanne needed any help with the casket. He'd heard at the lumberyard that she'd bought the wood and planned to build it herself. Kathy, who can't tell a mitered joint from a dovetail, said yes, but Joanne, the carpenter, shook her head and answered, "No, thanks." She said there was plenty of time.

We all went into the shop and looked at the pine one-by-twelves, one-by-sixes, and two-by-twos that Joanne still needed to cut, screw, and glue into a casket. Kathy said that if Joanne didn't get to work soon she'd miss the family dinner planned for that evening. Which I think is exactly what Joanne had in mind. Building the casket gave her an excuse to leave the crowded kitchen, filled with women and babies—Nedra's grandchildren and great-grand-children. The work helped Joanne sort it out, alone.

Joanne finished the casket about five hours before the funeral. She coated it in Danish oil instead of varnish, so it would dry on time. Julie and the motor home pulled into the driveway the night before, carrying a bolt of blue satin to line the coffin. Kathy tucked some quilt batting underneath it.

NEDRA WAS LYING comfortably inside the casket in plenty of time for the move in the old ambulance, which doubles as a hearse, to the Elks Lodge for the funeral. Even Kathy said that once the casket was done, time seemed to slow way down. The fi-nal hours before the funeral were empty. Getting everyone show-ered and dressed took less time than anticipated, especially with the motor home's extra bathroom. It was a warm, sunny April day. The very best kind of day. We sat outside in Nedra's garden, trying to keep the children clean and Joanne's energetic spaniel away from our good clothes.

Nedra's favorite hymn was the one about walking in the garden with Jesus. "And he walks with me and he talks with me and he tells me I am his own." At the funeral, Debra played it on the piano while everyone sang. I pictured a healthy Nedra alone with Jesus. What would Nedra say to him? My guess is she'd suggest a shave and a haircut, and then she'd question him about why he hadn't intervened in the more difficult days of her life. "Where were you," she might ask, "when all I had to feed the girls was mustard sandwiches?"

The ladies of the Emblem Club, dressed in black from gloves to stockings, conducted the service, taking turns at the wobbly podium overlooking the closed casket. Each woman carried a dark purple silk rose.

At the graveside, Reverend Jan Hotze said the final blessing, and the Emblem Club ladies each dropped a handful of dirt and a flower onto the coffin. Maisie Jones, who has buried a husband and several close friends, says it's good for the living: "When you throw flowers on the grave and say the Twenty-third Psalm, it does help. It helps us come to terms with the absence. Everybody feels serene about it afterward."

The Episcopal burial service includes a verse from John's gospel: "in my house are many mansions." In the obituary letter Nedra left for her daughters, she wrote proudly that her first home in Alaska was a fourteen-by-fourteen-foot shack on a mining claim in Talkeetna.

Nedra spent most of her life in the biggest state in the union in small, handmade houses. She wouldn't be comfortable for eternity in a mansion. Which is why her simple cabin of a casket, built with love and skill by her youngest daughter, ought to make her feel right at home in her new neighborhood.

DULY NOTED

On Monday about thirty Klukwan residents turned out at the Alaska Native Sisterhood Hall for an Elizabeth Peratrovich Day luncheon program honoring the legendary Alaska civil rights leader. A video of *Elizabeth Peratrovich,* a play performed at Hoonah High School a few years ago, was shown. The Klukwan School children read essays they'd written about Mrs. Peratrovich. Elsie Spud said, "It was hard for us to hold back tears because of the good job the kids did, both in the writing and the reading." She added, "We all left with important knowledge about why we celebrate the holiday." Elizabeth Peratrovich is credited with convincing the territorial legislature to change laws that once banned Native people from many public places, including movie theaters, restaurants, and stores.

———————

The last weeks of the school year mean trips and special events for elementary school classes. Kelly Pape's third graders went to Whitehorse on a two-day camping trip at the hot springs. Jansy Hansen's fourth graders took the water taxi to Skagway for a ride on the White Pass and Yukon Route Railroad and visited the Klondike Gold Dredge. Tim McDonough's fifth graders loaded up a school van with gear and left for two nights at Rainbow Glacier Camp.

———————

Local carvers John Hagen, Clifford Thomas, and Greg Horner have started work on a new totem pole commissioned for actor James Earl Jones. Alaska Indian Arts president Lee Heinmiller said the twenty-two-foot pole will take about a year to complete. "It's basically still just a log right now."

———————

A snowboard signed by members of the Teton Gravity Research pro ski team was Lucas Dawson's big present at his eleventh birthday party Saturday. The team of elite skiers and snowboarders from around the world stayed at the Dawson family lodge while they filmed extreme spring skiing adventures. "Lucas got to know the guys while they were here—and they got together and gave him the board," Lucas's dad, Jon Dawson, said.

———————

Everyone Knew Her as Susie

DUANE WILSON SLIDES open the glass door to his parents' house, adjusts his eyes to the darker inside light, and takes a deep breath of the warm, smoky air, scented with fish and fresh cedar. "Smells like an Indian house," he says, and we all laugh. On the table, a foot-square pile of dried smoked eulachon (pronounced "hooligan") rests on newspaper. Next to it is the remains of a sugary sheet cake. "Hmm. Cake and fish," Duane says, helping himself to both. The cake is left over from the potluck supper after the Alaska Native Sisterhood funeral of Susie Brouillette, a Tlingit elder who died earlier in the week.

I'm at the kitchen table, carefully chewing my own little dried fish and wondering if I should eat the fins and tail. It's actually better than it sounds. Much better than a similar dish my dad eats for breakfast—steamed kippered herring, or "kippers," which smells bad enough to drive a daughter to move to, say, Alaska when she grows up. Anyway, the reason I'm crunching the tougher parts of a eulachon and watching Duane snap off the shriveled eyeless heads into a neat pile is because I need Susie Brouillette's Tlingit name and the proper phrasing of her tribal lineage for the obituary.

This house is the home of the Alaska Native Sisterhood secretary, Marilyn Wilson, a happy woman with a round face and big glasses. She keeps good notes on her computer and has a fax machine in the back bedroom that she always offers to use when I call with a question. "What's your fax number?" she'll say, and I'll tell her I don't have one. I'd rather talk with Marilyn and her husband, Paul, in person. I like being in their house. There are usually puppies underfoot, grandchildren playing, and a nephew or cousin asleep on the couch. Marilyn and Paul's projects are everywhere. Today the television is on but no one is watching it.

While Marilyn and Duane, who is the president of the Alaska Native Brotherhood Haines Camp No. 5 and knows Tlingit better than his mother does, translate into English the Native words I've asked about, Paul carves a design on a yellow cedar canoe paddle and keeps me company. Paul doesn't greet me with any of the usual talk about when it will stop raining or if this summer will be warmer than last. Instead, the first thing he says is "I have missed many years of my culture."

Paul tells me he's learning the Tlingit language so he can *believe* the stories of his people, not just know the plots. When he was young, missionaries and the government prohibited Alaskan Natives from speaking their language and living traditionally. They often took Tlingit children from their homes and families, placing them in boarding schools as far away as Washington and Oregon. Now Paul is a grandfather and is committed to relearning a way of living that he says is not lost but rather hiding, just below the skin. He is proud of Duane and watches for a moment as his son helps his wife. "When I sing the old songs," Paul says, "it's like my chest is opened up and my heart is showing." Paul's words are poetry. I know because there is nothing I can say afterward. I just watch him resume his carving and try not to look too closely at the eye sockets of those dried fish. I recognize the movie on the television: *On Golden Pond*.

Meanwhile, at the other end of the table, Duane and Marilyn

have quietly sounded out the deceased's name, but they're not completely satisfied with the result. "I'll write *Taac*, but it's really *Taak'd*," my hostess says softly, emphasizing the throat-clearing ending sound. Tlingit names are based on the moiety, or reciprocal group, to which they belong. The term *moiety* is taken from a Greek word meaning half, and there are two moieties: Ravens and Eagles. In the old days, Ravens could only marry Eagles. Now Tlingits don't always observe that rule, and in fact often marry non-Natives. However, Ravens and Eagles still take care of each other. When a Raven dies, it is the Eagles who plan the funeral. Eagles sing songs to Ravens at potlatches. When a raven and an eagle are depicted together on silver jewelry or wood, the design is called "love birds" and is often circular, like the Eastern yin and yang symbol. They are different, but always complementary. The two halves make a whole.

The denotations don't stop with Ravens and Eagles. There are also what we call clans, although there isn't a matching word in Tlingit. Clans are more political and specific to an area than the Raven and Eagle identifications, which cover all Tlingits everywhere. Clans are what determine design, story, song, and property ownership. Unlike moieties, clans do have designated leaders.

Another grouping—are you still with me?—determines lineage. Houses are named for the place where the family initially lived, and link blood relatives. What makes it confusing is that, traditionally, newlyweds moved to the bride's mother's village and often lived in an uncle's house there. (The mother determines the children's moiety affiliation.) And sons were raised by their mother's brothers, not their fathers. Much of this has never been written down, and over time some of the finer points have been lost or changed. Often, so-called experts disagree.

Still more factors that make Tlingit families hard to track are adoption and the way names are used. Tlingits are generous with their culture and have adopted many non-Natives, giving them equal footing with birth relatives. They don't usually adopt them as babies and raise them as their own; instead, they adopt adults they like and who agree to honor Tlingit customs. Also, when an elder dies, his or her name is given to another relative (adopted or blood). This ensures that the family will have everyone they have loved with them throughout all time.

So you see, deciphering a Tlingit family tree, filled with the same names for many generations, gets confusing, even if you are Tlingit. I use the Tlingit names in obituaries because they tell who the person was and where they came from. But in the "survived by" category I stick with blood family lines. There isn't enough space in our little newspaper to write more.

Now Marilyn says that her friend Susie was a Raven. She thinks she was also in the sockeye, or Lukaax Adi, clan. "But don't put that in the paper," she tells me. "I'm just not sure." She does know that Susie was from Taac Dein Caan, or the Snail House, and that her name was Naa Goolth Claa. Marilyn watches me carefully spelling everything correctly. I repeat the way the words sound until she nods her approval. She suspects the truth — that I am trying to make up for past wrongs by people who look like me, who are part of my broad Christian-European-American heritage, by honoring her culture and her wisdom and her husband's open-heart poetry. After I get it all right, she smiles and says, "Everyone knew her as Susie."

All I can think of is the Beatles' song "Rocky Raccoon," where Magil was called Lil, "but everyone knew her as Nancy." I have a feeling Marilyn may have shared that thought.

Besides all the Tlingit stuff, I learn from Marilyn that Susie raised five children and two stepchildren. Her husband, a fisherman, was killed loading a log ship in 1965. Their youngest daughter drowned. One of Susie's friends from the Catholic church where she worshipped had already told me that, despite personal tragedy, "Susie had a gift for making whoever she was with feel special."

Before I leave the Wilsons', Duane hands me a pint jar of smoked eulachon. His father likes his dried, but Duane prefers to can them after smoking because the moisture comes back in the pressure cooker, plumping them up. They look like sardines. These first spring fish arrive sometime between March and May. The rendered oil is especially valued by Natives for both taste and health benefits.

This year the eulachon run has been strong. Beaches are noisy with hungry shorebirds. Sea lions cruise the shoreline with their mouths wide open. In the first few hours of the run, before the birds arrive to eat them, spawned-out dead eulachon litter the tide lines. As soon as word gets out that the eulachon are here, families such as the Wilsons reopen their fish camps along the Chilkat River. There are blue tarps strung between cottonwood trees for shelter and a shack or trailer to sleep in. Often there's an old couch or the bench seat from a pickup on the bank for elders to sit on. Some fresh eulachon are roasted over open fires, some are smoked, but most are buried in lined pits and left to rot for about three weeks. They smell so strong that when I'm riding my bike nearby I have to hold my breath. After the fish decompose, they are boiled outside in big pots until the oil can be skimmed off the top. When it cools, it's solid and white, like bacon grease.

Paul is eating some now, licking it off the spoon. He keeps it in a jar in the freezer and has it once or twice a day. "It's good for the heart," he says, offering me a spoonful. I try not to make a face. Paul laughs. He knows that eulachon, and especially the fat, is an acquired taste. I have a Native friend who won't touch the slimy little fish—not "boiled, roasted, or smoked," he says. He does help harvest them, though, because for him it's an annual reminder of the past, and an affirmation of the Tlingit culture's future.

The perfectly sealed jar of fish Duane gave me took the better part of a week to make—from netting on incoming tides to smoking for three days, and finally to sterilizing jars, checking lids, cutting and packing the fish, and staying close to the stove and watching the pressure cookers seal them for one hundred minutes at ten pounds of pressure. It is a generous and unexpected gift.

       I COULDN'T CALL Susie Brouillette's daughter Della and tell her I was coming over because she didn't have a telephone. I'd seen the red Trans Am she drives, but I hadn't been successful in flagging her down; she didn't pay any attention to my frantic waving. I had thought I was finished with Susie Brouillette's obituary when Marilyn gently insisted that I couldn't put anything in the paper without the immediate family's blessing. That would be Della. When I couldn't make contact with Della, I asked Marilyn where she lived. She told me, and said I could tell Della she had sent me. Marilyn also mentioned that Della was a private person and might not take kindly to a stranger. Then she added, "You'll do fine."

Cold rain blew as I knocked at the trailer door. When Della appeared, she was in her pajamas. It was almost noon. Marilyn had told me she was between jobs. Even surprised and rumpled, she was extraordinarily beautiful. I tried not to stare. I said Marilyn Wilson had sent me. She looked at me sternly and shut the door before I could tell her who I was or why I was there.

A long minute later, she reopened the door enough for me to finish my introduction and explain that the paper wanted to borrow a recent photograph for her mother's obituary. I also asked, quickly, if I could run the content by her, to be sure it was all correct. Silently, she took in my eager fair face, Patagonia jacket, and pressed khakis. For a second I thought she might throw me off the porch. Instead, she shut the door again and left me standing in the rain with a wet cat rubbing my ankles. I knew that her mother had been gracious, and that she was her mother's dutiful daughter, and that Marilyn had said I had to do this, so I waited, hopeful, under the wide eave of the firewood shed attached to the trailer.

When she reemerged it was to show me a photograph. I leaned inside the doorway to look. Actually, there were two: one was recent, her mother's long white hair instantly recognizable; the other showed a young black-haired Tlingit beauty, much like herself. She wouldn't give the pictures to me until she heard what I'd written. She was prepared to dislike it. Sometimes you just have to do things, like eat a eulachon, that you think you can't do. I read carefully.

Della was quiet. It was okay, she said. For me, okay was perfect. Then she said there was one thing she'd like me to take out. She asked that I not quote the nice old lady from her mother's church. "She doesn't like Indians," Della said. I mumbled something about not knowing that, which I hadn't, and scratched the words out dramatically.

Then Della asked that I use both photographs; the younger one was her favorite. I said I was sorry, but my editor (and good friend, Tom Morphet) would never print it. "No forty-year-old wedding portraits," Tom had told me the first time I'd brought one like that back. "No one will know who the hell it is."

I explained it differently to Della. "We can only use one picture," I said, "and since your mother was so well liked and respected by so many people who may not recognize her name but will know her face, it is important to show what she looked like, you know, *now*." But since she was dead, I added, "Sorry, I mean, *then*." Della had me flustered, and I suspect she knew it. My ancestors had never met hers, but that didn't absolve me of guilt about what my race had done and in many ways is still doing to Native Alaskans and Native Americans. I wanted Della to know I was respectful as well as trustworthy. It might not be much, but writing a good obituary for her mother was the best I could do. Printing an out-of-date picture, though, was impossible. She said she was disappointed but she understood. She shut the door without saying good-bye. I tucked her mother's photograph safely inside my coat and stepped off the porch.

Last time it had been Paul Wilson's heart that was showing; this time it was mine. I wanted to raise my hands and testify—thanking God for all these good people who forgive the past without forgetting it. I almost shouted *Thank you* right out loud. Thank you for Della's face, the Wilsons' kindness, eulachon, and for strong hearts beating in rhythm with ancestors. Thank you for Ravens and Eagles and halves made whole.

But I didn't. I never do anything like that. I am, as my mother likes to say, a "stiff-upper-lip" white Anglo-Saxon Protestant. That is *my* culture. So instead, I stood in the mud next to my car and realized that the only thing that keeps us going is love. I knew it then like I knew it was raining. I got a little off balance, the way you do when you're on a boat. I thought, It's as if we are all moving through this world on a big old ship, holding on to one another as we cruise up the generous river of life. The water that floats us is always new, yet it flows in the same direction, over the same old sand.

DULY NOTED

About seventy local fishermen, their wives, and guests celebrated the season at the Fishermen's Ball. The annual event was held at the Harbor Bar, with a big buffet spread on the pool table and live music from Skagway's Reverend Neil Down. The party lasted until the band quit at two A.M.

Kristin Bigsby and Frank White planned to spend the time between last week's gill-net opening and this one planning their August wedding. Instead they were mending Frank's net after a humpback whale swam right through it. "It was brand-new," Kristin said, "which made it even more of a bummer."

Gillnetter Norm Hughes is back from a Hawaiian vacation. He spent some time with other Haines vacationers, the Jacobson family, before visiting his mom, Colleen Hughes, at her home in Maui. Norm says he couldn't sit still on the beach so he took a diving class and is now a certified rescue diver.

Gold Medal Tournament basketball games were broadcast for the first time to Haines on Juneau's KINY radio station. The champion Haines Merchants team includes the Fannon brothers, Jesse McGraw, Danny Pardee, Stuart Dewitt, Chris Dixon, Andrew Friske, Daniel Martin, and David Buss, who all played for the Haines Glacier Bears in the high school state championship game not so long ago. Steve Williams called the games, which were broadcast to Angoon, Kake, and Yakutat as well.

The Sinking of the *Becca Dawn*

My older daughters, Eliza and Sarah, are working as deckhands on a gillnetter, fishing mainly for chum salmon eggs, or roe, which will be sold to a caviar company. The captain is a boy about their age who just graduated from Haines High School. They're learning a lot about fishing, and about life and death.

Gill-net boats, or gillnetters, are usually between thirty and forty feet long and catch salmon in nets two hundred fathoms long and thirty feet deep. A line at the top is threaded with oval corks to keep the net floating. A heavier lead line on the bottom keeps it straight, like an underwater fence. One end is attached to a drifting buoy, the other to a hydraulic reel. Some gill-net fishermen call themselves "fish chokers" because that's how the salmon die. The nets catch them by the gills and they suffocate.

It's seven A.M. on the first day my teenage girls have been home in four days. They arrived unexpectedly in the middle of the night. Their boat's net got tangled in the prop and torn and now needs to be repaired. While the captain and his parents were working on the boat the girls showered, slept a few hours in their own beds, and now have clean laundry tumbling in the dryer. At breakfast, they tell us all about their latest adventure. "It's like everyone is surprised that these blondes can be up to their butts in dead fish, working," Sarah says between bites of toast.

"Don't make eye contact, don't make eye contact," Eliza laughs, demonstrating how they quickly hand over the roe to the buyer's tender, without looking at the flirting crewmen. The girls pitch the salmon carcasses onto a barge that will haul them to a fertilizer plant in Washington.

When our friends asked if Eliza and Sarah could deckhand with their son, I said yes right away. We are Alaskans and live in a fishing town. They should know firsthand what that means. While I won't let the girls stay out all night with boys, when a young man is captain of a fishing boat it's different. He's in charge of $100,000 worth of vessel and permit. He has to make boat payments, buy insurance, and pay license fees—and maybe hopes to earn enough money to pay for college. He can't afford to mess up.

Eliza and Sarah have been to a fisherman's funeral. They understand that working on small boats in the cold ocean is serious stuff. The bloody business of killing fish is hard and dirty work, and there's not much room on the thirty-six-foot boat for privacy. Fishing around the clock leaves little time for sleeping or eating, and there's no shower. But, incredibly, they like it. Eliza pours tea and steadies herself against the stove. "Is it just me, or is the kitchen rocking?" Sarah reaches for the jam and shows us the new gash on her chin. It's from the gut-scooping spoon at the other end of her fillet knife.

Fishing is mostly about work, but there is some time to play. One evening, Sarah says, their boat tied up with some friends from town. They cooked spaghetti, walked on the beach, and played games that included hanging from the bow and seeing who could do the most one-armed pull-ups before falling in the freezing water. "But the most fun," she adds, "was firing the AK-47."

What was I thinking when I said they could fish? How much do

I really want them to know about life and death? "Relax, Mom," Sarah says, "we were just shooting a rubber glove, not *at* anyone."

I wish I knew the fisherman's prayer. All I can think of is part of the line on the memorial I've seen at the boat harbor: "They that go down to the sea in ships . . ." I have a feeling the rest of the verse is not very positive. Instead, I silently ask God to watch over my girls, if he gets a break from world peace and AIDS in Africa. It's a sparkling summer morning, which may be why the memory of a much more urgent prayer hits me like a bad wave and I have to leave the kitchen.

When the telephone rang at four on that November morning, I ran downstairs to get it, but the answering machine had already begun. I heard my friend Kathy say, "Heather, if you can hear me, pray." She said that the *Becca Dawn,* the Nash family fishing boat, was sinking—with three brothers and a friend on board. I didn't pick up the phone. I sat down on the bottom step and prayed that this was a false alarm. Then, just in case, I asked God to drop everything else and hold those boys in the palm of his hands. It was an outside shot, but I had seen enough three-pointers made by the crew of the *Becca Dawn* at the buzzer in high school and city-league basketball games to know that their odds of making it were better than you'd think.

Their parents, Becky and Don, are our son's godparents. Don is a fisherman and a carpenter. Becky is a quilter and teaches Sunday school at the Presbyterian church. There are six Nash children all together—Lee, Aaron, and Olen are biological and Yongee, Song, and Corrie were adopted from Korea. Becky refers to them as a six-pack of "half domestics and half imports." The Nash kids were raised on boats. Just out of high school, Lee and Olen both skippered their own trollers, which are bigger boats than gillnetters and use tall poles that drop out over the water trailing lines of hooks, with their brothers Song and Aaron as regular crew.

I woke up Chip, who headed straight for the Nashes' house with our neighbor Steve. Then I called Kathy back to learn what had happened.

As their boat foundered in fifty-foot seas, Lee, Song, and Olen Nash and their friend Jesse McGraw scrambled into neoprene survival suits, sent Maydays, and switched on the emergency locator beacon. They were thirty-five miles offshore with more than twenty thousand pounds of halibut on board. They were young, twenty to twenty-five, and, except for Jesse, experienced fisherman. They all knew enough about the sea to believe that without the life raft they'd never make it until daylight. It was unlikely anyone would be out looking for them in the storm. That's when a wave hit the bait shed that carried the life-raft canister and it broke up, blowing the raft off the stern.

Olen signaled over the din that he'd swim for the raft. He had been at the helm when the *Becca Dawn* had heaved over, and he may have felt responsible. He was the youngest, but the best swimmer. A lifeguard at the Haines pool, he liked to surf in the frigid waves on this same empty coast. He tied a line around his waist and secured the other end, so he wouldn't be swept away.

After Olen dove in everything went bad fast. The wheelhouse windows blew in, and the fifty-four-foot steel-hulled *Becca Dawn*, named for his mother and father (Becky and Don), sank bow first. Song yelled last Maydays into the radio. Lee couldn't find Olen's life rope, so he frantically cut every line in the tangle made by miles of halibut-fishing gear. About sixty coils one hundred fathoms long with big hooks every eighteen to twenty feet broke loose in the green water on the back deck. Lee had put his survival suit on over wet clothes, and the hooks punctured the foam rubber legs and feet. His numb fingers dropped the knife. Quickly, Jesse found another knife, and just as Lee thought they had Olen's line and were ready to cut it, the blade dropped and the *Becca Dawn* went down underneath them, sinking in the darkness with a weird glow. The lights were still on.

Olen was nowhere in sight.

Jesse, maybe because he didn't know better, was sure they'd be rescued. The big red-haired kid, who'd starred on Haines High regional championship teams and later on our town's Gold Medal championship basketball team, held on to the remaining Nash brothers as huge waves slammed them together and pulled them apart. He found a piece of plywood from the wreck and pushed Lee on top of it. While it wasn't enough to keep him completely out of the water, it did at least allow him to rest a little. Song, whose suit was too big, was puking seawater and struggling to keep his head above water.

The Coast Guard did hear the emergency beacon, and called Don Nash at his home in Haines to make sure it wasn't a false alarm. Don called Kathy's husband, Dr. Stan Jones, and Kathy called everyone else she thought should know. Bad news travels fast.

The Coast Guard sent a helicopter into the night, toward the emergency signal. Nearly three hours later, it found three of the boys tossing in the debris from the wreck. Jesse had managed to flip the switch of the strobe light on his survival suit with his teeth, never letting go of his friends. He had one in each arm. Lee was so tired and felt such relief he almost passed out. Jesse had to keep him from collapsing into the waves. Song saw the helicopter, but he had no idea how they would get into it. What they didn't know then was that the seas were too high, the winds too strong, and the conditions too deadly to send a rescue swimmer in to help them.

The Coast Guard practices these kinds of missions on calm days in tight-fitting wetsuits. The metal basket is lowered right to the role-playing "victims" who have tried this on land first. They climb easily into the metal basket bobbing on floats and sit with their knees against their chests for the quick ride up. In training, it takes minutes. In real life, it can take hours. In a recent rescue in the Gulf of Alaska, two helicopters ran out of fuel trying to pull up a boatload of drowning fishermen. A third helicopter finally saved what remained of the crew.

Song, Lee, and Jesse were cold, exhausted, and numb with shock, and they'd never tried this before. The wind screamed, spray stung their eyes, and the waves were taller than their three-story house. The Coast Guard crew had taped some glow sticks to the supports and the cable holding the basket, so it would be visible in the darkness. Later, Song said they should have had one of those lighted signs, like in an airport or on a big scoreboard, telling them what to do.

Song went first, diving for the basket, which was sliding sideways down a wave like a runaway toboggan on a snowy hill. He grabbed it but was flung back into the sea as it whipped up. It was lowered again, and this time Song held on tight and pulled himself in, because his life depended on it. After watching Song struggle, Jesse knew Lee didn't have the strength left to make it to the helicopter on his own. So he swam to the basket with Lee, heaved him in and jumped on top, crossways, to keep him there. They spun up to safety together. The Coast Guard rescue team continued to look for Olen until their fuel ran low, then took the boys to the clinic in Yakutat.

We didn't know all that when Kathy urged me over the phone, "Pray hard." I did, and then went in the kitchen to make cinnamon rolls to bring over to the Nashes. It was mostly men during the predawn hours because Becky was in Sweden, Olen's older sister, Yongee, was in Anchorage, and his little sister, Corrie, was on an exchange program in Australia. A fourth brother, Aaron, had stayed behind at the last minute with Olen's girlfriend, at the

Nashes' sportfishing lodge in Elfin Cove, where the *Becca Dawn* was based. It's hard to imagine a man with a wife and six children facing this without any immediate family near, but that's how it was. Women bearing casseroles and cookies would come later. Before Becky returned, they would clean the house and stock her cupboards.

The Nash home is rarely empty, and this night was no exception. Don's two hunting dogs slept on the couch, a cousin was staying in one of the upstairs bedrooms, and so was Jay, a guy who had hitched a ride with Don to the mainland from Elfin Cove. No one knew his last name or how long he planned to be there—but he was helpful, silently doing the dishes and taking out the trash as a steady stream of friends gathered around the woodstove in the kitchen.

Dwight, a friend of Don's who spends the better part of the year out on his own boat, the sister ship to the *Becca Dawn*, fishing with his wife and two young sons, pinned a map to the wall and traced the trail of the emergency position-indicating radio beacon (EPIRB). When activated, the floating emergency beacon sends a radio signal up to a satellite and relays its coordinates to the Coast Guard. This was how they knew the *Becca Dawn* was in trouble, how they found the crew, and how they hoped to find Olen. The Coast Guard figured the boat would drift in the same direction that a survivor or lifeboat would. Dwight didn't say much. Like everyone in the room, he hoped for a miracle. The Coast Guard searched the fishing grounds for two days, covering a thousand square miles, before they declared Olen lost at sea.

The next Sunday the bell in front of the Presbyterian church tolled twenty times, once for each year of Olen's life. Inside, slides projected on the wall showed baby Olen in his father's arms, Olen as a toddler on the boardwalk, and then all grown up—a handsome young man smiling in the rain, holding a tub of freshly filleted halibut. We all saw Olen snowboarding in the mountains above town, and holding a wounded kestrel falcon he'd rescued and fed with ducks he shot down by the river. The last slide, of the *Becca Dawn* trolling poles out in front of the setting sun, broke any hearts that weren't already cracked. Sure, everyone knows fishing is dangerous, and the perils of the Alaskan seas enormous, but a brave young fisherman is still a fine thing, a son any mother would be proud of.

After the church service, we walked through fresh snow to the fishermen's memorial, overlooking the boat harbor. Dr. Jones read a letter from the governor expressing his sympathy and praising Olen's courage. As he spoke, a crabber pulled into the harbor, gulls calling and diving in its wake. One of the wilder Nash cousins from Juneau walked out on the rocks. He turned his back on us and faced the sea, hitting a skin drum with his hand, in the same rhythm as heartbeats. It was too windy to light the candles Becky wanted us to hold, but we sang the Navy Hymn, a little wobbly at first, but clear and strong by the final verse:

> *Our brethen shield in danger's hour;*
> *From rock and tempest, fire and foe,*
> *Protect them wheresoe'er they go;*
> *Thus evermore shall rise to Thee,*
> *Glad hymns of praise from land and sea.*

Afterward the Alaska Native Brotherhood Hall was packed for a community potluck. The food was like that at a wedding: the best fishermen could offer, crab and shrimp. Becky thanked everyone for coming and invited us up to the microphone to share memories of the youngest and quietest of her sons. As did many people, I looked away. It was just too hard.

But Becky wouldn't give up. She asked us to please celebrate Olen's life, not mourn his death. "Olen died in a minute," she said, "but he lived for twenty years." Kathy made the first move. She marched up next to Becky and told us how Olen used to rearrange her Christmas decorations. It took her two tries to finish her story, to tell us how she has blocks that spell NOEL and Becky's son always made them spell OLEN.

A neighbor talked about the time Olen jumped off the house with homemade wings. When he didn't fly, he and his brothers went to the cruise-ship dock, which at low tide stands some forty feet tall, and he flapped off the end. He landed in the water, but he always insisted that he could have flown, if the dock were just a little higher.

After the funeral, after Olen's room was cleaned, after his graduation picture was framed and put on the wall in the kitchen, Becky found solace in her quilting studio above Don's wood shop, patching colorful fabric together into a wall hanging. She worked by eye, sorting colors and snipping shapes. She didn't let anyone see what she was working on for a long time. The finished quilt is wall-hanging size. The sea is all rough—blue and green triangles pieced together like in a crazy quilt. The *Becca Dawn,* its familiar shape and colors, lies askew in the fabric waves, with a heart tethered to it. Then up in the stormy sky on one side of the quilt are a Coast Guard helicopter and three orange survival-suited figures being hauled on board. In the other half of the sky, the same size as the helicopter, are a couple of angels, serene and white, holding another survival-suited figure. In Becky's telling of this story, all the boys were rescued, three by the Coast Guard, one by the angels.

NOW, STANDING ON the porch, I watch my own littlest angel, my son, Christian, casting his lure out into the water, and I listen to the laughter of my brand-new fisherman daughters in the kitchen. Salmon swim up this river every year to make more salmon and then die. Right now I want to stop time, to keep my son small and my daughters safe. I want to change the inevitable end to all of our stories. I want to go down to the shore and yell at those stupid fish, swimming so strongly to their deaths: "Turn around, don't do this—you'll all be rotting on the beach in a week." But I don't, because it wouldn't make any difference and because then there wouldn't be any more salmon, or any more fisherman, or any more angels watching over them.

Instead, after breakfast I'll help the girls take their fishy rain gear off the clothesline and throw it in the back of their captain's truck. Then they'll head out to the harbor again and to the boat that will take them out to sea. I'll tell them, and especially their skipper, to take good care of each other, and above all be safe. The girls will roll their eyes; after half a season deckhanding they're now old pros. But the young captain will look at me with all the gravity of a boy who is doing man's work and promise to take good care of my daughters and bring them home safely. Then he'll crack his boy-ish smile and say, "With any luck we'll all get rich." And I'll know by looking at him that he isn't afraid of the water at all.

Later, I'll look up the rest of the line from the fishermen's me-morial—the one about going down to the sea in ships. The whole verse is part of Psalm 107: "They that go down to the sea in ships, that do business in great waters, these see the works of the Lord, and His wonders in the deep."

DULY NOTED

Frank and Karen Wallace are back for the summer. Frank is working at John Schnabel's Porcupine gold mine. Karen is waiting tables at the Lighthouse Restaurant. This will be the seventh summer that the former mayor and his wife have returned to their hometown from their retirement home in Arizona. "The Alaska Highway gets better every year," Karen said.

More than one hundred people turned out for a taste of the Chilkat Valley's top potato salads and coleslaws in an Independence Day contest sponsored by the Elks Lodge. Marge Conzatti whipped up the winning coleslaw entry and Barbara Woods made the top potato salad. Each won a gift certificate for a steak dinner for two at the lodge.

Erwin Hertz and daughter Mary Hertz-Ake of Bend, Oregon, participated in the twelfth annual Gold Rush Days in Juneau last weekend. Mary took first place in the spike-pounding and hand-mucking competitions in the mining division and was named best all-around female miner. In the logging competition she took first in choker setting, log rolling, and hand bucking, second place in speed climbing, and was named "Babe of the Woods." Erwin competed in the spike-driving, hand-mucking, ax-throwing, and hand-bucking competitions.

Gretchen Folk finally went over the top this month, conquering Mount Ripinsky from the seven-mile saddle to elevation 3,920 across the north and south peaks of the mountain before descending into town. Gretchen trained for the arduous trek by hiking on Mount Riley daily.

Domestic Goddesses

I AM NOT SURE my friend Gail and I would have gotten to know each other if we hadn't lived on the same road and if I wasn't in a new place, with a new baby. It was our first summer in Haines. Chip and I had rented an apartment up at Fort Seward from Ted and Mimi Gregg. Their daughter-in-law Gail lived two doors down and had a baby boy the same age as my first child, Eliza. We were both a little lonely. While the two babies played, we got to know each other. Gail's house was full of paintings in progress, wood carvings, and costumes. Her husband was an artist, and she was a seamstress. Both were active in Lynn Canal Community Players and starred in that summer's melodrama about the Gold Rush, *Lust for Dust*, two nights a week at the Chilkat Center for the Arts. Gail played a Klondike-era madam named Lotta LaRue, as she was "a lotta" woman. The script was full of puns.

Gail met all the cruise ships dressed in Lotta's revealing cancan girl costume. She'd sewed her outfit from brown velvet, satin, and lace. She wore black fishnet stockings with spike heels. Her long black hair was wound up on top of her head, and her ample cleavage dusted with glittery powder. We made a funny pair—I am tall and a little stiff. My hair is short, and the only time I have had any cleavage at all was when I was pregnant or nursing babies.

Gail baked cheesecakes, fed dozens of people on her wide front porch, and taught me how to smoke the salmon Chip caught. We brined it overnight in Gail's downstairs bathtub, mixing water with brown sugar and salt until a raw egg floated, then slid in whole slabs of fish. In the morning, we pulled aside the wild-jungle-motif shower curtain, drained the tub, and Gail showered the slime off the fillets before laying them out to dry all over her big old house. We covered every flat surface with fish; some were draped on newspaper across the back of the couch. Gail hooked up electric fans to make the fillets dry quicker. She listened to George Strait and Randy Travis sing country-and-western tunes on the radio while the salmon smoked on her front porch in a row of Little Chief tin smokers borrowed from her neighboring relatives. We took turns dumping store-bought hickory chips into the hot plates in the bottom. When it was done Gail gave half of it away, served more to partying friends, and we froze the rest.

One night, a few summers later, Gail left Haines. She put her sewing machine in her Suburban and drove across the border into Canada with the new program director from the radio station, leaving her husband, two young sons, in-laws, a one-eyed cat named Precious, and big windows full of thriving houseplants. It could have been a country song. It was months before she called to say she was okay and living in Portland. She's still there. I had no idea she was so unhappy. I guess I just wasn't looking for signs of trouble. I know I wasn't the friend I should have been.

I STILL SPEND summer days and nights smoking fish, but with another friend now, in a much different setting. My neighbor Linnus and I share a smokehouse in my backyard that Linnus mostly built while I watched. She didn't need my help, but I like being with her, and figured I would provide moral support. Also, since Linnus never cooks, I fed her. Linnus and I usually brine our salmon together. In my kitchen, we cut the fillets in pint- and half-pint-jar-sized chunks and soak all of it in a mixture of water, kosher noniodized salt, and brown sugar in clean plastic pails. I like to doctor it up some, adding white wine and spices, but Linnus is a traditionalist. She isn't sure that adding anything extra is a good idea. We mix up a couple of different brines. Neither of us likes it too salty, so we don't let it soak more than a few hours. If the weather is cool and breezy, the salmon dries in the smokehouse, covered in cheesecloth until there's a shiny skin. It may take an afternoon or overnight. On hot days, we make room in our refrigerators.

Once the smoking begins, Linnus and I tend the fire almost every hour. We peel and saw up green alder branches for fuel. (The bark makes the smoke, and thus the fish, bitter.) We hang out around the smokehouse, sitting on upside-down five-gallon pails, talking about our husbands and children. Her younger daughter is in the Peace Corps in Mauritania. I know she worries about her, but usually she doesn't mention it. Now, because we have time, and because no one else is around, she does. "The life expectancy there is thirty-nine," she says. I'm forty; Linnus is ten years older. She is small and strong and moves like a boy. "Can you imagine?" she says. "We'd either be dead or very old there."

Linnus is a third-generation Alaskan, and she knows how to smoke fish. Our little operation is a model of efficiency and, because Linnus is an art teacher, aesthetically pleasing. The smokehouse sits next to the shore on the edge of a meadow of wild roses, fireweed, and bluebells. There's a board table on a stump, with a pail hanging underneath it that keeps our tools and matches dry. Light cedar-and-chicken-wire racks rest on finish nails so we can move them easily. In the base of the smokehouse, which is tall and thin, with a plank door and shed roof, there's a concrete slab with shells in it. I made it with the children, using a cardboard box as a mold. On top of that is a legless round barbecue grill Linnus found at a garage sale. The lid keeps the flames from burning down the smokehouse and lets enough air reach the coals to keep them smoking. A carved salmon above the door was made by Gail's artist husband—the one she eventually left. Gail gave it to me on my first Christmas in Haines.

A WHILE BACK, I hosted a dinner for a group of benefactors of our new library. We didn't know they were coming to Haines until a friend traveling with them called her friend here on a cell phone from the corporate jet they were on, just before we heard it fly over. Chip had been fishing, so we had plenty of sockeye. He uses a skiff with an outboard and a net about seventy-five feet long and four fathoms deep. Individual families are permitted to catch salmon this way, for personal use but not for sale. When you hear about "subsistence" issues in Alaska, this activity is part of what it means—our net is called a subsistence net. The greenhouse was full of tomatoes, and the brewery had fresh beer. I called a friend, who promised to make pies for dessert. Another said she could bake the bread. There were about thirty of us, so we ate with plates on our laps. One man didn't drink beer. He asked if I had any gin. I didn't but Linnus did, so we walked over to her house and she poured him a glass. When he indicated for her to fill it up, she suggested some ice, tonic, and lime. "No thanks," he said. "Gin will be fine." Linnus raised her eyebrows and I shrugged and we went back to the party.

Chip cooked the fish outside, but the rain kept the company indoors. One of the guests was the head of a large Native corporation in Anchorage. His was the only name I had recognized in the group. When he complimented me on the smoked salmon he was eating and asked where I'd gotten it, I told him I'd made it, and he asked to see my smokehouse. He stood in the rain and looked at it wistfully. He must be a millionaire now, and he has a fancy home that has been featured in several Alaska house publications, all logs and glass, overlooking Anchorage. He said he missed smoking fish the way he had done when he was a boy living in a rural village.

Village smokehouses are usually big enough to stand in and have barrel stoves on the outside that hold large pieces of alder or cottonwood. The pipe sends the smoke inside all day and night. Once the stove is going, it hardly needs tending. The larger operation still takes as long, but it smokes more fish with less work. I don't want a bigger smokehouse. Then I might not hear Linnus talk about Mauritania — they still have slaves there, she says, and it's 120 degrees. I tell Linnus about an obituary I just finished. The man had cancer and was in a lot of pain. His wife ended up telling me that she had let her nephew make her husband more comfortable with pot. They are a well-known Haines family, so she shared this with a stern "this is not for publication" warning. I get that a lot. At least half of what I learn writing an obituary is never published. I haven't told anyone this particular revelation, but I know Linnus will keep my confidence. The woman said her nephew made a bong-style pot pipe to blow the smoke into his uncle's lungs. "Did it work?" Linnus asks.

"Yeah," I say, "it did." It eased his pain and helped his appetite. We agree to remember about the pot if we ever get that sick.

Linnus and I smoke this batch of salmon for a day and a half before preserving it. We don't get the sterilized jars in the canners until after ten. We're tired and smell like wood smoke and fish. Everyone else has gone to bed. Instead of talking, we sit on the couch in companionable silence, drinking cold beer and half-watching a video — *Good Will Hunting* — that makes us both laugh and cry, while checking on the three pressure cookers hissing gently on the stove.

It was after one by the time we had the jars cooling on dish towels on the counter. The midsummer sky was already starting to lighten again when Linnus left to get some sleep. I stood and stared at those perfect pints, all shiny glass, brass-colored tops, and deep-orange fish, amazed and thrilled that I could make anything this good. I tapped the lids to know they were sealed properly and felt like a pioneer, a good mother and provident wife. Every single time I smoke salmon I feel the same way—as if it's some kind of a miracle.

When Linnus, who was born to all this, not a convert like me, notices my fish-filled jars lined up proudly on an open shelf rather than tucked inside a dark cupboard, she shakes her head. This is all as easy for her as walking. For me, it is like learning to speak a foreign language.

Next to my salmon are jars of jam, made from berries I picked with friends. In the fall, when our summer chores are done and when Linnus goes back to teaching art and the kids are all in school, I get a feeling that is the same as being homesick. My mother was a teacher, and I think she hoped I would be a professional woman of some kind. Instead, I got married, drove to Alaska, and had a big family, which I take care of. I can salmon, make jam, bake bread, and raise hens. I am able to prepare dinner for thirty in a hurry and serve it in a way that makes it look like no trouble at all. While my mother had her morning coffee in the faculty room, I have mine with friends at Mountain Market. She spent the first day of school selecting textbooks. This year I spent the first day of school picking blueberries.

Our aim was to gather berries for pies, jam, syrup, smoothies, pancakes, scones, muffins, and special cheesecake toppings. It takes an hour to drive out the winding logging roads up into the old clear-cuts on Sunshine Mountain. The berry patch looks a little like the one in the children's book *Blueberries for Sal*—all open, with stumps and bushes—except for the background. The panoramic view is full of snowcapped mountains and deep river valleys.

The distant slopes are all green, brown, and white. There are no people, houses, or even cars as far as you can see or hear. We have gallon pails on strings around our necks or on belts attached to our waists, so that we can pick with both hands.

To let the bears know we're here, too, one of the gals sets a boom box blaring show tunes high on a central stump. It is something my old friend Gail would have done. (Linnus picks berries with sleigh bells jingling from her belt.)

None of us can see the others over the brush, but we talk, loudly. "I've hit the mother lode," a voice yells over the peals of a love song from *Phantom of the Opera*.

"They're like clusters of grapes over here," hollers another.

"I'm pulling them down by the handful," someone else shouts.

We chatter on, in blueberry heaven, debating the merits of baking a pie today or freezing them to use in muffins—it takes six cups to make a blueberry pie; the same amount of berries will generously flavor ten dozen muffins. We also talk about books, movies, school, the weather—nothing and everything. We are speaking a kind of code. I say: I am glad the rain has stopped, that berries are so abundant, and I wish we didn't have to get back by three. I mean: I am so happy to be here, it is wonderful to have such friends, and I am not homesick anymore. I think about all of this, and I don't feel bad about not having a career or a real job. If I did, I wouldn't be here, and I wouldn't have had time to learn how to do all of these domestic things.

I like the idea of being self-sufficient, knowing that if I had to I could feed my family on what I grow, pick, and catch. We could heat the house with wood and get a hand pump for the well. Granted, we'd be leaner, and probably sick of fish. I'd have to work a lot harder at subsisting, but we wouldn't starve and we wouldn't freeze. We'd also have plenty to read when the power went out: I have all the Harvard Classics, a 1957 *Encyclopaedia Britannica*, atlases, dictionaries, poems, novels, biographies, art books, *The Ann Landers Encyclopedia A to Z,* and even old textbooks—just in case the world as we know it ends. Since September 11, that hasn't seemed as far-fetched as it used to. That day all planes were grounded, no ferries ran, and the border was closed. Haines was completely cut off from any other town or city.

I had stopped picking to stretch my back just as blue sky appeared above the fast-moving clouds. One of my companions yelled, "Get the camera, quick—I'm taking off my clothes while the sun is out." Everyone stopped picking and moved toward her voice. When we got there, we saw our friend wearing sexy blue underwear. She had arranged for another one of the ladies to take a picture of her in the lingerie while she picked matching blueberries as a present for her husband on their wedding anniversary. She made us swear not to tell anyone—"What happens on Sunshine Mountain stays on Sunshine Mountain"—then stomped up into a bright clump of heavily berried bushes, wearing nothing but bra, panties, and brown rubber boots. I hadn't seen so much of anyone in public like that since Gail left. On hot summer days, she used to wear a red bikini and sunglasses when she walked down the street to see me, a cool vodka tonic in her hand. Like Gail, my friend was a "lotta" woman.

The rest of us were so suddenly happy—from all the berries, our friend's unexpected boldness, and her generosity in sharing it with us—that everyone smiled big, goofy grins. The Andrew Lloyd Webber tape ended. The photographer, a Brownie troop leader acting just like Annie Leibovitz on a shoot for *Vanity Fair,* shouted, "Music, music, my model needs music!" Someone flipped the cassette. Our friend asked if she looked okay. "Am I too fat?" she said. We assured her that she looked better than okay. She was beautiful.

And then it was time to go home. None of us wanted to be late to pick up our kids on the first day of school. On the way down the hill we talked about what we had written on the school registration forms in the space labeled "mother's occupation." A couple of us had left it blank, one had put "homemaker," and another had written "housewife."

"I didn't like those options," the Brownie leader–turned–fashion photographer declared. "I wrote 'domestic goddess.'"

I still can't sew, and my girls bake better cookies than I do, but if I look back over my life since I left my parents' house all those years ago, it would not be incorrect to say that my primary job has been homemaker. It would also not be incorrect to say that I have taught myself, with the help of friends, to be a pretty good one. In a few months, on a dark Sunday afternoon, I'll open a jar of salmon, get out the cream cheese, jam, and bread, and bring everything into the living room for the family to share by the fire. It might look like an ordinary snack, but I know that the salmon and jam are preserved with more than smoke and boiling water. They are products of the love and skill of generations of women. As my thickest dictionary, the unabridged edition of *The Random House Dictionary of the English Language,* makes clear, *subsistence,* "the source from which food and other items necessary to exist are obtained," is also "the quality of having timeless or abstract existence." My friend was right. There is more than just a bit of the divine in food gathering and preparation. We are all domestic goddesses.

DULY NOTED

Joe Parnell is inviting friends to his college graduation party. Joe, who is graduating with a degree in general studies from the University of Alaska Southeast next month, said the May 5 bash will feature music by his rock band, Animal Rights; a performance of an original play, *Don't Bite the Man Who Feeds You,* by Joe's theatrical group, Querulous Theater; and a French-kissing booth. "I'm going to read some of my senior papers too," Joe said.

Presbyterian Pastor Pat Jeffrey had some explaining to do on Sunday morning when he stood in the pulpit with a black eye. The pastor, who plays for the Alaska Native Brotherhood team, said tournament play is intense. "It got a little rough under the basket Saturday night."

Ed Hays said the small house he built at Paradise Cove twenty years ago just isn't big enough anymore. So the former teacher is expanding to accommodate his wife, Yuko, and sons, Kai, four, and Mori, three. Ed, who taught woodshop at Haines High for many years, is back here after teaching English for ten years in Japan.

John Schnabel said he'll make it to his eightieth-birthday bash, scheduled for Friday at the Haines Elks Lodge, even if he has to go in a wheelchair. John is recovering from bumps, bruises, and broken bones suffered in a thirteen-foot fall off the roof of his Porcupine lodge Tuesday afternoon. John, who still actively mines his Porcupine gold claims, was shoveling snow off the roof of the log building when he slipped over the peak. He hooked his heels over the ridge cap and hung there for a while before letting go and sliding off the eave. "It's a long way down," John said. "You've got time to think about a lot of things."

Who You Callin' Crazy?

TOM EDITED MY first obituary for the *Chilkat Valley News*, and ever since then he's been the little voice on my shoulder saying, "Wait a minute, is that the whole story?" He also still poses the question in person, too, sometimes so loudly that we argue. Tom believes what they told him in journalism school—that all good reporters comfort the afflicted and afflict the comforted. I'm not sure this is the best approach when it comes to obituaries. And I tell him so. Often. We're still great friends. For my fortieth birthday, the newspaper staff gave me a T-shirt with TO HELL WITH YOU, TOM printed on it.

Tom grew up in Philadelphia, was educated in Catholic schools, and still wears his old Marquette sweatshirt. He worked in Anchorage at a big paper before coming to Haines and has edited the *Chilkat Valley News* on and off for fifteen years. Every few years he quits, determined to get either more of a real job or less of a real job. Lately Tom has been working for the United Fisherman of Alaska in Juneau as an information specialist. He researches fisheries issues and writes reports. (My neighbor Steve, the paper's other reporter, is serving as editor these days.) For now, Tom and his wife, Jane, live in Juneau, although they haven't fully moved there. Tom sees the out-of-town job as a way to pay for the improvements on his true home, the place at Rutzebeck Lake here in Haines that he calls Camp Weasel.

Tom built the cabin himself, more or less. He's not very handy. We learned that he couldn't run an outboard motor when we were fishing and asked him to drive while we fed the net into the water. *How,* we all asked, *can you live here and not know how to drive a skiff?* It seemed impossible. Tom has been building his dream home for a long time. Last year's Christmas-card photograph was pretty much the same as this year's: About half the siding is on. It's a ten-by-twelve-foot shed-roofed cabin with a loft and big windows in the woods off the same old logging road as our own weekend cabin. The last e-mail Tom sent from Juneau ended with "By the way, how's the Rutzebeck road?" What he wanted to know was whether he and Jane would need mud boots or snowshoes to get home next time they're here.

Tom's cabin is not a miniature log showplace. It's your basic plywood, shingle, and blue-tarp shack. I mean that in the best sense of the word. Like our cabin, there's no phone, water, or electricity. Tom doesn't have an outhouse, but there is a woodland privy area that's clean and secluded, and he has plans for a Japanese-style waste-composting system. Tom also built a substantial picnic table for guests.

He's no Henry David Thoreau, but sometimes I think the life Tom imagines at Camp Weasel is pretty close to the philosophy of living deliberately espoused by the reclusive New Englander. Thoreau's book about his own simple shack, *Walden, or Life in the Woods,* has never been out of print since it was first published in 1854. Tom isn't the only one, it seems, who likes the idea of a cabin in the woods.

Remember the Unabomber? Tom's cabin was winterized about the same time Theodore Kaczynski's attorney put the Montana cabin on a flatbed and drove it to California in an attempt to get

Kaczynski declared legally insane. They argued that anyone who lived in a place like that for twenty-five years must be nuts. The cabin looked all right to me. Moreover, as Tom pointed out with genuine admiration, it didn't fall apart when they picked it up and put it on the truck.

We moved Tom's cabin, too. Because he started it in the winter, when there's no direct sun on the hillside, he faced his window in the wrong direction. When summer came, he realized that he was still looking out into the shade. One morning a bunch of us jacked it up off its pilings and spun it around to catch the light.

Alaska probably has more cabin dwellers per capita than any other state. So when I read about Kaczynski's neighbor telling a *Washington Post* reporter that "he let things go" in the yard, it was easy to imagine the general disarray—the unstacked firewood ready for splitting, the crates of cans and bottles intended for re-cycling, the empty fuel drums, the old truck, the spare for parts. It's not Currier and Ives, but it is a familiar sight in rural Alaska. A cabin is also the first home for many of us, and for some the last. Now people Outside were suggesting that anyone who lives like that must be crazy.

Well, some of the craziest people I ever met weren't cabin dwellers at all, but lived in Alaska's biggest city. When Chip and I first came to Alaska we drove to Anchorage and, mainly because of a sled dog puppy acquired on the way, we couldn't find a place to live. We ended up sharing a split-level tract house in Anchorage with about eight other people.

Patty and Mark had left jobs in Florida for Alaska when they'd heard you could get $1,000 just for living here. Money from the state's oil revenues goes into a permanent fund that pays share-holders—every Alaskan man, woman, and child—an annual div-idend. That first year the checks were worth $1,000. They have been as high as $1,700.

Armed with a master's degree in forestry from Yale, Chip found work cleaning movie theaters at night (he used a high-pressure hose to blast gunk off the floors) and splitting firewood by the cord during the day. I applied for a receptionist job at a downtown hotel, and after I'd presented my résumé—Quaker prep school and Middlebury College graduate, sailing instructor on Long Island Sound—the woman in charge snapped her gum and said, "But honey, what can you do?" I didn't get the job. Instead, I worked as a waitress in the same place where our new housemate Mark was the bartender. That winter, Chip began working for a small rough-cut sawmill, then met a friend who got him high-paying manual labor in the North Slope oil fields. He helped lay out a ten-acre drilling pad at fifty below in total darkness. In between trips, Chip ran a loader and his friend drove a dump truck as they contracted to remove snow from shopping center parking lots.

Mark and Patty rode their motorcycles from south Florida to Anchorage with a Saint Bernard in a sidecar. Dressed in a snowmobile suit, Mark used the motorcycle to get to work all winter. Our other housemates were just as colorful but not as much fun. Jed drove a Cadillac Eldorado with steer horns on the hood. He wore cowboy boots and slicked back his hair. He worked up on the North Slope, too, at Prudhoe Bay. Whenever he came home, he bought us all New York steaks for dinner. The aging stripper who stayed with Jed every now and then and sometimes lived in his room when he was working had a deaf son who supported them by stealing TVs and stereos. The other housemates, Karen and her two young children, spent a lot of time with her boyfriend, Mickey, at her (our) place, because he had a wife and kids of his own across town.

As soon as we could, we got out of there.

We found a cabin for rent south of the city, overlooking the water and mountains on the other side of Cook Inlet. It was so high on the mountainside that the only trees were scrub spruces that grew like a bonsai forest. The cabin had a woodstove and electricity, but no water. There was a propane toilet in the closet that actually burned human waste. Don't ask. We took showers at a Laundromat in town and filled jugs of water for drinking and dishes at a fire hall on the way home.

We could ski out the back door, and in the spring, we hiked up to Rabbit Lake. We liked that cabin enough that a decade later we built our own in Haines, up at Rutzebeck Lake, about a quarter mile from Tom's place. It took two summers and a pair of hired carpenters plus me to finish off the twenty-four-by-twenty-eight-foot timber-framed cabin. The kids all have bunks in a loft and Chip and I have a small bedroom, and there's another little one for company. Downstairs there's a wood cookstove and a fireplace. We now have a little electricity. Chip attached a generator to an exercise bike that has a battery wired to it so that when you pedal you charge it enough to listen to a small CD player and radio. He also hooked one small reading light to it. Otherwise it's kerosene lamps and propane wall lights. Chip also figured out a way to pump water from the lake to a holding tank in the eaves so that we have gravity-fed running water in the summer. In the winter, we haul it in buckets from the stream.

We have seen bear cubs run down the trail past the woodshed, and moose climb out of the lake and walk by slowly in the woods, their great antlers somehow avoiding all the branches around them. We have whiled away hot summer afternoons drifting in the canoe and skated waving sparklers at midnight on New Year's Eve. We don't live there full-time, but we are crazy enough to want to.

I GUESS THE truth is that there are crazy people in the woods and crazy people in the cities and crazy people in between. Recently I wrote an obituary for Speedy Joe, who did live out in the woods full-time. Joe, who was forty-eight, had apparently been dead for weeks when he was found frozen in his bed. Most likely he'd been on a drinking bender. He lived in a cabin at 38 Mile and worked odd jobs; he was a sometime mechanic and drove a truck. He wore a red union suit all the time, often with nothing else but boots and a wide-brimmed hat. He never took off the hat, not when he slept and not when he got his hair cut. "Uncle Joe was a very unconventional guy," said Kristina, his niece from Anchorage, in what Tom and I agreed was the understatement of the week.

Speedy Joe was born in Washington and came to Haines with his father. He attended grade school here for a few years before moving to Wrangell. Joe returned to Haines in his teens and after his father's death made the upper valley his most permanent home. He was nicknamed Speedy Joe because he never did anything quickly. But his physical pace belied a mental quickness. "He was a good mechanic, and real sharp," said his friend Henry. At the 33 Mile roadhouse, where Joe was an irregular customer, Kathy, the owner, felt bad when she heard the news. "Joe had his problems," she said, "but I always enjoyed talking with him." Speedy Joe came and went, sometimes for years at a time, sometimes visiting his nieces in Anchorage or friends in Juneau. Other times no one is sure where he went. Kristina and her sister, Shaunna, were Joe's only family. Kristina said her uncle was a true hermit who would be out of touch for months at time. Now at least she knows where he is: in heaven, making St. Peter smile just to look at him in that hat and those long johns. "It's like he was born in the wrong century. He just didn't fit in this world, even as bright as he was. We loved him, but I don't think anyone really understood him."

I ALWAYS GET a little kooky myself when the first snow-flakes mix with rain in September. Winter is coming and suddenly this little town seems too small. I want to get out of here, but the firewood hasn't been split or stacked, and the boat is still in the water; I haven't gotten around to covering the garden with seaweed yet. I'm still in bed, stewing about all this, while Chip is singing in the shower across the hall. It's a B. B. King tune. "I gave you seven children . . ." he wails ". . . and now you give them back." Christian knocks on the door telling B. B. King to hurry up. I should have made my own bathroom when we built this house.

Before everyone leaves for school, Eliza, who spent the summer kayaking around Kuiu Island and has just learned she'll be traveling with the Haines High debate team to Hawaii this fall, stands on the porch holding a mug of herb tea with both hands and looking out across the water at the mountains asks, "Why would anyone want to be anywhere else?"

I want to be somewhere else — for just a few days. In fact, if I don't go somewhere else soon, for at least a little while, I'm going to lose what is left of my mind. Once I realized, months ago, that Eliza would be home through the first week in October, when the lumberyard slows down enough for Chip to leave, and that she could watch the other children, I dropped hints about just the two of us taking a trip. In twenty-one years of marriage, Chip and I have spent seven weekends away from the family. Six were to run marathons and one was for his laser eye surgery. When I first suggested that we could leave town without running twenty-six miles or having a medical emergency, Chip looked confused. This had never occurred to him. When I brought it up again, hoping he'd think of Seattle, Chip said we might as well head up to the cabin. Our cabin is eight miles from home. We can run there. But it was still better than nothing. On Tuesday, when I told him that spending the weekend at the cabin would be a fine vacation, he grinned and looked down. "We're leaving town Friday morning and we won't be back until Monday night and I'm not telling you where we're going."

And he didn't tell me we were going to Vancouver, British Columbia, until we were halfway to the airport in Whitehorse. Driving as fast as we wanted through one of the wildest places on earth, where it wouldn't be surprising to see a mastodon or even Mr. Bigfoot himself walk out of one of the glacier valleys, I thought about how this 260-mile trip always makes me feel like Elizabeth Taylor in *Giant*. Especially when I have sunglasses on.

In Vancouver, our room was on the eighteenth floor of a downtown hotel. It was an urban treehouse—two walls were glass, and we looked out on high-rises and rooftops. After the first day, I was convinced that when the kids grow up we should come here for the winter—or longer. In our children's wedding announcements, we would be the "Lendes of Haines, Alaska, and Vancouver, British Columbia." How hip would that be? A lot hipper than we are. The town has running trails, boat harbors, great ethnic food, stores, museums, music, brewpubs, fresh fruit, and a ski area. But the best part of Vancouver was that the streets were full of people we didn't know. We did notice all the homeless people; they seemed more familiar than the well-dressed city folks and tourists. One gray-bearded raving man in a Greenpeace shirt looked just like a certain tireless Haines environmentalist. A saxophone player made us think of our friend Pizza Joe. If he'd been on that corner playing music and giving his passionate speeches about litter and manners, people who didn't know him might have made the same wide arc that we gave the sax player.

On our way to a Thai restaurant, we observed two young Natives—or, since we were in Canada, I should say First Nations men—sitting on the sidewalk carving cedar. Few people stopped to see their work. They had long hair but didn't look much different from Haines's master carver Wayne Price. I thought of the young Native men Wayne had recently taught to carve a traditional Tlingit canoe, and wished these Vancouver guys could meet him.

Not all of the people talking to themselves around us were on cell phones. Some were having imaginary conversations. There's a boy like that in Haines. He sometimes hears things the rest of us don't. Once when I was in the beauty parlor he came in looking for a cigarette. He was frantic, so everyone dropped what they were doing to find him one and then stood outside with him while he smoked it, making sure he was all right. It took so long that my hair, which was supposed to be highlighted just enough to cover the gray, came out blond.

In Vancouver, I started to avoid a man walking toward me talking about Jesus, but then I thought about Raymond and nodded hello. Raymond never has to walk far in Haines. He flags down passing vehicles. The first person who has room for him usually stops. The last time I picked up Raymond, he greeted me by saying thank you in German, Tlingit, Japanese, Hawaiian, Haida, and Spanish. Or so he said. "It's important to say thank you to God for all our blessings," he told me. Despite his crazy ways, Raymond is so popular that he was the grand marshal of the Southeast Alaska State Fair Parade last year. He was driven down Main Street in a classic car, wearing a crown, waving, and tossing candy to the children. In Vancouver, I watched as Raymond's double approached another stranger, who backed away.

Some of the people on the streets of Vancouver were sick, and held cardboard signs asking for money for medicine. Apparently no one knew them well enough to organize a fund-raising auction and dinner, as we would in Haines. Coming out of the Godiva store with a box of chocolate for the children, Chip gave the change to a little old lady using a walker. She looked like Hazel or Louise, the old friends (very old friends—Louise is past ninety and Hazel looks older) who attend every potluck, open house, and community event in Haines. No one minds saving seats for them or helping them to the car.

BACK IN HAINES, on my way to town the morning after our trip, I give Raymond a ride to the grocery store. Before he climbs out he says, "You are a beautiful lady." I blush. "And you have a love-i-lee day, you hear?" he adds. In this pretty little town, full of such good people, how can I help it?

When Tom e-mailed me, asking about the trip, I told him Vancouver is nice, it's a great place to visit, but I'm more at home in a cabin in the woods. I have a feeling that when we are old, Chip and I will indeed be crazy enough to live in ours full-time. When that happens, we will walk by Tom's place every time we go to town, maybe even with a grandchild or two in tow, and I'll tell them how the old editor of the *Chilkat Valley News* is a bit like Thoreau, that he dreamed of a quiet place in the country and he built one. Then we'll probably stop in and help Tom with the shingles, or maybe even a new water system. There's a Buddhist saying that when your house is done your life is over. I hope Tom works on Camp Weasel forever.

DULY NOTED

Offering prayers "for assistance and focusing for the people of Haines," Georgia Haisler and a group of Baha'is and friends gathered in the rain on Election Eve at Lookout Park. Georgia said she is concerned about all the decisions that are being made in the next few weeks—from local and state elections to the vote on unification and the appointment of a new magistrate. "A lot is happening in Haines right now," she said, "and so we prayed for guidance."

Homeschooled Caitlin Stern of Haines is one of four recipients of the Alaska Conservation Foundation's 2001 Wilcher Award. The foundation recognizes students who are "thoughtful, energetic, and educated stewards who have made long-term outstanding contributions to the conservation movement in Alaska." Caitlin, now a Harvard freshman, was honored for her work as a field biologist in the Alaska Chilkat Bald Eagle Preserve here.

The local band the Truffles have made Juneau radio station KINY's top ten this week with their song "Clear as the Light." It is number three on the capital city station's chart, just ahead of a song by Elton John. Haines High senior Lesley Rostron sings, plays the piano, and wrote the words and music. Lesley's father, Mike, said he and guitarist Rich Cooper "Pretty much stand there and play for her on that one."

Jennifer Norton is home after spending eleven months as a meteorologist with the National Weather Service up in Barrow. Although she described her time on the Arctic Ocean shore as a "great experience," she said she's glad to be back where "there's trees and stuff."

Learning Moments

THERE ARE NOW two weekly papers in Haines that just about everybody reads, sometimes twice. The *Chilkat Valley News* has been published since 1966 and is the paper of record. It's where my friends and I work. I'm completely biased, but I think it's a great paper.

The new *Eagle Eye Journal* is a weird, right-wing sort of publication that prints the cable TV guide, Dr. Dobson's "Focus on the Family" column, and redneck jokes off the Internet in "Bubba's Corner." It was started by a developer who thought the *Chilkat Valley News* wasn't pro-business enough. After we reported on a fine he had received for destroying wetlands, he got mad and tried to buy the paper. When our publisher, Bonnie Hedrick, told him it wasn't for sale, he started his own paper, hoping to put her out of business. Recently, a private pilot who was also a reporter for the *Eagle Eye* was killed when his plane disappeared between Haines and Juneau. I had to write his obituary for the *Chilkat Valley News*. Dave McKenzie hadn't been in Haines very long but was well known.

Because of the uneasy relationship between the two papers, his friends were suspicious of the treatment he would receive in my obituary. I think they warned his wife, who had just come up from

California, where she'd been living while he worked here. The day after they called off the search for Dave's plane, I phoned her, explaining that her husband had known many people in Haines and deserved a proper obituary. She reluctantly agreed to meet me at his house, first thing in the morning. I brought over a sack of muffins, freshly ground coffee, and a pint of half-and-half. We drank coffee and visited. A friend of Dave's was there too—no doubt to make sure I was nice. After about half an hour, the friend left and we were alone.

We talked about life and death—in general and this one specifically—in a room full of boxes and empty shelves, while Dave's widow sorted things to throw away, ship down south, or give to the Salvation Army. I helped her pack up Dave's belongings while she wrote down the spelling of their children's names. She lent me a photo of her husband standing in the snow by his plane to print with the obituary. She told me a psychic had called and said her husband was alive. The psychic had wanted a lot of money to help her find out where he was. It made her sad and angry, and she even felt a little guilty for not agreeing to pay. What if the woman really did know where he was?

When we had finished talking and just about everything was packed up except his office area, she asked me if I wanted her husband's books on writing. She said he had admired my stories in the Anchorage paper and *Alaska* magazine and had even mailed some clippings to her. I was surprised. "Please take them," she said, filling a box with books. "He'd want you to have them." Which is why *Arizona Marketplace for Writers and Photographers* and *Writing Crime Fiction* are now on my reference shelf. I see them every time I sit down to write. When I do, I think about the differences between papers and people and what it means to trust each other. One of Dave's books was Annie Dillard's *The Writing Life*. It's hard to believe that someone so conservative could like her writing as much as I do—especially like it enough to carry the book all the way to Alaska. It's small, but even so. In it, she writes, "How we spend our days, of course, is how we spend our lives."

There are some weeks when I spend part of every day in community meetings—for my church, the library, or the school. At one of those meetings—a special meeting in the high school library—Annie Dillard's writing and Dave McKenzie's politics came to mind and I realized how critical it is to teach our children that people think differently, and that there are ways to act on our beliefs without demeaning others who don't believe the same things.

This meeting was called because earlier in the week a list of the twenty "nappiest bitches" in school had appeared on the lunch tables and had been posted on bulletin boards. The girls were labeled *whore, gothic, lesbo,* and *skanky,* among other even less printable names; a freshman was singled out because she's Jewish. Two boys were caught and suspended for ten days. Now concerned parents, community members, and teachers were meeting with the girls to figure out what could be done to make things right. A big girl with strong shoulders sobbed, "Since I came to Haines people told me to get tough. I'm tired of it. I don't want to get any tougher." Another girl, also red-faced from crying, put an arm around her. The adults looked on helplessly as more students explained how it feels to be picked on, every day, at school.

One of the girls said her father raised her to turn the other cheek; she planned to buy the boys a Bible and tell them to read the *list* in there—the Ten Commandments. The Presbyterian pastor's wife nodded her support. So did Howard Hoffman, the minister of the Port Chilkoot Bible Church. But when the girl said she would get her GED rather than return to our school, no one smiled. Mothers looked like they'd been slapped. Fathers, standing in work clothes with their caps still on, gripped the backs of chairs tightly to keep from punching something. The home economics teacher started to cry. One woman said that meanness is not just a school issue, it's a community problem. "Haines isn't a very tolerant place," she declared. That hurt almost as much as the girls' tears.

Before the meeting adjourned, we learned that one of the boys who had written the list was a member of the Haines High varsity basketball team. The team is full of boys from good families, nice kids who make the honor roll and sing in the choir. Their parents acted swiftly to distance the rest of the players from the incident. Another suspension would jeopardize our chances of a berth in the state championship tournament. Reverend Hoffman, whose son is also a starter for the team, said he was concerned for the boys who wrote the list. "Think of them for a minute. They need our help, too. In my experience, people who are unhappy themselves often show it by this type of behavior. Has anyone talked to them?"

That Friday night, fans filled the gym to watch the home game. There were elders in wheelchairs, newborn babies on laps, and the night patrolman in his uniform. The smell of popcorn drifted from the snack bar, and the cheerleaders clapped and kicked. Everything was as it always is on game nights during basketball season. Haines looked for all the world like the quintessential American small town supporting the home team.

Except there was no music. The Pep Band, which includes some of the targeted girls, wasn't in its section of the bleachers. Bob Krebs, the bandleader, kept them out of the gym in silent protest of the week's events. Eliza plays the clarinet. Although her name wasn't on the hateful document, she was proud of her teacher's action. She said other students weren't taking the girls' response to the name-calling seriously enough. Bob told me he hoped that this could be a learning moment for everyone in Haines. In good conscience, he said, he couldn't let it pass.

I thought about all those "learning moments" in my life that I'd passed up. Mainly they were "little things," like ignoring a racist party joke. Some were bigger. Just this fall, during the Southeast Alaska State Fair, a couple of men spoiled the annual parade by heckling people on a float. One of the hecklers threw rotten vegetables. The float, created by environmentalists, parodied the Royal Caribbean cruise ship that had been fined millions of dollars for dumping photography chemicals, dry-cleaning fluid, and other bad sludge in Lynn Canal, between Haines and Skagway, and lying about it. The daughter of one of the organizers was hit in the face with pieces of flying tomatoes.

Although charges were filed against the assailant, who is the owner of a gift shop, dozens of Haines residents, including two school board members, signed letters to the court testifying to the man's good character. They like his wife and children, his in-laws and cousins—and they don't like the environmentalists who made the float. The magistrate, who is new in town, gave the tomato chucker the judicial equivalent of a ten-day suspension from school.

I have learned from trial and error that the secret to long-term survival in Haines is knowing which battles to choose. I thought the parade incident wasn't mine. Our family talked about all of this, loudly, over several dinners. I asked Sarah why she didn't speak up about the meanness at school—there are only about a hundred students in the whole student body and she's on the girls' basketball team, so I figured she had to know more than she was saying about the list's origins. She said, "It's not easy to rat on your friends. You didn't say anything about the tomatoes at the parade."

At the meeting, I had seen the pain in the hearts of both the victims of this latest so-called prank and their parents. The boys suspended from school aren't the only ones responsible for the awful list. It's not the basketball team's fault either. I have a feeling that Haines isn't the only place where every day someone hears a snide comment or sees a flippant gesture. It may even be the thing left unsaid. Most people of goodwill are like me; we don't do anything about it unless it's aimed directly at us or people we love.

I decided to take the music teacher's advice and make this a learning moment. I joined a school committee planning to use the list, and the reaction to it, as an opportunity to teach tolerance. After much discussion, we agreed to bring in some guest speakers and sponsor three days of lectures and workshops called "Reaching for Respect." One of the areas of intolerance we all agreed should be addressed was homophobia, especially the name-calling variety displayed in the halls at Haines High. I volunteered to work on that part of the program.

I knew that Mildred Boesser, the wife of the Episcopal archdeacon of southeast Alaska, Mark Boesser, often spoke on this topic. They have four grown daughters; the oldest describes herself as a lesbian. They're members of a group called Parents and Friends of Lesbians and Gays (PFLAG); they carry the organization's banner in the Juneau Fourth of July parade. The Boessers are well-respected, longtime Alaskans. Mark officiated at the funeral of Alaskan corporate and cultural leader Morris Thompson and his wife and daughter, who were killed in a plane crash. I thought that this kind, elderly, Christian couple would be perfect to broach the subject of tolerance toward gays and lesbians at Haines High. Turns out some people in the community didn't agree.

After reading a *Chilkat Valley News* article (written by my daughter Eliza, who happened to be an intern at the paper at the time) describing the half dozen planned workshops, a couple of school board members and other apparently influential members of Haines's so-called Christian community got very upset about the homophobia workshop. Residents who believe homosexuals are deviant pedophiles and certainly will be going straight to hell dominated the "Letters to the Editor" pages of both the *Chilkat*

Valley News and the *Eagle Eye Journal*. Some people expressed support for the school's handling of the problem. But enough influential people called the superintendent of schools in protest that he canceled the Boessers' presentation without public discussion. The committee was told about it the next afternoon, during our last planning session. Some committee members were angry, some were sad—as I was—but I don't think anyone was completely surprised. We'd all lived in Haines long enough to know how these things happen. This time I decided not to let it go.

I wrote and read a commentary on the radio explaining why I thought the workshop was important. Not for NPR or even Alaska statewide news. It was just for us and was broadcast only on KHNS, the local public radio station. If everyone who gets the signal had their radios on and their family gathered round, three thousand people heard it. I also paid to print my opinion in the *Chilkat Valley News*. I chose this battle, fully expecting the wrath of my neighbors and my children's teachers. Chip supported me, even though we both knew carpenters who might boycott our lumberyard.

But what happened instead was a surprising display of public support for my position. It was as unexpected as discovering that I would have liked Dave McKenzie had we ever talked about writing and our favorite authors. People waved to me from pickup trucks while I was running. One guy yelled, "Right on" out his window. I received over a hundred positive phone calls and a handful of letters from out-of-town newspaper subscribers. One elderly couple actually bought something from Chip because of what I said; turns out they have a gay son. It was unbelievable. I had only one negative reaction—an anonymous hate letter, from someone who was smart, articulate, and knew my family very well. It gave me the creeps. Chip said to ignore it—if they didn't have the guts to sign it, they weren't worth my time. I wish I could. Instead, Steve taped it to the wall at the newspaper office, where it remains to this day. Once every couple of weeks I read it, and spend an afternoon looking at my friends more closely. I know it's silly, but I can't help wondering where it came from.

I hoped that all the support, coupled with my public arguments for the workshop, tempered by reason and love, and backed by the Constitution of the United States and even the Pledge of Allegiance ("with liberty and justice for all"), would change the opposition's minds. I had visions of the superintendent himself sitting bolt upright in bed, thumping his hand to his forehead, and waking up his wife with a shout: "Heather's right! I'll put that gay workshop back!" But that didn't happen.

So there I was, defeated, perhaps knocked down a rung or two on the Haines social and political ladder, but back in the school library for the monthly meeting of the Parent Advisory Team. A different parent group. I was not saving the world this time, just going over the student handbook with other parents, page by page. I was asked to report on the thoroughly uncontroversial section devoted to school buses. There are two.

At the end of the meeting one of the parents said she really thought we should weigh in on the current controversy surrounding the homophobia workshop. Everyone either looked at me or pretended not to. "You all know how *I* feel," I said, and they laughed, a little. Then Kathy said, "Homosexuality is a sin. Some studies say it is biological, but just as many say it's a choice." She's the same Kathy whose son is the captain of the gillnetter on which my daughters crewed. The Kathy who called me in the middle of the night when the *Becca Dawn* was sinking. I know her. I like her. We have a lot in common.

I took a deep breath and decided to observe everyone as an anthropologist would, from a scientific distance. I didn't get mad. I explained that for me the workshop wasn't about the origins of homosexuality. "It's not about why," I said. "It's about being nice to people, about loving your neighbor as yourself." Kathy agreed that this was important. The school counselor, who is part of the Parents Advisory Team, told us she had been at an emotional faculty meeting earlier that had showed the school staff as divided as the community. Several teachers had threatened to quit if the workshop was reinstated. Others had threatened to quit if it wasn't. Nobody can afford to lose one of the best jobs in Haines, so I doubted any teachers would really walk out, one way or the other. But I didn't say so. The counselor observed that any room in town with ten people in it would not be able to come to a consensus on how and when to talk about homosexual issues in school. Echoing the sentiment at an earlier meeting, she said, "Haines isn't a very tolerant place."

When the meeting was over, I gave Kathy a ride home and asked her what she would do if one of her children turned out to be gay. "I'd be sick," she said. "I'd love 'em, I'm their mother, but I tell you, I'd be sick about it." After I dropped her off, I couldn't stop the tears rolling down my face.

To shake off things like this I need to move — outside. I used to exercise for my body, but these days it's more for my soul. I strap on my snowshoes and go for my daily outing. I rarely see anyone, and I look forward to the hour or two alone in the woods and ridges above town. I stomp up the trail, thinking, talking to myself, even rewriting the workshop saga. In my head the Boessers come and talk with everyone. They get a standing ovation. Half a dozen students come out of the closet and form a gay student union. Flash forward to years later: one becomes the United States representative from Alaska after the notoriously conservative Don Young retires. I'm feeling much better when I break out into a clearing and look down over the water, mountains, and this tiny place barely hanging on to a cold country.

I'll never be a nature writer, because my favorite part of any hike is looking down on homes and boats. From two miles up the trail, Haines seems like a toy town. I try to find my house. I can't quite see it, but think I spot smoke from the chimney. I can see Chip's truck parked at the red lumberyard on the waterfront, and the school, the boat harbor, Main Street, and Fort Seward. I think of all those people in all those little buildings, spending their days and thus their lives at work, school, or home, trying to do the best they can to take care of themselves and the people they love. I look right and left and see snowy mountains repeating all the way into the haze over Glacier Bay, whitecaps on Lynn Canal, and the braided channels of the Chilkat River weaving into the sea. I say thank you to whoever is listening and head back down the trail with a much lighter load.

HERE'S SOMETHING THAT happened a few years after the ugly incident at school. It happened in the windowless basement kitchen of the American Legion, Lynn Canal Post No. 12. It confirmed what I had suspected for a while — that I was no longer an outsider looking in but an insider looking out. For all the flaws, Haines is my hometown now. I was one of the cooks for a fundraising dinner for my daughter's friend Haley and her family. Haley was in seventh grade, and had been in Children's Hospital in Seattle for five weeks with a ruptured appendix. Her dad is a musician and carpenter. Last winter he built a sailboat, a wooden cutter. It's in the harbor now. He has a rock band with his other daughter, Lesley. They're called the Truffles. They play at the bars and have made two CDs. Lesley went to Los Angeles instead of college, but she's home now, making sandwiches and lattes at Mountain Market. Haley's mom grew up here and works at the post office, so they have insurance. But the emergency Learjet flight from Juneau to Seattle cost over $20,000, and they just don't have that kind of money. Few people here do.

The post commander ended up doing much of the cooking. After the other volunteers and I took one look at the ancient black commercial stove and feared it would either catch on fire or blow up if we turned the wrong knob, we called him for help. He arrived a few minutes later and showed us how to work the stove. Then he decided to stay and put on an apron, and began sautéing onions and peppers on the griddle.

The commander had lots of opinions about what to put in the spaghetti sauce. He'd never used a recipe, he said, and wasn't going to begin now. I never do either, but dinner for two hundred was so daunting we had figured that the best approach would be to multiply out a *Moosewood Cookbook* recipe. "Moosewood?" said the commander. "Never heard of it." Then he dropped a handful of chili powder and handful of salt into each of the five bubbling pots.

The butcher, Clint, came in to inspect the cooking. He had on a cowboy hat. He tasted the sauce and in his Texas twang said it needed wine. "Should we have wine at a fund-raising dinner?" someone asked.

"Not to drink," he said. "To put it in the sauce. Go out and get a nice big bottle of burgundy—that'll do the trick."

The commander said he didn't know why guys don't join the Legion anymore. He's the youngest member, he told us, and he's fifty-three. One of my friends chopping peppers next to the commander is married to a Vietnam vet, but her husband never says anything about the war and doesn't have a flag decal on his pickup. He definitely wouldn't want to share war stories down at the Legion. She didn't say anything, just finished her task and left quietly. The other volunteers wiped the dishes, hung up their aprons, and went upstairs to set the tables and organize the auction. That left just me and the commander, stirring sauce and boiling noodles for the next two hours.

I learned that he was in the navy in Vietnam. He said he got in trouble for not making regulation spaghetti sauce. "The navy sauce had no spices, just paste, tomatoes, meat, and one bay leaf for, like, twenty gallons. It was bad." So he added all kinds of things—onions, garlic, oregano, basil, and lots of salt and pepper. "Guys came back for seconds—that's when the cook knew I'd done something. He was not happy. I got in trouble for that one."

The commander showed me his discharge papers; he keeps them folded in his wallet. He earned three awards—I don't remember which ones—and told me about his broken back. I said he must have gotten a Purple Heart for that. "Nope," he said. "Gotta bleed. No blood, no Purple Heart." I joked that if he cut his thumb slicing mushrooms I'd give him a cook's Purple Heart. Then he felt the edge of my knife, which I'd brought from home, and said that it was too dull to cut much of anything and started sharpening it. He told me about his heart attacks (two) and his wife ("If she even has a sip of a margarita she gets tipsy"). And how proud he is of the Legion Hall's new paint and flooring, real improvements done on his watch. We talked about movies, too. We both liked *Nobody's Fool*, with Paul Newman and Jessica Tandy, about a good guy in a small town who doesn't seem to do much of anything but who really takes care of his friends and neighbors.

It was close to five, and the Legion's bar was filling up. A woman with a raspy voice was bartending, and a handful of regulars sat on their stools. Country music played on the jukebox, and whenever anyone opened the door, warm smoky air went out and cold damp air came in. The flags above the porch were in a wet tangle around the pole. The snow had changed to rain.

The sauce was finished and we had noodles waiting in warming pans and garlic bread wrapped in foil in the oven. The Bamboo Room Restaurant, across the street, sent over donated salad and dressings. Upstairs, the long folding tables were covered in white paper, and Haley's friends and their parents were gathering to help serve and clear. Chip was there, too, with the kids. They had already poked their heads into the kitchen to say hello.

Debbie, who was the main organizer along with the post office crew, came into the kitchen. "I haven't slept in a week, I'm so worried," she said. "Do we have enough food?"

"Yes," the commander said, in an of-course-we-do-dear-take-it-from-me-I-know-these-things voice.

"Will people come?" she asked.

"Yes," the commander said again.

"But I want it to be really big, a real success. I want it to mean something."

"It will," the commander said, taking off his apron and heading toward the bar.

Two hundred and forty people paid ten dollars a plate for spaghetti, garlic bread, and salad. Some, seeing the line out the door, wrote checks and went home without food. Some came during the intermission of the arts council's annual film festival, the Panhandle Picture Show, featuring local videos. They were laughing over one video made by Doug Fine, a KHNS radio station reporter who hosts a popular call-in show called *Talk Around Town*. Doug's video, which he dubbed *Talk Around the Cave,* poked fun at his own show and our predictably polarized politics. In it, early Haines cavemen fight about everything and there are always two distinct camps—exactly the same way we fight today. You can see it in arguments over bear hunting or the benefits of tourism—and in the uproar over a homophobia workshop—and our opinions are always reflected in the letters to the editor in the *Chilkat Valley News* and the *Eagle Eye.* Apparently, one grunting guy in the video does suggest that they all take a break from arguing and share some mastodon meat, but the others caution that while that may sound like a good idea, "it's not so simple."

By eight-thirty the commander, who had been in and out

throughout the evening, had given his last order in the kitchen and was smoking in the doorway, inspecting the cleanup from the fund-raising dinner. The stove had been wiped to a shine, the floor mopped, and the pots washed, dried, and put away. I'd worked extra hard on the stove. I wanted it to be cleaner than I'd found it, and I also wanted to prove that I'm not all bad, and that just because I may disagree with the folks at the Legion on some issues, I am still respectful.

You see, I am someone who some folks at the bar at the Legion don't think they like. I may even be someone the commander himself doesn't think he likes. A while before the fund-raiser, I had run for the school board and lost the election to the former Legion commander by fifty votes. He said I was antitourism because I wanted helicopter tours regulated, some wilderness areas set aside as noncommercial, and I don't think riverboat guides should feed eagles herring so tourists can get better pictures of them. My opponent also brought up the homophobia workshop debacle. He warned of what he called "the new tolerance." He told the *Eagle Eye* I had both gay and environmentalist friends. It wasn't a compliment. When one of my friends told me I had to contest that, I said, "Why? I even have *gay environmentalist* friends." He laughed, but we both knew it wasn't that funny.

The *Eagle Eye* supported my opponent. The new editor from down south, a man I had never met, called me—and Chip, which really hurt—slackers and hypocrites in several editorials. The *Chilkat Valley News* didn't come to my defense, because they've been in business long enough to know better than to ever endorse candidates.

Until Haley's fund-raiser, I had never met the new commander, but I saw the recognition of my name move across his face when we were introduced. He didn't say, "So *you're* Heather Lende." To his credit, he never mentioned that he knew exactly who I was as he told me all about his wife, his navy life, and his cooking philosophy. He never mentioned it as we laughed about the scene we both liked in *Nobody's Fool* when Paul Newman drives his pickup down the sidewalk and the overzealous small-town cop shoots at him. I also kept my feelings about more controversial subjects to myself and genuinely enjoyed my day with the commander.

Every now and then a curious legionnaire poked his head into the kitchen to see who the commander was talking with, only to twitch at the sight of me. Or maybe that was just my imagination. At the end of the evening, everyone complimented *all* of the cooks.

Annie Dillard is right about days adding up to make a life. My afternoon and evening with the commander was a good one. A life spent working and living in a small town with people I may disagree with has taught me a lot about humility and forgiveness. And when to keep my mouth shut. Some lessons have been more painful than others, but my days and my life are richer because of them.

DULY NOTED

Don "Bosh" Hotch said that memories of his Vietnam service are clearer after a recent visit with a former platoon mate. Bosh, who served as an infantryman for about six months in 1968–69 before being injured jumping out of a crashing helicopter, just returned from a North Carolina reunion with fellow Vietnam veteran James Featherstone. Bosh said Featherstone's was the only name he could recall from his days in Vietnam, since most of the soldiers went by nicknames. "They called me Cold State because I was from Alaska," he said. It had been thirty-one years since he'd last talked with a buddy from his war days. "It felt good to know I could talk with somebody from my company. We went through a lot of the same things," Bosh said.

About eighty residents turned out for the Emblem Club's annual community service auction on Saturday, contributing nearly $6,000 by bidding on donated goods, services, and unique crafts. The fund-raiser supports a wide range of local programs and activities, from youth softball to the food bank. Auctioneer Joanne Waterman kept the bidding lively. Items on the block included beadwork by Joyce Thomas, a nightlight by Dave Black, and a birch jewelry stand with a mirror made by Don Braaten. A gold nugget from the Big Nugget Gold Mine was won by Diana Lapham in the raffle.

More than seventy snowmobilers participated in the annual Chilkat Lake Fun Day on Sunday. Drivers started at the steel bridge, then traveled up Clear Creek and around Chilkat Lake. The event, sponsored by the Gross and Hess family businesses, was a great day in the sun. Snowmobiling conditions on and around Chilkat Lake are ideal, said snowmobiler Diana Lapham.

Angels All

NOT LONG AGO a friend asked if I would take her daughter to my church. She said her daughter was curious about it, and their family didn't belong to any religious congregation. I agreed that our church was a good introduction to organized Christianity because it's so traditional and historical. There's the Book of Common Prayer, Holy Communion, and all the robes, crosses, and even incense on special occasions. She was shocked. "You're kidding, right?" She'd thought Episcopalians were liberal.

My mother says St. Michael and All Angels is very "western." When I was young, she took my sisters and me to a formal old brick-and-oak-timbered church designed by Stanford White. Behind the altar was a Tiffany stained glass window depicting a bearded God in a flowing robe, light shooting out all around him. The caption, in gilt letters, read "God Said Let There Be Light."

St. Michael and All Angels Episcopal Mission meets Sunday morning at ten-thirty in the lobby of the Chilkat Center for the Arts. The altar spends the week in the theater's ticket booth. Before church we roll it out and cover it with white linen. Behind the altar are floor-to-ceiling plate-glass windows. You can see the backyards of some Soap Suds Alley homes, the streets leading to the cruise ship dock, and fishing boats in the harbor. But your eyes are drawn beyond the clotheslines and old trucks to the blue-green water of the Chilkoot Inlet and the mountains beyond. I've seen light stream down from clouds just as it did through the stained glass window in my old church many times, but every time it happens, I still think it might be God.

We don't have any churchy decorations or big stone sculptures, but we do have a small porcelain statue of the Virgin Mary. It doesn't seem right to leave her in a box in the closet all week, so we take turns bringing her home. I have some friends who worry that I may become too religious on them someday. They were especially concerned the first time they saw Mary standing on the piano in my hall, but now they're used to her.

About twenty of us attend St. Michael's regularly. We arrive early to set up chairs, get robes on young acolytes, and plug in the coffeepot for after church. We don't have Sunday school, so the little children play with toys in the back during the service. Our senior member is Maisie Jones, a widow who has an English accent. She always dresses up and sometimes wears a hat to church. When I had knee surgery, Maisie took the opportunity to get me acquainted with opera. She lent me videos of *Carmen* and *La Bohème* and then came over and watched them with me, just to make sure I understood the story lines.

Maisie brought an armload of red and yellow tulips from her garden for the most recent baptism: Shadow, a young woman from Klukwan, had just joined the Army National Guard and wanted some extra protection before heading out of town for basic training. Our priest, Jan Hotze, lives and works in Klukwan, where she runs the health clinic upstairs in the Alaska Native Sisterhood Hall. She's also a volunteer firefighter. Growing up, we always called the priest Father, but my kids—and everyone else's—just call ours Jan. She delivers short, informal homilies without notes that always seem to come around to the power of God's love to change us, and the world. She has a rich alto voice and chants much of the service in plainsong.

Bill O'Neal is the best lay reader. He stands up front, one hand in the pocket of his jeans, the other holding the Bible, and delivers the Old and New Testament lessons with the authority of an elementary school principal lecturing spitballers. He has a clipped gray beard and doesn't take off his hat, which is usually a wool cap with earflaps. He is grouchy enough that when he speaks we all sit up straight and listen. After a life of military regimentation, including combat duty in World War II, Korea, and Vietnam, the freedom of wild places is what lured Bill to Alaska. He still carries himself like the air force sergeant he was, but after retiring, Bill wanted to get as far away as possible from that life. Lines from a poem he wrote say it best: "Ah, the far-off places I would see . . . / High across the great plateau / With none to order 'stop' or 'go.'"

Music is a big part of our worship, mainly because the congregation includes Nancy Nash, a concert pianist; Bob Plucker, a retired college choir director; and Bob Krebs, the school district's music teacher. We also have a lot of members who like to sing. When the Lynn Canal Community Players put on *Angry Housewives*, a musical about three stay-at-home moms who enter a punk-rock band contest and write funny songs with bad words in them, some churches threatened to picket the performances. Jan encouraged us to attend because three of the four leads were from our church; the other was a Mormon. Margaret Sebens sang a song called "Eat Your Fucking Corn Flakes." Pam, a grandmother who teaches math at Haines High and spends summers in the Peace Corps in Kazakhstan, surprised us all by rocking out in the stage punk band, adorned with Magic Marker tattoos and colorfully dyed hair. Nancy directed the band and played electric piano in a miniskirt and blue wig.

BILL O'NEAL LEARNED he had colon cancer before Thanksgiving and asked Jan to announce it in church between Christmas and New Year's. His funeral was just after Easter. When initial treatments in Seattle weren't promising, he decided to come home to die. For a while he continued to read the lessons at church, but often he left before communion. Then Jan moved him to her home, converting her office into a sickroom. In the beginning he was brave and stubborn. In the middle he was angry and frustrated. And in the end he was resigned and ready. I sat with Bill on his last day, from after lunch until about five-thirty. I read aloud to him from *Naked*, by David Sedaris. He didn't respond, although some of the passages were so funny I cried trying not to laugh. Or maybe I laughed because I was trying not to cry. It was hard listening for Bill's last breath. He was already halfway into the other world by then, and the only one Sedaris's humor distracted from the death-watch was me.

After an hour or so of reading and wondering if Bill would die that day, I moved from his room to a chair by the window in the living room. It was very quiet, and Bill's mouth was open, so I could still hear him. I got up a few times to moisten his lips with a glycerin-coated Q-Tip, the way Jan had instructed me before she went back to work. He didn't even move when I touched him. He slept with one eye open and the other closed. I was scared. Before she'd left me with Bill, I had asked Jan what I was supposed to do if he died while I was there. She'd given me her prayer book with the commendatory prayer bookmarked and said to read it out loud over Bill, then call her. I really hoped I wouldn't have to do that. What if I panicked and forgot? Or ran out of the house sobbing and Bill didn't get into heaven? I know it's silly now, but it seemed really important just then. Somebody with more authority than I had should send Bill off to the great beyond. If Bill had been in a hospital room, I could have pressed a button to call a nurse or chaplain for help. But he was not in intensive care. He was stuck with a well-meaning amateur who might faint if he stopped breathing.

Bill must have had the same concern, because he waited to die until about an hour after I left, when Jan was home. The volunteer undertaker, Paul, told me he was sorry I'd missed Bill's exit. "You've been present at the beginning of life," he said. "It's really good to be there at the end, when another door is opened." Jan and the church treasurer, who was also with Bill at the very end, said he went out well. It was peaceful.

I guess I had hoped my last day with Bill would be packed with deathbed wisdom. I even brought a notebook to write it all down. I went as much for me as for him. But Bill didn't tell me the Meaning of Life—or Death—or if he saw God, angels, and all his buddies from the war, who were whole and young again, urging him to join them in heaven's poker game. He slept the whole time. My friends said that maybe I was getting so eager on my obituary beat that I'd taken to visiting people just before they died to get a last interview.

When you think about it, it's no wonder Bill chose to go gently into that good night. The people sitting with him in his last hours were an obituary writer, an undertaker, an accountant, and a priest.

Before he got sick, Bill walked up to the Bamboo Room for breakfast from his apartment in the Haines Senior Village (he called it the Wrinkle Ranch) almost every day. Around here, we think we know a person's politics by his appearance and habits. A long-haired journalist with a kayak on the Subaru is a liberal environmentalist. A seventy-six-year-old retired air force sergeant who goes to church and eats eggs over easy, white toast, and bacon every day at the Bamboo Room—that's our man Bill—must be a right-wing conservative.

Guess again. His friend Albert said, "He thought Clinton could do no wrong, even in the middle of his sex scandal" and that

President Bush "could do no right," even after September 11. Bill didn't keep his opinions to himself. He was a great letter-to-the-editor writer, and once suggested that all the street and place-name signs be changed from English to Tlingit. Haines, he said, should go back to calling itself Deishu, or "End of the Trail," its original name. Over his morning hot chocolate (Bill believed coffee was bad for you), he told Albert, a Tlingit, that he was going to "come back as an Indian and raise hell with the whites."

Just looking at Bill, you'd never guess he was such a liberal. I don't think he saw himself in the same camp with the activists in town, the crowd my mother refers to as "aging hippies." If you asked Bill, he would no doubt say that he was an American patriot, true to the original principles on which our country was founded. Just as Jan might say there is nothing radical about her church — nothing more than following a man who told us to love our enemies.

When cancer first slowed Bill down, I offered to read to him or help transpose some of his stories. Bill had written a rambling, un-published novel about Bylville, an imaginary town a lot like Haines with a hero a lot like Bill. He declined, saying he'd rather watch CNN. By then people from church were taking turns visiting him. Some had more success than others. He got along well with Paul, who was about his age and helped bathe him. But a sweet first-grade teacher originally from South Carolina who adored Bill's grumpy ways refused to see him any more until he got dressed. Bill had quit wearing pants because he had trouble getting to the bath-room. "I want to help, I love Bill, but I just cannot be in the room with a man who won't cover himself up," she said. He met her halfway and draped a towel over his lap. But when that fell off one too many times, she quit. When the accountant was with him on one of his hard days and he asked her why God wasn't taking him, she got angry and told him he wasn't nice enough. "God doesn't want you," she yelled. He yelled right back. Then he apologized and cried. She did, too, and it was better between them after that.

The week before he died, Bill called the newspaper office and wanted to know why the houses in Haines didn't have numbers on them. The fire department had mapped the town a few years back and assigned every building a proper address, in case of an emergency. Since we all pick up our mail at the post office, and since we all know where everyone lives, the street addresses hadn't caught on. Bill wanted to know how much the numbers cost and why no one was making sure they were posted. He told Bonnie, the paper's owner, that she should write a story about it. She listened, said she'd look into it, and told Bill she hoped he was feeling better. Later she wondered what it was that drove Bill to worry about street numbers when he was dying. I told her that sometimes thinking about small things keeps your mind off big ones. I think he'd also wanted to talk to Bonnie one more time and had needed a reason to call. He may have been complaining about street numbers, but what he was really saying was "Good-bye, I've enjoyed your company."

A few years ago a young man came to St. Michael's and asked if he could camp on our property. We had purchased a six-acre meadow on the other side of town with the hopes of building a church someday. He wanted to stay there until he had enough money to buy a ferry ticket to Bellingham. We struggle to meet the rent at the Chilkat Center, give Jan a small stipend, and make land payments. We all dream of building a real church but agonize over the benefits of a nice building versus doing good things with the money it would cost. We had just given five hundred dollars to Bulgarian orphans instead of putting it in the building fund. We'd almost bought new hymnals, so we wouldn't have to share on crowded holidays like Easter and Christmas, but had given a check to the food bank instead.

We knew this young man. We had all read his name in the court report in the paper when he was arrested for possession of pot and then again for drunk driving. He'd met another wayward soul and they'd gotten married and had a baby. Afterward, she'd quickly realized that she needed more security. Her mother had agreed and had flown her and the baby home to the Lower Forty-eight. We knew all that, and though it was sad, thought it was probably best, for now anyway. She looked so young. He was almost thirty.

While everyone else had cake and coffee in the lobby, the vestry, which is the church leaders and included Bill and me, stood in the narrow ticket booth we used for storage and debated the young man's request to camp on church property. Jan said the shed out there had an oil stove in it, so there was heat; he could stay in there instead of in a tent. Dwight offered to set up a portable boat toilet. They were trying to make it work. I was thinking that this was a terrible mistake. The Episcopalians were already on the edge of the Christian community here. Some of us had left other churches, and our priest was a woman. Nationally the Episcopal Church has been vocal about environmental issues—it opposes drilling for oil in the Arctic National Wildlife Refuge (something most Alaskans want) and logging in the Tongass National Forest (something half the people in Haines want). Then there were the gay issues. We might be an old denomination, but we were new to Haines. I thought, What if something bad happens and the other churches make it difficult for us to build ours someday? I suggested we simply explain that we didn't have camping facilities; that we were sorry, but it wouldn't work. I looked to Bill for help. Surely he'd put his foot down to a freeloader who had never even come to our church before. But Bill only asked Jan if we had insurance. We did. Then Bill reminded us that we were Christians, "part of a faith community that is supposed to love our neighbors, especially the difficult ones." Of course, he was right. Didn't Jesus himself hang around with guys just like this?

Dwight had an idea: Ask the young man to be our caretaker. We could give him fifty dollars a week and a place to stay in exchange for some chores. It was the perfect solution. We called the young man into the ticket booth to tell him. For this interview, he had dressed neatly and taken out the nose ring, cut his hair, and shaved. There wasn't much room. Standing shoulder to shoulder, Dwight told him our plan. Bill looked stern and emphasized that this wasn't charity; it was a way to save up for his ticket, earn his keep, and help us out. "This isn't what I had in mind," the young man said, about three times. We assured him it would be great for everyone.

Chip isn't on the vestry. I told him about our meeting on the way home from church. He couldn't believe we'd do something so foolish. "What if he burns the building down or gets arrested on church property? What were you thinking?" I didn't want to get in a fight about it. I was still embarrassed for not thinking kinder, true Christian thoughts about the whole situation to begin with. Chip knows how impractical and softhearted I am. I think that's why he loves me. He also knows that the rest of the St. Michael's vestry are, too, and I think that's why he comes to church.

Three days later Bill and I were sitting next to each other at the beauty parlor, in matching plastic capes, having our hair trimmed. There's only one hair shop in Haines. Bill said he'd heard at the Bamboo Room that the young man, who had just begun working for us at the church, might be leaving. Sunday morning—a week after we'd hired him and done our great good deed—we learned he had already left without telling anyone. And he'd kept our key. If Bill was disappointed, it didn't show. "It could have been worse," he said. *Oh,* I wanted to shout, *but it could have been so much better.* The young man could have turned our six wild acres by the stream into an English garden with a boxwood maze for meditation, a wide green lawn, and a tidy gravel driveway. The old shed could have been transformed into a chapel. Bill could have walked down there each morning and barked out instructions, supervised the progress, and reported back to the vestry. The honest outdoor work, our kindness, and Bill's guidance could have brought out the best in the lost young man. His family could have returned. He could have gone to school, become a teacher, and started a camp for troubled youth. Maybe the campers could have built us a little timber-frame-and-stone church. Instead he hadn't done much of anything, had left without saying thank you, and had stolen our key.

I asked Bill how he felt about it all, if he would make the same decision again. "Sure," he said. And we left it at that.

At Bill's memorial service, the Chilkat Center was full of his friends, dressed in jeans and flannel shirts or fleece pullovers. There wasn't a suit in sight. A sign on the door said that no one wearing a tie would be admitted. It was Bill's last wish. Nancy played "St. Patrick's Breastplate," Bill's favorite hymn, and we sang all seven verses. Nancy pounded the final verse out so loudly the whole room shook. Maisie wore a black dress and matching hat; the acolytes had on their white robes. There was communion and incense. Jan gave a short sermon without notes about God's love and its ability to find us anywhere, not just in church. She came around to the power of God's love to transform us, and thus the world, and wished us all the peace of the Lord, which, she said, "passes all understanding." She was interrupted a couple of times by the small children playing with toys in the back, but nobody minded. I sat there looking out the big windows, half-listening to the prayers, thinking about Bill, God, and angels—and how we all fit together.

I also thought about something one of my friends had asked when she'd heard I'd been with Bill the day he died. She wanted to know if he'd given off a death rattle. That's when your breathing goes all noisy and erratic just before it stops for good. Apparently, it's quite a moment to witness. Like a drum roll for a high diver. If it's a good death, you see the soul take flight. No, I didn't hear Bill's death rattle. And I'm glad. I have a feeling it would have been unforgettable, in an awful way. At his funeral, when I looked out the big windows facing the backyards of Soap Suds Alley, the inlet, the mountains, and the cloudy sky that God sometimes peeks down from, I saw a lone bald eagle circle higher and higher until he was gone.

DULY NOTED

Rob Goldberg and Donna Catotti hosted a picnic at their Mud Bay Road home with traditional Bulgarian food and hot dogs. Their son, Aihan Catotti-Goldberg, is originally from Bulgaria, and Rob and Donna are adopting another little boy from Bulgaria.

James Alborough and nearly three dozen other Southeast residents took the U.S. oath of allegiance in a citizenship ceremony on July 19 at the Dimond Courthouse in Juneau. James, a native of South Africa, lives in Haines with his wife, Sarah "Tigger" Posey, and two children. James said the citizenship ceremony capped off sixteen months of paperwork and study, including exams on civics, U.S. history, and the English language.

One of the tiniest Haines residents carries a hefty moniker. Newborn Dante Salvatore Bonaccorso is named after his great-grandmother and great-uncle, said mom Justine Starzynski. Harry Johnson Sr. is the proud papa. Bonaccorso means "good path" in Italian and was the maiden name of Justine's maternal grandmother.

Since Canadian customs officer Marinka Darling is originally from the former Yugoslavia, she speaks Slovenian. "It is as different from Albanian as French is from English," she said this week, which is too bad, because Canadian officials were ready to fly the Haines woman to Montreal to help translate for ethnic Albanians from Kosovo seeking refuge there.

The fourth annual Tlingit Cultural Awareness Month wrapped up September 30 in Klukwan with a potluck at the Alaska Native Sisterhood Hall. The tables were loaded with, among other things, beach asparagus, deer stew, roast goose, smoked salmon, and herring eggs. The Klukwan School children danced and the Alaska Native Brotherhood and Alaska Native Sisterhood honored their lifetime members.

Mother Bears

It takes four flights to get to Bulgaria: Haines to Juneau, Juneau to Seattle, Seattle to London, and then London to Sofia. When we get there, Eliza and I will pick up my newest Lende, Stojanka, from an orphanage. Since it may be a once-in-a-lifetime trip, Chip encouraged us to spend a week in England on the way. He is staying home, running the store and taking care of the rest of the family. Chip's sister, who spends part of the year in England, has promised to entertain us.

With each flight, I gain confidence. When we descend into Heathrow, in our British Airways socks and sleep masks, I feel rich, like a world traveler. Eliza and I get through customs and take a train downtown. We follow my mother-in-law's directions to an apartment—a flat, as she calls it. It belongs to a friend of hers who is away but has left a key with the manager.

We spend the next few days sightseeing. We take a water taxi down the Thames, making stops at the Tower of London and Buckingham Palace. We go to a Rembrandt exhibit at the National Gallery. At Westminster Abbey, the guard at the door says, "This is a church service. The Abbey is closed to tourists now." Eliza and I are Episcopalians. We are not tourists, I tell him, we are pilgrims from America, and he lets us in. It's an Evensong service. The music fills the ancient chapel, and I feel as if I'm standing in my own past. I pray that Stojanka will like us and that everything is all right at home.

We get lost one night after seeing a play. I cry, at midnight, in an underground station, trying to figure out how to get back to the apartment. I hope we won't be murdered and thrown in the river. We take the stairs to the street and walk quickly from the empty alleys near the station to a busy intersection and hail a cab. "Let's not tell Dad," I say to Eliza. "Let's pretend we did just fine without him."

After four days in London, we take a train to the Cotswolds and visit Chip's sister, Karen, and her husband, David O'Connor. They are Olympic equestrians and are training at a farm there. Eliza and I walk through old villages named Upper Slaughter and Lower Slaughter and browse in churchyards, reading the verses on ancient headstones and memorials. The last night, we all get dressed up and go to Lord and Lady Something's house. He is called Froden, which may be his last or first name. There is a pond filled with huge trout. They are "pet trout," Lady Whatever says. They wouldn't last long if Christian and his friend Wayner were here, I think. Froden cooks outside. He calls it mixed grill. When he's done, everything is laid out on platters on the buffet table in the dining room. Sausages, lamb chops, hamburger patties, tomatoes—all burned black.

Captain Mark Phillips, Princess Anne's ex-husband, is a guest, too. He is Froden's neighbor and also coaches the U.S. Equestrian Team. We all stand when he arrives. He is pleasant and unassuming, although everyone is on their best behavior around him. We wait until he sits to be seated, and until he takes a bite, to eat. Eliza doesn't mention her vegetarian preference. She chews the blackened meat slowly. The captain has a wandering eye, so I have to concentrate to look in the proper pupil.

For dessert, Froden has made cherries jubilee. He carries the saucepan to the table, pours brandy on the cherries, and lights the whole thing on fire. Everyone claps at the swirling blue flame. When it's done, he serves it with vanilla ice cream. Froden forgot to pit the cherries, so the captain carefully takes each seed out of his mouth, placing them in a row around the edge of his wide-lipped bowl. I do the same; so does everyone else, figuring this is proper British cherry-pit etiquette. When he's finished, the captain looks up and, with a sparkle in his good eye, sings a little song. It's sort of like our "she loves me, she loves me not," only this one counts the cherry pits to predict when you will marry. "This year, next year, sometime, never," the captain sings, pointing to each pit with his spoon.

WAITING IN HEATHROW for the flight to Bulgaria, I think about that odd, friendly meal. The food was awful, but no one minded because of the company. I also think how strange it is to dine with almost royalty one day and be on the way to rescue a Gypsy orphan the next. Suddenly I miss home, Chip, and the kids, and our friends and neighbors who walk into the house without knocking, who help themselves to leftovers or a cold beer, depending on the time of day. In a way, this new child is making all of us even more of one big family. Steve and Linnus have promised to be Stojanka's godparents. I put their names on all the school forms that ask for an emergency contact and next of kin. All our friends were interviewed by the social worker, who wanted to ensure that we'd take good care of Stojanka. Tonight Steve's probably making pizza while everyone is arguing loudly—especially if Tom is there —about the new playground at Tlingit Park and why the high school basketball team hasn't won a game in two seasons.

Some time ago, when I was writing Lillian Hammond's obituary, Tom insisted that I separate her blood relatives from the rest of her extended family. It was impossible. She didn't think that way.

Lillian was a Tlingit elder who lived in her clan's communal home, the Raven House. Her biological son Charlie said his mother liked nothing more than feeding everyone and keeping them safe under her roof. Over the years, Lillian and her husband added to their household by adopting children and adults, Native and non-Native, into their family. Some have brown skin and dark eyes; others are blue-eyed blonds with no Tlingit blood at all. Charlie said his mother believed that "with numbers comes strength."

I think Lillian's tragic childhood made her determined to rebuild her culture and her family in any way she could. She was born in a traditional Tlingit village, but it had disappeared by the time she was an adult. Most of her family members and friends had died of diseases such as chicken pox and measles introduced by white men, or they wandered—like Bulgarian Gypsies—around southeast Alaska. Like the Roma, Stojanka's people, they were not always welcome in schools or restaurants. Missionaries convinced Native mothers that their babies would be better fed and better educated if they put them in church-run orphanages. Sometimes these children were reunited with their families; often they weren't.

When I explained to Lillian's son that the newspaper needed to differentiate in the "survived by" list between the biological and adopted family members, Charlie looked puzzled. What Tom had actually said was that I could include only her real family. "What's a real family?" Charlie said. "If a bear cub's mother is shot and another sow allows him to suckle, she protects that young one the same as the one she birthed. That was my mother. She was a mother bear. We were all her children."

I hope I will feel the same way about the daughter I didn't conceive. I hope I'll love her like the others, and I hope she'll love me back. Maybe these doubts trouble me more than I'd like to admit, because on the Balkan Air jet from London to Sofia, my fear of flying returns. The safety-procedures talk looks like a sketch from *Saturday Night Live.* The stewardess, in a tight, shabby old uniform, smirks as she drapes the flat would-be life jacket over her shoulders, as if to say, "We all know this will only help them find your body." When the FASTEN SEATBELT sign goes off, most of the passengers light up cigarettes. So do the flight attendants. The engine is so loud that Eliza and I have to shout. One of the tray tables is broken; the other is sticky. Everything is rattling. Eliza looks at me for reassurance. I pretend all's fine, as if I have taken this flight a thousand times. "This is how it always is on Balkan flights," I yell. We both laugh, but I do wonder why my friends Rob and Donna, who made this trip to adopt their son, didn't warn me about the plane. For dinner we are given cold cuts, a chilly brown roll, and a strong-smelling sheep's-milk cheese wrapped in cellophane. There is free wine. We drink it.

AFTER TWO DAYS of waiting in line and getting documents stamped and approved in Sofia, we head out across the country on empty freeways to pick up Stojanka. You can't rent a car or buy gas in Bulgaria, so we have to hire a driver. Which makes me feel rich again. I've never had a driver before. It's all starting to seem like an old movie. Doc, who works for the American adoption agency in Bulgaria, is also with us. A better character actor would be hard to find. He is short, round, and bossy, and he tells us Bulgarian history between Elvis and Beethoven tapes.

"They have proven," Doc says, "that Bulgaria is one of the oldest societies in the world. In Sofia they found tools seven thousand years old." He speaks of the Middle Ages as if they were a few years ago. "The Bulgarians invented the alphabet," he says, and he makes us memorize the names of the two ninth-century monks responsible so we will be sure to tell Stojanka when she grows up. "Cyril and Methodius," he enunciates, making us repeat after him, pronouncing the hard *C,* rather than the familiar sound we use when we say Cyrillic. Doc weeps when he speaks of the five hundred years of Turkish oppression. He makes us promise never to forget the great patriot Vasil Levski, the revolutionary who is credited with overthrowing centuries of Turkish oppression. He planned an armed overthrow of the Turks but was caught and killed before the uprising in 1876, when twenty thousand Bulgarians were massacred by the Turks in front of an American journalist whose name Doc didn't make us remember. (He must have assumed we knew, this being part of *our* history, too.) After the story broke, world opinion changed and the Turks had to get out of Bulgaria.

Not only did Doc tell us all this, and much more, but he insisted on quizzing us. Out of the blue he'd yell, "Vasil Levski," and Eliza would shout back, "Great patriot." He didn't say much about the Gypsies except to remind us that although they are treated badly by his countrymen, the Bulgarians still didn't let the Nazis take them to the gas chambers, the way they did in other places. He tells us they came to Europe a thousand years ago and were called Gypsies because people thought they were from Egypt. "India is their real home," he says. "They are Indians."

Doc cries again when he tells us that he could have cured Beethoven's deafness. A retired ear, nose, and throat doctor, he was sent to Ethiopia to work during the Soviet Union years. When he returned, he earned less per surgery than the plumber was paid to fix his sink, he says. Eventually his medical credentials, combined with his language skills and bulldog attitude, landed him a job with All God's Children, an American adoption agency based in Portland, Oregon. At seventy, Doc is a man with a mission: to match families with the children he thinks they are meant to have. In his single-minded pursuit of building families, he reminds me of

Lillian Hammond. He also knows that the mostly Roma children who fill the orphanages have little hope of thriving in Bulgaria, even the new, democratic Bulgaria. Doc doesn't share his countrymen's prejudice, but he understands that the brown-skinned, dark-eyed children of the long-wandering people may never be embraced here.

With no segue, he asks my opinion of Graceland. When I tell him I've never been there, he refuses to believe it. He's visited Elvis's shrine twice and knows all of his songs. After a stop to pee on the side of the road, he shouts, with a finger in the air, "Elvis has left the building!" and we pile into the car and are on the road again.

I think we are going to an orphanage to pick up Stojanka. Instead, we meet her at a Shell station on the side of the highway somewhere between Sofia and Dobrich. She is with half a dozen people Doc says are from the orphanage. He says they have been camping. I don't believe it. I suspect she has been working in nearby fields. I don't want to argue about it. I'm so happy and relieved to finally see her, although we don't cry with joy and jump up and down. It is a much more subdued introduction. I touch her hair, smile, and gently squeeze her hands. I don't want to frighten her.

Doc tells me I'm supposed to buy everyone lunch at the Shell station grill. I am ill from the car ride. Eliza has been sick to her stomach since our first day in Bulgaria. I'm getting weary of Doc. I want to grab this child and fly home — now. But I can't even talk to the driver. He doesn't speak English, and I don't speak Bulgarian. I also don't want to upset Stojanka, especially since she doesn't know a word I'm saying either. Still, when I sit next to her at the table, I feel different than before we met, extremely maternal. Eliza is on her other side, and I can feel her shift into big-sister caring mode. We make a good team. I am no longer a passive, slightly confused foreigner. I am a mother bear with two cubs.

Doc orders grilled chicken and beef kebabs for all of us. The chicken is raw. I object, but Doc says that's how they like it, rare. When I won't eat it, he tries to give it to Stojanka, who has already finished her beef. She was an orphan a few minutes ago but is my child now, and I cannot let her eat it. I will not let her risk salmonella. She is so thin; I want to feed her, but not raw chicken. Doc protests, but this time I don't let him decide what's best. I take the chicken off her plate and put it back on the platter. Everyone laughs and grabs the pink chicken kebabs. I think less-than-kind thoughts. I hope they all get really sick.

We spend the night in a hotel with a portrait of Lenin over the front desk. Doc and the driver have one room, and we girls have another. Stojanka is all I hoped she'd be, and more. She can read and write in Bulgarian, which is a surprise; we were told she had no schooling. We have an English-Bulgarian phrase book, and know how to say critical sentences, such as "I love you" and "Do you have to go to the bathroom?" Eliza is better at Bulgarian than I am, and she and Stojanka can communicate pretty well. Actually, we all can. I don't understand how it's possible, but Stojanka is as trusting with us as a newborn, and a lot easier to care for. She takes a long bath, by herself. Eliza and I think it may be the first time she has ever been able to soak in warm, soapy water. Afterward she puts on the pajamas that her new sister J.J. picked out for her in Charlotte's store in Haines. They are both almost nine. Their birthdays are a month apart. People who haven't met them, who only know that I have two girls the same age, will ask if they are twins for the rest of their lives. At first, I'll explain that one is adopted, but after a while I'll simply introduce them both as my daughters, and leave the inquirer to wonder how that can be—how one child can be so fair and the other so dark.

IT HAS BEEN almost a year and a half since I first saw the photograph of Stojanka that was being passed around in Haines, and a year since we saw the videotape of her. When people ask why we added a fifth child to an already busy household, I don't know what to say. When they ask what about the risks of adopting an eight- or nine-year-old — the nature-versus-nurture argument — I also don't know what to say. It isn't a logical thing to do. Chip and I adopted Stojanka on a feeling, a good hunch. We like children; we had an extra bed and plenty of ice skates. When other friends in Haines who have adopted Bulgarian children — Kathy and Dr. Jones have two Bulgarian daughters and Rob and Donna have one Bulgarian son and another on the way — asked me to think about it, I really did. When Kathy gave me a picture of Stojanka and asked for my prayers, I gave them. When she brought over a video-tape, I asked Chip to watch it with me.

In the tape, a voice I now recognize as Doc's interviews Stojanka from a position offscreen. She wears a Disneyland sweat suit and holds a huge Winnie-the-Pooh stuffed bear, no doubt donated by an American church group. She has very short hair, cut that way, I'm guessing, because of head lice. She is pretty, cheerful, and sweet. They speak in Bulgarian and Doc translates. He asks her what she wants to be when she grows up and he tells us she says a doctor. We learn that her favorite color is yellow and that she likes goats. What's her favorite game? "Construction," Doc says. "She likes to build things." We own a lumberyard. Chip whispers, "Finally, someone to take over the business." Doc asks if she'd like to sing a song, and she does, verse after verse until he cuts her off. She reminds me of Little Orphan Annie. Then there is a spirited argument on the tape. She and Doc go back and forth — and she wins. "She wants to tell you something," Doc says.

Stojanka looks right at the camera and speaks slowly and care-fully, in English. "Hello, Mommy. Hello, Daddy. I cannot wait to meet you. I love you."

• • •

ON THE WAY back to Sofia the next day we stop at what appears to be an abandoned school but is really an orphanage for some one hundred Bulgarian children. While Doc is inside videotaping them for prospective adoptive families, Stojanka and I walk around the parking lot. It's ninety degrees and the air tastes like bus exhaust, but there are no buses in sight, just an old Soviet military ambulance and our hired car, a late-model Volvo. The driver is leaning up against the hood smoking. Eliza sits in the back seat with the door open, hoping for a breeze.

I spend my life finding meaning in small, everyday things—an afternoon of fishing, a walk on the beach, cooking a nice meal. Now, in the middle of a really big thing, I can't quite get my bearings. Maybe it's the heat, but I'm a little woozy. Stojanka and I make quite a pair. To impress the Bulgarian officials, I dressed in slacks, a silk shirt, and good shoes. Stojanka wears jeans, a T-shirt, and sneakers, an outfit she chose from a bag we packed for her in Alaska two weeks ago. She is pretending to be an all-American girl and I'm pretending to be a Middle-Aged Woman of Means. A purse has replaced my regular backpack. I look like my mother.

By the third loop around the deserted parking lot, I start singing an old country song.

Well I gotta get drunk and I sure do dread it . . .

Stojanka squeezes my hand and smiles, so I sing a little louder.

Oh, I gotta get drunk and I sure do dread it . . .

I end with a flourish in front of the car. Eliza looks up from the back seat. "Are you sure that's appropriate?"

"She doesn't understand the words."

But on the next lap I switch to songs that are more American, like "This Land Is Your Land," until I forget which verse goes where. After beginning "The Star-Spangled Banner," I quit on the high notes. Then I try "Alaska's Flag."

> *Eight stars of gold on a field of blue—*
> *Alaska's flag. May it mean to you . . .*

I am about as far from Alaska as I can get, as far from home and the rest of the family as any of us has ever been. All I want to do is get out of these ridiculous clothes and go home.

On her new American birth certificate, my daughter's name is Stojanka Antoanetova Stephanova Lende. It's a big name for a small girl. I am listed as the mother and Chip is the father. Her birth date is the same day and month as on her Bulgarian birth certificate, but the year listed corresponds to when we adopted her, rather than the year of her birth. Her first name is unusual—it's the name given to a child who survives after a mother has many miscarriages or stillborn babies. It means "special gift" or "blessing." The second name is her mother's family name, and the third is from her father's family. Stojanka is in the Lende family now, and no one here calls her Stojanka anymore. When she first got here, my father had trouble pronouncing Stojanka on the telephone. When he came to Haines to meet her, he kept calling her Solzhenitsyn. Then one day at the newspaper office, Tom and Steve decided that Stojanka was close enough to Stolichnaya, the name of a brand of vodka that no one can pronounce either, and that everyone just calls Stoli instead. They nicknamed her Stoli—and she liked it.

Back when I was writing the obituary for Lillian Hammond, I learned that she, too, had an unusual nickname. The distinguished Tlingit elder was called Storehouse Mama. The name was given to her by friends impressed by her cooking and especially her well-stocked pantry. She had other names, too: Shalee Tlaa was her

Tlingit language name. She was also Mrs. Hammond and always Sister Lillian when she rang the Salvation Army bell at Christmastime in the Pioneer Bar; but the people she loved best of all called her Mom.

THE OTHER DAY Stoli and I were the only ones home. The tide was high and the water calm, so we decided to take the kayak around Pyramid Island. Paddling away from the beach, she asked what her mother looks like. "Just like me," I started to say, but that wasn't what she'd meant.

"She's probably tall, dark, and pretty, like you," I said. All I really know is that she left her three-week-old daughter with a special name in an orphanage and never came back. I told Stoli that her mother hoped she'd find a family like ours, that she loved her and wanted her to have a good life.

"Mom," she said, "I wish I had a picture of my mother."

I wished I'd read those adoption books more carefully. Luckily, her attention shifted to what we thought was a seal but turned out to be a log. The wind picked up, and the way home was difficult. I paddled hard to keep the kayak upright and level. We got wet. Stoli asked if everything was all right, and I assured her we would be fine. Then I guided the boat with my precious cargo through rough water to the safe shore, because that's what mothers do.

DULY NOTED

Spelunker Kevin Allred helped scientists find some of the oldest human remains in North America in a cave on Prince of Wales Island recently. Paleontologist Tim Heaton says the bones date back ninety-two hundred years. He believes the discovery could prove that people lived in southeast Alaska before the Bering Land Bridge was formed, which means the New World may have been settled by people who traveled here in boats, rather than walking from Asia, as was previously thought.

Ever wonder where all those tourists come from? This summer the American Bald Eagle Foundation's Dave Olerud has talked with people from Israel, Europe, Asia, and the Lower Forty-eight, including a busload of teenagers from Detroit. Dave said visitors generally appreciate the Alaskan wilderness. "This country has so much space they can't believe it."

About sixty Haines residents attended the Rachel Carson Day festivities Sunday. The celebration included an organic potluck, a reading from Carson's book *Silent Spring*, and the showing of a movie adaptation of that same book. "The highlight of the meal was an outstanding cake," said coordinator Fiona Campbell. The cake, decorated by George Figdor, depicted scenes of environmental destruction. "It was really an exceptional evening," Fiona said.

Haines High School graduate Cody Loomis recently received his airplane mechanic certification from the Federal Aviation Administration. Cody is back home after making the dean's list at the University of Alaska in Anchorage. He plans to work as a sportfishing guide in Elfin Cove this summer.

Peculiar Awe

THE OTHER DAY I had a near-death experience. I'm exaggerating—a little. I flew from Haines to Juneau in a small commuter airplane, a Piper Aircraft Company Cherokee Six. The planes have low wings and usually seat six, including the pilot. This one had seats for four; the two in the back had been removed to make room for mail. The weather was good and the flight uneventful. It's just that I don't like flying. Planes make me scared and sick. When I was pregnant with Christian and J.J., I flew to all my prenatal appointments in Juneau. Our little Haines clinic had stopped delivering babies by then. With two other small children at home, I couldn't be gone overnight, which eliminated the ferry as an option. I always flew with the same pilot, Barb, a middle-aged New Zealander. She was cautious and brave and made me feel completely safe. Then she died. In a plane crash. Her plane hit a snowy mountaintop between here and Glacier Bay. Later I heard that one of the passengers may have had a can of bear-repellent pepper spray that exploded.

Now whenever I fly to Juneau I prepare for an unexpected landing. And I'm not the only one. The FAA has been running public service announcements on KHNS, informing rural fliers of passenger responsibilities. They actually tell you to dress for the weather and carry emergency survival gear, to be aware of "pilot fatigue," and to pay attention to any hazardous conditions. Like bad weather. If that doesn't make a nervous flier worry, I don't know what will. You'd think the pilot or airline would determine if it were safe to take off, not me.

So I made sure to dress carefully for my flight to Juneau. I wanted to look nice for the meeting I was going to and still be able to survive on a cold mountainside or wet beach until the Coast Guard rescued me. Before I left the house, I stuffed a zip-locked bag with a Power Bar, a lighter, paraffin, a space blanket, and a Swiss Army knife into one pocket of my coat, a jacket with a fleece lining and a waterproof shell. In the other pocket were gloves and a hat. I did have on a nice shirt, but I wore jeans, wool socks, and running shoes. I'd change into a skirt and clogs in Juneau.

At the airport, I climbed into a plane about the size of a Subaru station wagon. It was just me and the pilot. I'd never seen him before, and he was young. I like old pilots. They've lived longer. To reassure me after the stomach-dropping takeoff over the river flats, he shouted something about a narrow strip of beach we could land on in an emergency. He tipped the plane so I could see what he meant. I didn't look down. A few minutes later he announced that we were four thousand feet up in the air and moving through it at 140 miles an hour. I asked if we could fly lower. He said once you're over five hundred feet it's all the same. "The death spiral would just be less dramatic."

The death spiral? I was hot. It was a warm day, and I was wearing too many layers. Moisture beaded up on my forehead. I was flushed with fear and nausea. I felt a pulse in my stomach. I put my head between my knees and breathed in and out, slowly. The pilot asked if I was all right. "Fine," I shouted to the vibrating floorboards over the whine of the engine. We hurtled through the air for what seemed like hours but was actually about forty minutes. There was a light sort of dip as the pilot steadied the little plane above the end of the runway and a jolt when tires met tarmac. After a short taxi to the terminal the plane stopped.

The pilot tapped me on the shoulder to see if I was conscious. Still in a tuck, I looked up. He grinned and said, "The most dangerous part of this flight is when we get out of the plane; you can slip on the wing and hit your head pretty easily." He was teasing, but I heard concern in his voice, even pity.

Hold it.

I play shortstop for a softball team called the Diehards. I have run six marathons. We were on the ground now. Terra firma. I sat up, looked my pilot right in the eye, pulled down on the latch above me, and popped open the door with as much authority as Beryl Markham. Then I crawled out onto the wing, slid off on the seat of my pants, and stood, dizzy but successfully deplaned. Inside the terminal, I raced to the bathroom and threw up.

I'm sure Mr. Cave never got airsick. He loved to fly. The first time I saw his plane land on the beach was when we were still building our house and the Caves were thinking about buying the one next door. It was, coincidentally, the same home my capable Kiwi pilot had owned before she'd died, a few years before. I was painting upstairs when a small blue-and-white airplane went right by what was going to be our bedroom window — just beyond the spruce trees at eye level. I thought it must be a crash landing and I thought about Barb. I didn't want to see what that looked like. My heart beat fast and I ran outside in my coveralls, pretty sure I was going to witness a terrible, fiery explosion. Luckily, the landing was right side up. But I still sprinted to be sure the pilot was okay, see if he needed help getting to town or calling whoever you call when your plane is on the ground someplace other than an airport.

I don't understand how planes, big or small, stay in the air. I mean, I know about lift and thrust and air moving over wings and propellers and jet engines and all that, but I don't trust something so heavy to fly for long. However, I do think pilots are exceptional people. Mr. Cave didn't disappoint. He climbed down from the pilot's seat, smiling, and assured me that he was fine. Finer than fine; he'd landed his plane here on purpose. Mr. Cave didn't look like a bush pilot. He was dressed like an insurance salesman, in pressed slacks, a golf jacket, and clean suede Hush Puppies. Here was a man who could land a plane on the beach so confidently that he didn't dress for "the unlikely event of an emergency" landing. He was so sure he wouldn't get his feet wet that he didn't even wear rubber boots. I was awestruck.

At dinner, when I told the family all about it, Chip was equally impressed by our potential neighbor-to-be, but the kids didn't see what the big deal was. They assume that all planes land safely. The next few times Mr. Cave flew in, they watched him land the plane, but after the Caves bought the house, we all got used to seeing them fly in and out of our backyard.

The last time I saw the Caves was the weekend before Eliza and I flew to Bulgaria to adopt Stoli. Mrs. Cave came over while I was weeding the garden. I gave her some lettuce, and we talked about our families and my big trip. She was interested. She said she'd like to volunteer in a foreign orphanage some day. The nature of the Caves' visits—weekend getaways—made them a different kind of neighbor than my Haines friends. Our relationship was more formal. Mrs. Cave said to call her Shirley, and I did, sometimes, but I never called Glenn Cave anything but Mr. Cave. We didn't talk about the weather or birds. We didn't walk into each other's kitchens without knocking. The Caves left for Juneau later that afternoon. My nephews were visiting from New York and thought a plane taking off from the beach was pretty cool. It was clear and calm when we all went out and waved them off. My sister asked if this was dangerous. She and the boys had come up from Juneau on a small plane, and she hadn't liked it. (She and her husband also try to fly on separate jets when they travel, just in case.) I could understand her concern, but I told her they do it all the time.

Halfway down Lynn Canal the Caves landed at a church camp on Berner's Bay for dinner with friends. Afterward they offered their friends' newlywed son and daughter-in-law a ride back to Juneau. Near the airport, they ran into clouds and couldn't see where they were going. The guess is that Mr. Cave tried to turn around over the water but became disoriented in the clouds. He hit a wooded hill on Douglas Island instead. All four of them died instantly. My sister was more stunned than I was when we heard the news. The kids couldn't believe it, and still don't quite understand what happened. But they don't think it has anything to do with airplanes.

There is risk to getting around in this country, and you can't let fear of flying (or boats or even wild animals) keep you from it—or you might as well live in New York. My sister doesn't let her boys out of her sight except in supervised school or club activities. The highlight of the first trip my five- and seven-year-old nephews took here was walking from our old apartment above the lumberyard down the road to Mountain Market for bagels and back without a grown-up. The store was out of bagels, so the boys went past the library, school, and shops on Main Street to the bakery and came home with doughnuts instead.

After I heard the news about the Caves, I talked to my neighbors Don and Betty Holgate. They are no strangers to tragedy. If their only son had lived, he would be forty-two now. Close to my age. Don and Betty could have had a whole pack of grandchildren, just about my kids' ages. They talk about Jonathan a lot. He drowned with three other young people from Haines twenty years ago, when their boat sank while they were halibut fishing. Once I asked Don if it was hard, remembering. He said it was. Some people couldn't see why he and Betty stayed in Haines after the accident. Especially, they reckoned, since this wild country took his son's life. After he told me this, Don shook his head, baffled that anyone would blame Alaska. "There really is no place like this, anywhere, is there?" he said. "Besides, where else would we go?"

Now Don and Betty—she's a former flight instructor and he's a veteran pilot—wondered out loud about Mr. Cave's experience flying with instruments. Don said that in the clouds you can't rely on your senses. What feels like up may be down. When I got home, I read Psalm 139, for the Caves, and for Betty and Don: "If I take the wings of the morning and remain in the uttermost parts of the sea; even there shall thy hand lead me, and thy right hand shall hold me." At dinner we said a special prayer for the Caves. My sister said, "Big planes are fine—but not these little puddle jumpers." Then Sarah told the story about another fatal crash, this one over the Davidson Glacier, two sightseeing planes ran into clouds. One pilot turned around and came back to the airport; the other said over the radio that he was sure he could make it to the "other side." The joke then was that their new slogan was "From Here to Eternity." That's how we deal with these things around here. Laugh nervously and change the subject. Chip tried to be more serious, assuring Kathleen that the regularly scheduled flights between Haines and Juneau never crash. "I can't think of one," he said. Neither could I. But Kathleen decided to take the ferry to Juneau on the way home, instead of flying out of Haines.

After the dishes were done, I went out in the garden and looked at the Caves' house. Mr. Cave had been building an addition, a big sunroom, and he had left his ladder up. He must have planned to fly back the next day. God, it was just so awful. The crash made the

Chilkat Valley News, but the Caves' obituary was in the *Juneau Empire*. They didn't really live here. I'm glad I didn't have to write it.

Their house was empty for a year. I wasn't sure if anyone would live in it again, ever. The Caves' grown children had scattered their parents' ashes in the backyard, making it almost impossible for them to let go of the property. Then one night when I was tucking the girls into bed, we saw lights from the windows next door. Someone was in the Caves' old house. I hoped it wasn't another pilot. They say bad things happen in threes around here. Deaths are even supposed to line up that way. I've tried to keep track, but it depends on when you start counting. You can always make it work or not. Turns out our new neighbors were the Caves' friends from the church camp. A pastor and his wife. The same friends who'd lost their son and daughter-in-law in the plane crash. They were going to spend the winter in Haines. In that house. Stoli asked about the Caves and the new couple next door. The accident had happened before she'd arrived. I told her how the Caves used to be our neighbors before she got here, but that they had died when their plane crashed. "Now do they live in heaven?" she asked.

"Yes," I said, and hoped heaven has a runway on a beach just like ours so Mr. Cave can take off and land all he wants without ever getting his feet wet.

The Cave children never did sell the house. Those first tenants became the new pastors at the Port Chilkoot Bible Church and moved to the parsonage. The place was vacant for a season, and Pastor Hicks, from the Assembly of God, moved in when his apartment in the church was needed for meetings and Sunday school. But before his second stormy winter, he, too, moved to a more protected location. Now another church-affiliated older couple is house-sitting.

John Muir wrote about a trip he took in southeast Alaska in

1879: "No words can convey anything like an adequate conception of its sublime grandeur, the noble simplicity and fineness of the sculpture of the walls. . . . Still more impotent are words in telling the peculiar awe one experiences in entering these mansions of the icy north." Wild places are reminders that the world doesn't revolve around us. It doesn't care about our little successes or smashing failures. The tides ebb and flow and the seasons change regardless of how we live or die. That, I think, is what Muir meant when he wrote that his first view of glaciers prompted a "peculiar awe." It is both inspirational and humbling. I like that feeling. I think most people who live here do, or they wouldn't stay.

So, despite my fear of flying, when Ken, who used to be "the new millionaire" in town, and maybe the only one, but is now a friend and very good neighbor, called and asked if I wanted to fly out to Yakutat to see the Hubbard Glacier close off Russell Fiord, I said yes. He knows I don't like to fly but thought I should see the glacier make a new lake from an old inlet. It could be a once-in-a-lifetime opportunity. The sky was unbroken blue, there was hardly a breeze, and it was sixty-five degrees. "It's a perfect day for flying," he said. Ken also knows how curious I am about everything that goes on around here, both natural and manmade. So I said yes, because I really wanted to see it—and because I trust Ken.

We fly 131 roadless miles north of Haines over raw mountainsides covered with snow, ice, and wide, mostly gravel river valleys. When we get near the Hubbard Glacier, Ken drops down to a thousand feet for a closer look. The Hubbard is six miles wide and over seventy miles long. The front wall stands up four hundred feet above Disenchantment Bay. It's big and impressive. Of course, in this setting, with ten-thousand-foot peaks rising out of rivers of ice on all sides, everything you see is big and impressive. We are mostly silent, trying to take it all in. I murmur "wow" a lot. Russell Fiord is a deep teal. It is startling in this brown-and-white world. Disenchantment Bay is so thick with debris from the calving glacier that it looks like a terrazzo floor. I strain to see any boats. There are none. There are no planes or helicopters either, just us. The glacier hasn't closed the fjord off to seawater yet, but the dam of ice and mud that it's pushing forward has. All that's left is a roiling river, about thirty feet wide, running out the bottom of the pile of rocks.

The residents of the nearest town, Yakutat, are worried that the backed-up fjord will overflow into Situk Lake and Situk River, wrecking sport, commercial, and subsistence fishing and flooding the airport. But they can't do anything about it. Trying to stop a glacier is, well, like trying to stop a glacier. In the not too distant past, a hundred years ago, a nearby Tlingit village was destroyed by another advancing glacier.

On the way home, we take a friendlier route along the coast. There are set-net camps dotting a long, sandy beach. Instead of using big boats, Yakutat fishermen anchor gill nets on the shore and float them out into the bay, tending them from the beach with small skiffs. A group of rafters, at the end of an eleven-day Alsek or Tatshenshini River trip, wait on the shore of Dry Bay for their flight back to civilization. Just beyond their camp three bears play in the waving green grass. We head up into Lituya Bay, to see the new trees marking the line from a giant wave that filled the bay after an earthquake nearly forty-five years ago. It was the largest tsunami recorded in modern times. Then we fly up over the Johns Hopkins Glacier and down the other side into Glacier Bay. Two cruise ships look like bathtub toys. From here, it's a short hop over the Davidson Glacier to the familiar landmarks of home: the red cannery, muddy Chilkat Inlet, our house, and the Haines airport.

When Chip asks about the trip that evening, I tell him the glacier was magnificent, too grand for words, really. Everything was so rough, new, and foamy white; it looked as though God had just shaped piles of rocks into mountains and valleys with a bulldozer and a backhoe and filled the gaps in with shaving cream. Chip would love the beaches of Yakutat. I also realize that I wasn't afraid at all, and didn't feel sick except way up high above Lituya Bay when we were climbing over into Glacier Bay between the pointy peaks above the ice fields. When we hovered up there the only thing I could think of was that Patsy Cline song "I Fall to Pieces," which is what happened to her when the plane she was in crashed. I have got to quit listening to so much country music. What I should do is ask Ken to show me how to steer the thing next time we go up, so that "in the unlikely event of an emergency" I'll be able to soar east with the dawn and west with the night, or at least get us back to Haines.

DULY NOTED

Maisie Jones, Nowyta Badgley, and Joan Snyder are back from a trip to Greece and Turkey. Everyone's favorite place was the Greek island of Thíra. Maisie hiked to the top of the Acropolis on her birthday. (She'd rather not say which one.) She did say the trip was "wonderful," though the ladies are all "extremely glad" to be home.

———

Klukwan residents Lani Hotch, Marsha Hotch, Ruth Kasko, and Denise Kahklen recently completed training at the Sealaska Heritage Foundation's Kusteeyi Institute. Lani and Marsha learned methods for teaching Tlingit language lessons to adults and children. Denise and Ruth took part in Chilkat-blanket-weaving and spruce-root-basketry classes.

———

Mimi Gregg, director emeritus of the Alaska Community Theater Festival, and her daughter K. A. Swiger of Ketchikan attended the International Community Theater Festival at the Mendel Center of Lake Michigan University. The festival featured fifteen plays, including a Russian *Romeo and Juliet* and a French version of Chekhov's *The Marriage Proposal.* Mimi says not knowing what the actors were saying wasn't a problem. "The plays were so well done you got the gist of it." Mimi is busy reading scripts and scores for the Lynn Canal Community Players, who are hoping to stage another musical this fall.

———

The next time you fire up the hot tub, give Elsie Mellot a call. The octogenarian was honored with a gift of a bathing suit at last week's Chilkat Valley Historical Society meeting. Members gave Elsie the aquamarine one-piece suit after she used the old "no bathing suit" excuse when begging off a soak at a previous historical society meeting.

———

Grand Old Dames

ABOUT TEN YEARS ago I traveled to the Kenai Peninsula with Mimi Gregg for a state community-theater festival board meeting. We flew to Anchorage and rented a car for the two-hour trip south to Soldotna. On the trip, we talked about marriage and family, and Mimi told me that her long marriage to Ted was not an accident. He always let her try new things, and whenever they had a big fight her rule was, Will this matter in ten years? Usually it wouldn't. "Take the long view," Mimi said. "It works." Mimi drove that wet, winding road through Turnagain Pass like Mario Andretti, chatting as if we were at her kitchen table. I thought I was going to die. I begged to take my turn at the wheel, pleading the case that my young children needed a mother. Mimi called me an "old fuddy-dud." She was seventy-four.

Mimi's friend Mildred Meisch also used to drive fast. She would cruise around town in her vintage Mustang or, later, silver T-bird and invite tourists to come for a ride, promising to show them the sites for free. She may well have been Haines's first tour guide, spiriting delighted and no doubt increasingly alarmed tourists to her friend Nowyta's place ten miles from town. "She *druugg* more people into my cabin than I can count," Nowyta declared in her Texan drawl. "She knew any friend of hers was a friend of ours, and everyone was Mildred's friend."

Mildred, whose own Texas accent, heavy silver jewelry, tight red leather pants, and cowboy boots made her hard not to notice, died of congestive heart failure. She was eighty-eight years old. "That little woman was all heart," Clint, the butcher and Mildred's fellow Texan, told me. He said he knew summer had arrived when Mildred came in and ordered her chili beef. Mildred first saw Haines when she was eighteen. She came from Texas with her cousin, a military doctor, to care for his children while he was assigned to Fort Seward. She fell in love with another army doctor, H. M. "Doc" Meisch. They were married four years later in Texas. The Meisches returned regularly on vacation. When Doc died in 1980, Mildred decided to spend more time in Haines. As her friend Lola says, "She was a guest who came for the summer and stayed twenty years."

After visiting Haines with Mildred and Doc, Nowyta (pronounced No-*wheat*-ah) decided to make Haines a permanent part of her life, too. Nowyta and her husband, Abe, summered here until he retired from Exxon, and then they moved up for good. When Abe died suddenly, Nowyta was lost. He was the love of her life for fifty years. She had to learn how to make the bed, she told me, because she had never done it by herself before. She sold their cabin, called "Happy Ours," and now spends part of the year in Texas with her daughter and the rest in a rented house on Officers' Row, next to all the Greggs, with an entourage of southerners—friends and relatives from Texas and the Mississippi Delta.

Every July they host the Mississippi Blues Party. Which may explain how I ended up singing "The Beer Barrel Polka" with a retired public health nurse, the Episcopal priest, a tourist from Mississippi, and a friendly guy I'd never seen before who was wearing a T-shirt with a picture of an automatic rifle on the front commemorating some sort of militia warrior weekend. My guess was that one of these old gals around me picked him up hitchhiking to town from the ferry terminal and invited him for supper. We were the opening act. I was there without the rest of my family partly because they all went to a fund-raising spaghetti dinner at Mountain Market. Another reason was that my children are shy about attending a party where the youngest people were Nowyta's nephew Fireman Al, his wife, and me. There was one teenager from next door, but she didn't stay too long. Al is the son of Nowyta's husband's identical twin brother, Babe. Abe and Babe, and their families, lived in matching log cabins on the beach out at Lutak.

It rained all day and was still wet when Nowyta's party began, so while some hardy souls had mint juleps, iced tea, and home-fried salty pecans on the front porch, most of us crowded into Nowyta's living room, balancing paper plates of exotic southern food; no local moose, salmon, or halibut here. Instead, we ate black-eyed peas, sweet-potato salad, spicy okra with rice, jalapeño relish on corned beef, pecan tarts, pralines, and Ritz crackers with a sweet lemon spread (it tastes better than it sounds). It wasn't a potluck either; they made all this themselves.

People were dressed in whatever we Alaskans think Mississippians look like. One guy wore a wide straw hat and new denim overalls. Several women had big hairdos. Nowyta was in a long flowered skirt and matching shawl, a southern belle, her tanned face accented with bright lipstick and shiny earrings. Like her friend Mildred did, Nowyta has a double-take kind of style that the hokey costume couldn't disguise.

The Mississippi Blues Party is participatory. You can't just sit there and drink and eat. Guests provide the entertainment, though some are more prepared than others. Nowyta divided us into sections, counting off one to eight. There were four or five in each group. When none of us in Group 1 volunteered to go first with a song, joke, or story, we were assigned "The Beer Barrel Polka." She handed us the music. Our hearty attempt loosened up the crowd, and the rest of the evening's entertainment rolled forward.

Erma Schnabel and her friend Helen Tengs, representing the crew from the Schnabels' Big Nugget Gold Mine, sang "You Are My Sunshine," holding dancing battery-powered sunflowers that hummed the tune. Maybe it was all the food, or maybe I drank my julep too fast, but I started thinking about another remarkable old dame who really could have stolen this show.

Josephine "Porcupine Jo" Jurgeleit, a one-legged lady gold miner who died last year, was a great storyteller and especially loved to talk about her adventures. She and the Schnabels owned the only active placer mines in the historic mining district on Porcupine Creek, north of town. Jo threatened to settle most of her disputes with a rifle, and just about all of them were with John Schnabel over their mining claims. For years, Jo kept up a running feud with the Schnabels. The bullets she fired whizzed passed John's head on many otherwise still woodland evenings. When she failed to kill him, she took John to court. John says he never had much chance against "a one-legged widow," even if she was well known for her grit and independence.

Jo was profiled in numerous publications, including *National Geographic*. When she was seventy-three and still digging for gold, Jo told the *Alaska Geographic Society Quarterly*, " I love the mining game. . . . I feel sorry for people who live in the city and never go out in the woods." During one illness, Jo even got a get-well card from tycoon J. Paul Getty. How he met her, I'll never know.

Jo was almost killed six years ago when she backed her pickup truck off a cliff while moose hunting near her claim in Porcupine. She was eighty-five then. John rescued her. I would have loved to have seen the expression on his face as he stood over the ravine looking at her truck hanging on a tree and realized that her life was in his hands. John called his crew, and they got a winch and a loader and hauled her truck up and pulled her out of the crushed cab. John drove the twenty-five miles to town as fast as he could while Erma sat in the back of the pickup with the bleeding Jo on her lap wrapped in blankets. Jo might have died that day if the Schnabels hadn't been there. Instead, she took her last breath a few years later in an uncharacteristically ordinary way, at a rest home near her daughter's house in Soldotna.

Jo never had a prosthesis. Waiting to cross Main Street, she sometimes whacked the side of a truck with her crutch to get the driver to stop, while one empty pant leg flapped in the wind. I used to imagine the story she would tell about losing that leg. Maybe, I thought, it had something to do with a bear attack, or a rockslide, or even a shootout. The truth wasn't nearly as interesting. Writing her obituary, I learned that a misdiagnosis had led to an infection and the leg had had to be amputated. It must have broken her rugged heart.

But it hadn't slowed her down much. "Telling Jo she couldn't do something," her sister Hazel told me, "was like putting a red flag in front of a bull." Jo came from a pioneering Haines family. She and her siblings were so similar that we just called them all by their maiden name: the Vermeire sisters. Besides Jo and Hazel there was Emma, Clara, and Mary. With Jo gone, Hazel is the only one left now. She still lives alone in a picture-perfect farmhouse with a steep gable and a front porch. Sitting in the spotless living room last year, Hazel told me all about her sister, peppering her speech with *goddamns* and *sons of bitches*, and lewder expressions that didn't match her appearance. One unrepeatable story made me laugh, and she smiled, enjoying the "Did this nice little old lady really say that?" look on my face.

Like her sister, Jo had a quick wit and a sharp tongue. The most polite way to describe her was offered by her friend Jane, a retired shopkeeper who gets her white hair done at the beauty parlor and dresses up for lunch at the senior center. She and Jo used to go "four-wheeling" together in Jo's truck on old mining roads in the Yukon. "Many of Josephine's stories were risqué," Jane said, "and her language was colorful." That is how you put something that some people might consider a criticism into an obituary that you want the family to still be able to clip and save. You get someone who loved the deceased to say it. Then it becomes a compliment.

Jane was at the party, sipping a julep and talking with Mimi on the sofa. They both looked so small. All these great old dames make me want to be like them when I grow up. I want to spend my life in the same place with the same friends and, after all those years in the same community, still surprise people. This crowd at Nowyta's bash had me looking forward to old age. I can't wait to peer wisely over the top of my glasses, shake my gray head, and share contrary opinions punctuated with an occasional expletive. I'm going to bring down the house at parties like this when I'm eighty. I may even wear lipstick and get some red leather pants.

Laughter from Father Jim's awful religious joke brought me back to attention. It was about a group of missionaries from several different denominations who were caught, cooked, and eaten by cannibals. "The next morning," the Catholic priest said, "they had the first ecumenical movement." Everyone groaned. A banker from Fort Worth made balloon animals and hats, and then a Haines elementary school teacher who is also an opera singer belted out "Summertime."

Nowyta called the next day, to make sure the *Chilkat Valley News* would cover her party in "Duly Noted." She told me they'd had a memorial service in San Antonio for Mildred. Her ashes will be mixed with Doc's, and half will remain in Texas, but the rest will come back to Alaska and be scattered over Haines. No doubt Nowyta will host the party afterward.

"I love ya, darlin'," she signed off in her singsong Texas lilt.

"I love you, too," I said.

DULY NOTED

Martha Jones may need a vacation to recover from her summer visit with daughter C. J. Jones. Martha flew into Anchorage on June 10; then she and C.J. spent two days driving to Haines, where Martha volunteered at the museum and for the chamber of commerce. For Martha, the highlight of her trip was volunteering as the race marshal for the last checkpoint of the Kluane-to-Chilkat International Bike Relay. "Mom had a lot of fun being a marshal," C.J. said. "She just enjoyed everything."

An unexpectedly quick onset of labor led to a relatively rare home birth in Haines last week. Emmanuel Raymond Hansen was born on Thursday to Valina and Scott Hansen at the family's Cathedral Peaks home. "We had planned to have a home birth down in Washington, but when I went into labor we decided it was best not to go anywhere," Valina said. After a doctor's consultation, family members, including sisters Felicia and Victoria and brother Scotty, as well as two helpful friends, brought Emmanuel into the world. Everyone is doing well, Valina said. "You work when you can and nap when you can."

Scott and Mandy Ramsey welcomed about thirty-five family members and friends to their outdoor wedding ceremony at Moose Meadow on August 9. Neil Ramsey, the groom's father, married the couple. The newlyweds don't plan to honeymoon anytime soon. Scott is busy working as a mountain and rafting guide until September. The couple thank all the friends who provided skiff transportation to the meadow and erected the wedding tent.

Black Mariah's Lunch Date

IN THE OLD *Joy of Cooking,* the recipe for fish chowder began with fish stock. To make it, you take a fish head, bones, tail, skin, a cheesecloth bag of special herbs, a cup of good dry white wine, a twist of lemon zest, six white peppercorns, four cloves, a shallot, a celery stalk, and a carrot. You add two cups of water and simmer everything for fifteen minutes. Cool, strain, and then clarify it by adding a beaten egg white and the crumpled shell. Simmer it slowly until the whites and shell make a crust on top of the liquid. Don't stir it. After an hour or so, let it cool and strain it again through a wet cloth into a clean pot. Now you are ready to start making the chowder.

Some people would say this is an awful lot of trouble for a bowl of soup. They might even say to themselves, "Oh, forget it, I'll just make an egg salad sandwich." Be warned: The perfect egg salad sandwich takes even longer to make than fancy fish broth. Especially if you are home alone on a cloudy late August day.

First, you need hens. You do not need a rooster to have eggs. Hens are like women; they ovulate with or without a mate. If you want to grow hens from baby chicks, you can keep them for a week or two in the cardboard box—the one in which they were mailed from a farm near Anchorage—safe in your daughters' bedroom.

Soon, you will smell them when you walk in the house. If you let them out of the box, they poop everywhere and are harder to catch than you'd think, especially if they get under the couch. If a curious dog picks one up, the chick dies instantly of fright.

Free range doesn't mean homeless. It means they walk freely in and out of their sturdy coop into a fenced pen and on nice days get to peck around in the woods, yard, and driveway before you shut them back securely in the coop for bed. Which for chickens is clinging to a roosting pole four feet off the ground.

You need to feed and water your hens, keep their house clean, and make sure they are warm and dry. Every day you check on them, and shovel out the soiled sawdust and sprinkle new shavings on the ground. To get the chickens out of the coop when you are cleaning it, you dump a pile of kitchen scraps in the pen, and they eat them all. You also make sure their feed container is full and that they have clean water. In the winter, when the water freezes, you use two watering tins. The frozen one thaws in your mudroom while the fresh one freezes in the coop. You care for them like this for six or seven months before they lay the first light brown, surprisingly big egg. When you find it in the straw-lined box that you have made just for this purpose, it is as exciting as if you laid the egg yourself. It is a minor miracle. Soon poached eggs for breakfast and egg sandwiches for lunch are regular fare. But the perfect egg salad sandwich can't be made until the end of August, because that's when you have fresh lettuce and red tomatoes in your garden. The timing is good, because you need an egg salad sandwich most right then. August can be a melancholy month. August is the end of summer in Alaska, a time of beginnings and endings, regrets and thanksgivings. School starts and it rains a lot.

You have plenty of time today. You get dressed in running clothes; it's raining, but a wet run out to the cannery and back will make you appreciate that sandwich even more. Before you can leave the phone rings. It's Christian, who's forgotten his trumpet and needs it for band class. You find it and drive over to the school. On your way out of the building, a teacher calls your name. Sandy is concerned about the budget cuts the school board has to make. She knows you care about school issues. She asks if you have a minute. You say sure, and sit on the bench in the hall with her. She tells you about the lack of support she perceives the new superintendent is showing for her department, special education. Twenty minutes later you say you really have to go, you have a lunch date, and remind her that the new superintendent used to be a special ed teacher and is probably more sympathetic than she thinks. "I hope so," she says.

Driving back home, you swing by the lumberyard to say hi to Chip. He reminds you to keep the culvert that channels a creek down to the beach clear of debris so the excess water can run off, rather than overflow and fill the cellar. When you get home you put on rubber boots and go check. Spruce needles have clogged the wire mesh in front of the big pipe. A puddle is growing into a pond in the woods. You get a shovel from the chicken coop and keep the culvert clear for an hour, until most of the water is drained. Before going back inside you step into the coop and grab a pocketful of warm eggs. You check your watch and decide to postpone the run until after lunch.

So you walk over to the garden and pick the lettuce, then across the beach to see how well the culvert is working (great—the muddy water is running out) and back up the path to the greenhouse for a ripe tomato. Inside it's musty and warm. The waves from the beach are muffled; all you hear is the weak tap of the last raindrops as the tail end of the storm blows through. In Alaska, tomatoes are much harder to grow than lettuce. You can plant them in five-gallon buckets and put them in a sunny window in early spring. If you don't like the way the vines block the view, build a greenhouse. That is what Chip did after he got tired of the tangle of vines. Now the tomatoes grow in a trough two by two by twelve feet filled with dirt and chicken manure. Even young chickens make plenty of it.

Back inside you pull off your boots and pad into the kitchen with your harvest. You get out the half-and-half, an essential ingredient for the perfect egg salad sandwich. The house is clean and quiet. For the first time in a long time, you are home alone. The geraniums have been moved from the porch to the windowsills; the dogs are sleeping in a pile by the woodstove. You are a little behind schedule, but should still have time for a run before the kids get home from school.

The phone rings. It is your editor at the newspaper. "Black Mariah," he jokes, "you've got a cold one." An older woman who had been dying for a while passed away, he tells you, not kidding anymore. The family is ready to talk about her obituary. Right now. He told them you were on the way. You put everything for the perfect egg salad sandwich in the refrigerator and change from running pants to khakis, throw on a nice shirt, comb your hair, and brush your teeth. You grab a steno pad and pen and stuff them in your coat pocket. The rain has stopped, and the sun is starting to break through fast-moving clouds. It looks like the run is off, so you ride your bike. On the way up the hill, the chain falls off. You swear and try to put it back on without getting too greasy. Up at the house you apologize for being a little late and ask if there's a place to scrub your black hands. Turns out it's a good introduction. They are surprised, and happy to help. They offer you coffee, but you say no thanks, unless they are having some. They are, so you take a mug, too, and drink it black, even though you always have milk, because the last thing they need to do right now is get you anything.

You listen and write as they talk about their mother and wife. "The way she saw it, the Lord was going to heal her or take her, and either way she won." She was born in Norway and her early years were hard. When she was eight years old, she traveled alone on a steamship from Vancouver to Juneau to live with her father, a gold miner. She spent the rest of her life in Juneau and Haines. She raised six children, and when her husband and son-in-laws bought an albacore fishing boat she sailed on it through the Panama Canal. When they took it to the South Pacific, she met them in places like Fiji and the Cook Islands. Recently, she took a trip back to Norway. But her daughters don't say their mother was a world traveler. They say their mother loved her family, husband, home, and garden. They offer you some spicy Japanese dried peas, but you decline. You are late for a lunch date. You don't say it's with yourself.

As you skid into the gravel in your driveway, you think how great that sandwich is going to taste. You are just stepping in the door when a car pulls in. It's Jan, the priest. What day is it? Oh God, how could you forget you promised to go over the rental agreement for the Chilkat Center with her? You pretend not to be surprised and ask her in. She says she'd like some coffee, so you make a pot. A half hour later you've cleared up the few sentences in the lease you were uncomfortable with. You both agree that since the borough, not the church, plows the parking lot, the church can't be held responsible financially if someone slips and falls in it. You promise you'll present the church's concerns at the next Chilkat Center board meeting and ask her to remind you the day before, in case you forget.

As Jan is leaving, J.J.'s little dog, Phoebe, jumps into the priest's car. Jan reaches in the back seat, but Phoebe jumps into the front seat. You tell Jan you can get the dog, and say, "Stay," firmly. Phoebe leaps away from your hands. Then you say, "Good girl, come here," gently, and the damn dog does the same thing. Each time you think you have her, she escapes over or under the seat. You open the doors and both you and Jan reach for the dog from opposite sides.

She jumps off your shoulders up onto the back of the seat. You dive toward her and she flies to the ledge below the rear window. Jan takes her soft briefcase and pins Phoebe like a bee against the glass while you grip the dog's back leg and softly tug her out. Jan quips, "All creatures great and small, the good Lord made them all" and says she'll see you Sunday morning.

It's two-thirty. The kids will be home from school in an hour.

This, finally, is how you make the perfect egg salad sandwich: boil two eggs, rinse them in cold water, and peel them. Add some half-and-half, a pinch of salt, and ground pepper. Mash it all up with a fork and spread it on toasted sourdough bread. (Buy it from the bakery; it's better than you can make, and you've spent way too much time on this sandwich already.) Lay on lettuce leaves, then a thick slice of tomato. Spread some mayonnaise on the other piece of toast and place it on top. Cut it diagonally; put it on a china plate, next to a cloth napkin and a cup of hot tea. Take a deep breath and say a little private grace.

DULY NOTED

On Sunday a group of volunteers cleaned up the Mount Riley trail, cutting fallen trees that were blocking the route, adding plank bridges, and filling in eroded areas of the popular hiking path. Dan Egolf says they carried spruce timbers all the way up to the meadow near the summit and plan to rebuild the boardwalk through the swamp there. "We need to do a better job of protecting the fragile alpine muskeg," he said, adding that hikers should "please stay on the trail and use the new bridges."

Members of the American Bald Eagle Foundation enjoyed halibut fish and chips from the Bamboo Room Saturday afternoon. Foundation director Dan Hart says the catered event at the natural history museum will be held annually. Teenage trapper Stuart DeWitt was recognized for his donations of specimens for the wildlife display, especially a rare fox with half its winter (white) coat and half its summer (brown) one.

An account has been set up at the First National Bank of Anchorage to help defray medical expenses for store owner Dave Shackford, who is recovering from injuries received in a goat-hunting accident. Dave is back home after an extended stay in Anchorage. His wife, Dot, said that although he still suffers double vision as a result of his fall, he's happy to have visitors.

Alaska Division of Fish and Wildlife Trooper Ike Lorentz received the Southeast Trooper of the Year award from the Department of Public Safety. Ike, a twenty-two-year law enforcement veteran, said the award was a surprise. He noted that his presence here helps keep a lid on poaching and other wildlife-related crimes in the Chilkat Valley. Ike said he's also proud of his involvement in hunter and wildlife safety programs.

Leaning into the Light

I AM NOT A HUNTER. I am not a big gun person either. But on the first anniversary of the sinking of the *Becca Dawn* I agreed to let Don, Chip, and their friend Craig take ten-year-old Christian on his first deer hunt. Chip had a lot of work to do before they left, so I ended up at Craig's house helping Christian find the right gun for the task. The guns in Craig's cabinet are jammed in every which way, some spilling out onto the floor, like the books in my bookcases. Craig helped Christian try several. One rifle had even been his mother's. When I asked if she had used it much, Craig said that she'd taught him everything he knows.

Craig is witty and handsome, in a rogue kind of way, with gray hair and blue eyes. He's a sportfishing guide. "Why work when you can fish?" he says. Over dinner one night he told us he'd joined the navy right out of Haines High School. Craig is not a follow-orders-and-salute kind of guy. "Was the other choice jail?" Chip asked. "Heck no," Craig said. "I was already in jail." He may have been telling the truth.

It was snowing lightly on the dock the next morning when I kissed Chip good-bye and hugged Christian, who ducked out of my arms. It will take them all day to cruise down Lynn Canal and across Icy Strait to Elfin Cove and Don's lodge, where they'll hunt. I try not to worry, but between the winter boat ride and the hunt, there seem to be so many possibilities for disaster—and that's not even counting the date. Don says Olen's death is not an anniversary to be marked, but everyone is thinking about it, and I have a feeling the hunt was scheduled for that reason. It was the guys' way to be with their friend when he would need them, without coming right out and saying so.

I was relieved a few days later when Chip finally called to report that everything was fine. Then he put Christian on the phone. He told me he'd shot his first deer. I could hear him smiling. I knew just how he looked. Christian said he hadn't killed it with the first shot, so he'd had to shoot it again, up close. "You would have cried, Mom," he said. I hoped Christian had had a moment's pause before taking the life. At the same time, I was glad that he was hunting with Chip, Don, and Craig, and happy for him that he'd shot his own deer. I want my son to hunt for the same reason I encouraged my daughters to deckhand on a fishing boat. I want my children to really be part of this place.

It was dark and raining at the harbor when they returned a week later. Christian spit off the dock. I asked Craig if he'd taught him that. "No way," Craig said. "I taught him to do it like this," and he made an awful sound in his throat and spit a gucky glob in a high arc into the water. Christian copied him and they laughed.

The tide was out and it was hard pushing the loaded carts up the ramp. I offered to help Christian, but he said he could do it himself. Chip gave me a proud "that's my boy" look and I knew the hunt had been successful. In a week, it seemed, Christian had grown years. Craig and Chip heaved five Sitka black-tailed deer into the back of the truck, holding them by the legs and swinging them with a "one, two, and three." The carcasses hung in our garage until the hunters came back a week later to skin and butcher them.

I couldn't bear to watch, so I left with my dog, Carl, for a trail run in the woods.

When I got home, they had a pile of legs, ribs, and dark red meat two feet high on the butcher-papered kitchen table. Craig and Chip trimmed roasts and back straps at the counter, tossing sinewy scraps in a bucket for a trapper to use as bait. Christian wrapped the meat in plastic and then white butcher paper and labeled each package for the freezer.

Don stood at the stove in one of my aprons, frying up the tenderest medallions of venison, with hash browns and eggs. The whole house smelled of meat, raw and cooked. Walking in from the clear outdoors made me dizzy. Craig was already eating, with both elbows on the table. He chewed slowly and groaned, "Man that's good." Before I could take off my wind jacket, Don handed me a big greasy plate, saying, "Isn't this great?"

I wasn't sure I could eat in full view of the dead deer—or what was left of them. I would have preferred a private meal, just Chip and me and perhaps a glass of wine or two. But I didn't want to let down Christian and, especially, Don. In the year since Olen's death, his boyish face has aged. There were new lines around his eyes, and a kind of wisdom just behind them. The steak was so tender I cut it with a fork. It really was good, and I said so. The men laughed. Christian smiled at me, then looked down, just like Chip does when he's pleased. Don got the camera and asked me to take a picture of him and Christian in front of the meaty table.

Focusing the lens on Don and Christian, my heart tilted toward them. I hoped the hunt had helped take Don's mind off last November's tragedy. At the same time, though, being with a little boy, and teaching him about life, death, and the great wide world, has got to remind him of other times spent on those wet beaches and mossy hills when his own sons were young. The picture I was taking reminded me so much of the photos on display at Olen's memorial service that I had to shut my eyes. I realized that this same scene has been repeated over and over again since our ancestors scratched images of a bison hunt on the walls of a cave. Maybe killing animals is as fundamentally human as telling stories or breaking bread and sipping wine. Maybe it's as instinctual as conceiving children.

CHRISTIAN IS THE REASON Chip took up hunting. Our son was spending more time with his friend Wayne, who's called Wayner (it's a family thing, his uncle is Jimmer), than with us and we missed him. Since their mother left them, Wayner, his brother, Daniel, and their dad have maintained an all-male household. Christian loves hanging out over there. They take him hunting for ducks, grouse, and even squirrels. So Chip taught himself how to hunt with books from the library, videos, and hours at the shooting range. He likes to hunt now more than he used to enjoy hiking or rock climbing. I think it is because he has a purpose. Hunting is not play, although it's not work either. The November deer hunt has now become an annual event.

Christian and Chip have also been hunting closer to home for mountain goats. Chip watches the goats all summer with his spotting scope from the sunroom window, studying their habits and browsing patterns on the mountains across the way. In the winter, he brings binoculars when skating on Chilkoot Lake and scouts the ridges above it for goats. His first goat hunt was with our friends Roger and Steve and Roger's son Payson and Christian. They came back two days later with a muddy billy goat that they had dragged whole down a mountain. They skinned and quartered the animal in our garage. I did some inquiring among hunter's wives — even though the guys swore it would be great, I don't always trust their judgment — and was told that goat meat was either inedible or so tough you couldn't digest it. One woman said I could can it like salmon, in pint jars in the pressure cooker, and that would make it soft enough to chew, "if you can stand the smell." She also said that if I sniffed the carcass I'd get a hint of the odor. I went out to where the men were cutting up the meat and took a whiff. It smelled like steak. I sniffed again, thinking there must be a mistake, but it still smelled fine, and the deep maroon meat was virtually fat free.

I asked Chip to cut me off two rump roasts and I put them in a pail and carried them to the kitchen. I rinsed them off and dredged them in flour and salt and pepper, then browned them in a cast-iron pot with onions, poured a whole bottle of good red wine over them, chopped up garlic, tossed in a handful of rosemary from the greenhouse, and put the lid on and let it simmer all day. I invited the hunters and their families over for dinner, making a vat of mashed potatoes, as well as steamed carrots, popovers, and a big salad just in case the goat meat lived up to its awful reputation. It didn't. It was so good that not one bit was left over. Since then, goat has become my favorite "company" meal.

The only problem with goats is that I can't look at them, cook them, or eat them without remembering Sam. Though that may be a good thing. Sam Donajkowski was a friend of ours when we first came to Haines. About our age, he was young and active like we were. Sam worked for the Alaska Department of Fish and Game at Chilkat Lake. He ran marathons and he and Chip raced each other in the annual triathlon. Sam usually beat Chip. Sam married his sweetheart, Mary, one year in May, and died goat hunting the following September. He slipped and fell down a scree slope as he was retrieving the goat he had shot. It was a stormy day, and shortly after he fell, a mudslide buried his body.

Knowing what had happened to Sam was part of the reason I went mountain goat hunting for the first time. Chip was planning on going alone in a fast, hard one-day hunt up above Chilkoot Lake. He didn't want to be held back by someone who wasn't in good enough shape to climb a mountain and pack down a heavy load with him. Right after he explained all this to me, we both realized that I could do it. Chip said it would be fun to hunt together. And I agreed, because it would be safer if Chip had a partner.

I've also been worried that lately we've turned into Wilma and Fred Flintstone. Chip has become a hunter while I've been waiting in the kitchen for him to bring home supper. Even though I love cooking game, I'm not wild about this new pattern in our marriage. I'd never thought I'd become a stereotypical middle-aged homemaker while he was out in the woods all day with the boys. So I was thrilled when Chip asked me to hunt with him. I wasn't as sure about the killing part. I have never seen anything die except a fish or a baby chick. I don't know how to shoot a gun. This would be not just my first goat hunt. It would be my first hunt—ever. There is a running joke at our house that my chickens will die of old age and be buried in the backyard before I'll ever chop off one of their lovely heads.

I'm pretty sure that Chip also wanted to show me something that he thought I should know about him, and about hunting—something big that neither he nor Christian was able to articulate.

We left at five-thirty the next clear morning. The navy blue sky was all stars. The night before, our neighbors Steve and Linnus had promised to check on the kids and stay with them in case we didn't get back on time. I'd half-joked that Linnus shouldn't call the Coast Guard until we'd been gone three days. A Coast Guard helicopter had tried to rescue Sam from the gully he had fallen in. It was raining hard on that late September day. Avalanches of mud had threatened to block the Haines Highway. The saturated hillside was too unstable for the mountain search-and-rescue crew to risk it on foot. While the helicopter hovered over Sam, the earth shrugged and he was covered by a ton of rocks and mud. His hunting partner told us later that he believed Sam was already dead by then, that the fall had killed him.

I made sure Chip and I packed overnight gear. If the weather turned, or we got into any kind of trouble, we would be able to camp on the mountain. We drank coffee and ate eggs and toast before loading up the truck and driving ten miles to the end of Lutak Road. As we stumbled through the dark, unfamiliar woods, I asked Chip how he knew where to go. "Easy," he said. "Just keep heading up." It wasn't so easy. I tripped and fell through two big spruce trees that had blown down in last winter's winds and hung there by my armpits, with my headlamp shining toward the sky and my pack hooked on a broken branch.

Half-stuck in the hole, I didn't yell for help. I pulled myself out and caught up to Chip. I was determined to be a good partner. Two hours later we were above the tree line, creeping silently and paying close attention to everything we heard, saw, and smelled. We knew there were goats one slope over; Chip had seen them earlier in the week. But getting to them would be dangerous, and if we did shoot one near the cliffs, it might fall out of reach. I reminded Chip about Sam. He whispered that I was being too cautious, but we did climb a ridge in the other direction. It was about fifteen degrees colder on the mountain than it was down in the woods; also, when you hunt you don't move quickly enough to get warm. Hunting is slow and thoughtful, with a lot of sitting very still. We stopped to put on warmer clothes and eat an energy bar. That's when we saw the lone billy goat walking down a rocky trail toward us. He picked his way to within about four hundred yards before Chip left me to crawl around close enough to shoot him.

I sat perfectly still, using a rock to prop up my binoculars. The billy goat looked at me and I looked at him. He was white and fluffy, with a funny long face and black button eyes. The fur on his legs looked like pantaloons. In such a rugged place, this fancy fellow looked as odd as I would have right then in a wedding dress. I liked him. I could have saved his life by waving my arms. I could have whistled and spooked him without Chip ever knowing what had happened. I could have, but I didn't. Instead, I sat perfectly still, holding my breath, as the billy goat kept walking.

When the shot finally cracked across the cliff, it didn't startle me. I knew it was coming. What I was completely unprepared for was the violent death. The goat stumbled from the impact of the bullet, slumped, and started to fall on his knees, then leapt forward right off his perch, bouncing off the rocks three times before slamming dead onto a ledge, blood staining his white outfit. I looked away and exhaled. Chip was running toward the goat, calling for me to get the packs. It looked close, but with one pack on my back and another in my hands, it took a while to get there. I chose to go through a cluster of small trees rather than across the loose scree. My legs were shaking. The trees were dwarfed by wind and altitude, and their roots were wrapped around big boulders. I kept falling down between them. I was having a hard time with the unfamiliar terrain, both outside and in. Chip had killed a goat, and it was horrible. Yet I was proud of him. I had wanted him to get the goat, and he had. A branch whacked me in the chest, knocking the wind out of me, and I cursed and sat down, trying not to cry. This was not any fun at all. It had been a huge mistake. I wanted to go home.

Then I heard Chip calling my name and I yelled back; we did that for a few minutes until he found me in the bushes. He helped me up, took his pack, and asked why I'd chosen the hardest route. I mumbled something about being a little distracted. He was so happy, he didn't notice my distress. I didn't tell him. He wanted to know if I'd seen him shoot the goat; he said he couldn't believe that the goat hadn't seen him and had kept walking in his direction; he said it was big, maybe even trophy size. Then he said something I'd heard Don say before, about how the fun part was over once the animal was down: "Now is when the work begins."

When we reached the goat, it was on an ice-covered ledge about a foot wide above an old avalanche chute. We needed to move it, or we could slip and fall trying to cut it up. Chip grabbed the back legs and pulled, but the goat was too heavy. I pulled, too, and between us we dragged it to firmer ground. I watched as Chip cut the hide off. It peeled away smooth and dry, like a paper label off a jar. Without the fur covering, goat legs look almost human, with their muscled thighs and calves. Chip said I didn't have to help him if I was uncomfortable. I walked a few yards away and sat down and thought about it while taking in the view only angels and mountain goats usually get to see. I owed it to Chip to finish what we'd started. I thought, I am just as much of a hunter now as if I'd pulled that trigger myself, and this is what hunters do.

Chip looked relieved as he handed me rubber gloves to pull on over my wool ones, and a sharp knife. We dragged a hindquarter farther away from the icy ledge to a safer place. Slicing steaming meat off bones is hard on body and soul. But not as difficult as I thought it would be. I dug around in the warm muscle tissue until I could find a bone, then gripped it with one hand and cut the flesh off it with the other.

At first I tried not to get blood on my good hiking clothes, but the steep slope and the slick meat made that impossible. I slipped as I carried a hunk of shoulder roast to the game bag and ended up clutching it tightly against my chest to keep us both from falling. It sounds corny, but just as I had an obligation to help Chip, I also felt that I owed it to the billy goat's soul not to drop that meat. I held on as if *my* life depended on it. Chip and I worked for three hours in near silence, filling muslin game bags with the meat and then dropping them in our plastic bag–lined backpacks. After Chip helped me shoulder mine and I steadied his pack so he could lift it, I wondered if we'd make it down the mountain before nightfall. It was difficult balancing the load on the steep, trailless terrain. Between us, we had about 130 pounds of meat. The hide was in a duffel bag with a rope tied to it that we tossed down ahead of us or dragged behind.

My thighs twitched from the strain and the fear of falling. I could see now how easily Sam had slipped to his death. Sometimes I refused to look down, especially when we traversed a gully, holding on to the alder branches and rappelling like rock climbers with our backs to the inlet below. The last hour through the forest at the bottom was the longest, with the worry of darkness and my knees aching from going downhill so long with such a heavy load. I watched Chip sway a bit in front of me and heard him curse as he slipped, climbing over a log.

When we reached the truck, we were both punchy. We had been gone ten and a half hours. We lay down on the tailgate to make it easier to slide out of our packs. Chip reached for my hand and held it. Chip's hunt was successful, and I had helped make it so.

Later, when I called my father and told him about our hunt he said, "What did that goat ever do to you?"

Barry Lopez explains this conundrum best in *Arctic Dreams* when he struggles to reconcile his feelings after witnessing the "blood," "horror," and "darkness" of a walrus hunt with his Alaskan Native friends. "There are simply no answers," Lopez wrote, "to some of the great pressing questions. You continue to live them out, making your life a worthy expression of leaning into the light."

We killed the goat, and we will eat it gratefully. Any hunter will tell you it's better to take responsibility for your own food than to leave that task to others. The hamburger you buy in the grocery store, he'll remind you, was killed by someone; you just don't know who, where, or how. That meat loaf was once part of a tail-swishing sloe-eyed steer. Hunters will tell you all this over a big family dinner the same way pastors will tell newlyweds, in front of all their friends and relatives, to be "fruitful and multiply." The truth is,

Chip hunts because he likes it. Being with him right after I'd seen him kill something felt a lot like the morning after a wild night of lovemaking, when it's hard to believe that the Chip and Heather having breakfast with the kids and going over the spelling-test words one more time with J.J. are the same people who romped under, and sometimes on top of, the covers the night before.

As we were about to head home from our hunt, one of the residents of the small settlement at the head of Lutak Inlet stopped his pickup truck to talk with us. Frank had given Chip permission to cut through his property and was curious to see how the day had gone. I listened as Chip told our hunting story, never describing the actual death. The killing part was reduced to "While Heather waited I crawled around and got a good shot." Chip doesn't talk about the naked part of our marriage, and when I do, he blushes. Maybe it's the same thing. Frank is a hunter, too, so he could see it all in his mind's eye. Maybe the reason he was looking at me differently was because he knew that now I could see those images, too.

I watched Chip show Frank the pictures I had taken on the digital camera of him and the dead goat. Then Chip looked down and smiled, and I remembered the picture I'd taken of Christian and Don after that first deer hunt. My husband and son are so much alike. They have the same quiet ways, the same smile, and the same pink flush on their cheeks, although right then Chip's was buried in grime. Talking to Frank, he was trying not to smile.

He was trying hard to act as though all of this was no big deal.

DULY NOTED

Haines tours were among those most highly recommended by passengers aboard Princess and Norwegian cruise lines in recent surveys. The Chilkat Guides, Chilkoot Charters, and Alaska Ice Field expeditions were commended by Princess for their excellent customer service. Norwegian Cruise Line listed twenty-five Southeast tours on their most recommended list. Seven were from Haines: Sockeye Cycle, Chilkat Guides, Haines-Skagway Water Taxi, Alaska Nature Tours, and Alaska Icefield Adventures. Lenise Henderson of Chilkat Classic Cars said her company has made the grade with Alaska Airlines customers as well. She's been so full lately she's had to hire extra drivers for her fleet of old cars. "In one day," Lenise said, "I had a group who said they couldn't live in Haines for forty-eight minutes or they'd go nuts and another car where everyone wanted to know how to buy land here. Go figure."

Before he was an artist and shopkeeper, before he served as Haines borough mayor, Fred Shields was an afternoon radio host on KHNS. Last week Fred met one of his hero's wives, Mrs. Carl Perkins, wife of the late rockabilly star. Valda Perkins and Carl's cousin visited Fred and Madeleine Shield's Fort Seward art shop. Fred played some of the country legend's music on the stereo, and Valda autographed the shop wall. Madeleine said the Perkinses "were really fun."

Kathy Franks was the top winner in the Chilkat Valley Preschool's getaway raffle. Kathy won her choice of $1,000 cash or a travel package including two round-trip tickets to Seattle plus three nights of hotel accommodations, car rental, and $200. Nelle Greene won airfare for two to Juneau, and Jill Closter took third prize, two tickets on the water taxi to Skagway and back.

Just Say "Unknown"

WE SPENT THE better part of a year building our house. Like most homes here, it has a colored steel roof (green) to shed the snow and rain. The weathered shingles help make it look like an East Coast house. Since we're from there, it makes us feel good. In fact, the house looks a lot like the house I grew up in, with porches and gables and even blue walls in the living room, but light blue, not navy.

There's a chimney for the woodstove and window boxes on the south side full of nasturtiums and geraniums. We built it with three carpenters from the Covenant Life Center, a Christian community twenty-six miles out the Haines Highway. The 150 or so members took over an old homestead, so they, and we, usually just refer to their place as "the Farm." The ladies all wear skirts, sensible shoes, and makeup. The Farm men are all clean-shaven; they're not allowed to grow beards. They are nice people who work hard and, besides being builders, own the bakery. When the Farm carpenters drop a hammer, they say, "Shoot" or "Gosh darn."

I worked with the carpenters on our house every day, hauling material, staining exterior trim, and sanding and finishing all the interior woodwork. Chip bought whole units of one-by-four-inch Douglas fir that I belt-sanded and coated with a water-based polyurethane. I used red paint on the front door. After I'd done the last cleaning up in my dirty coveralls and the table saw was carried off the porch and packed in the carpenters' truck, it was time to say goodbye. I teased the Farm men that I would have to hire a Farm woman to answer the door wearing a dress, the house looked so good.

The house I spent most of my childhood in had an acre of manicured lawn and garden surrounded by high, trimmed hedges and big old rhododendrons and azaleas. My yard now is mostly a tangle of long beach grass, fireweed, wild roses, spruce trees, and gravel paths. There's a fenced garden with three big strawberry beds, peas, lettuce, onions, carrots, zucchini, and some sorry-looking beets. There's a smokehouse for smoking fish that looks like an outhouse and smells like alder wood and salmon, and in the greenhouse behind it there are tomatoes, cucumbers, herbs, and hot peppers. In the chicken coop are seven laying hens and a rooster.

Living in this house has made me think hard about the bonds we have with our first homes, and what I want my children to remember from theirs. When Eliza and Sarah were babies, I didn't really think about what it meant to raise them far from their grandparents, aunts, uncles, and cousins. It hit me about five years later, when my sister Kathleen was visiting from New York with my nephews. All six of our kids (Stoli wasn't here yet) were running up the Rutzebeck road in front of us, and Kathleen looked at them, all tumbling together, so much alike, and said she was sorry we didn't live closer. I was, too. We had come to Alaska on our honeymoon—and ended up staying. We hadn't planned it, but that's what had happened. Chip and I make sure our children stay close to their East Coast relatives with regular visits. Their grandparents all come every summer, and they take turns visiting with aunts and uncles on their own or with us. Often, one or two head back with one set of grandparents and return with another. It's not perfect, but there is a family chemistry that gels whenever we're together.

Friends also become like relatives, and on holidays, our house is as full or fuller than mine was growing up. Chip and I both make the connection with objects from our past, too, and like to live surrounded by old things that wouldn't pass as antiques and aren't valuable to anyone except us. Recently, both my family and Chip's sold the homes in New York and Massachusetts that we grew up in. Last summer a huge container arrived here full of everything no one wanted back East. Aside from a few broken lamps, all of it is now in our new home.

I scrubbed the iron bed that came from my grandmother's house with a wire brush and gave it three coats of creamy oil paint. I'd slept in this bed the night my grandfather died, back when I was a teenager. We had arrived at my grandparents' home in Pennsylvania a few days earlier, when my grandfather was put in the hospital. He fell into a coma, and we waited. The phone rang in the middle of the night, during the kind of thunderstorm they only have in the Allegheny Mountains. My aunt ran to my grandmother and led her in the Lord's Prayer. They shouted the words above the rain and thunder. It's funny, but I have no recollection of the funeral. None. I do know that my grandfather was prepared for death. Before he got sick, he cleaned the garage, attic, and basement. He gave away or sold his hunting and fishing gear. By the time he was in the hospital, only one suit hung in his closet, along with a clean shirt, underwear, and the socks and shoes he wanted to be buried in. His household records were all in order, his bills all paid.

My grandfather, my mother's father, had an Alaskan connection. When he was born, his mother died in childbirth. Family lore goes that his father, Charlie Smith, was so upset that he left the baby on his sister's doorstep. But I wonder if that is really true. He must have at least knocked on the door and handed the baby over. Then again, maybe not. That would explain what happened later. Charlie Smith, my great-grandfather, headed west for the Klondike

Gold Rush. He was in Alaska from 1898 or '99 until 1952, when he came home sick and old. He lived in my grandfather's house for about a year, until he died in the very same old iron bed that I am cleaning up and painting for Eliza to use.

My mother, who was a teenager then, says she knew him only as "Uncle Charlie" and thought he was a distant relative. She knew he'd been in Alaska because he talked about it. She remembers that he took a lot of photographs, and shared them with her. Now she wishes she'd kept a few. When Charlie died, my grandfather took his father's belongings and burned them in the backyard. His trunk, clothes, and any record of his Alaskan life went up in smoke. I have tried to find where Charlie may have lived, but it's difficult. First, there's the name. A lot of gold seekers changed theirs to the name he already had — Smith. Charlie was just about as popular, so finding *my* Charles Smith was not easy. He did have a middle name, Lawrence, which is why I think he was in Skagway — records there show a receipt for taxes made out to a Charles Lawrence Smith. He may have been in Nome, too, because a Charles L. Smith was fined for something there. Other than those two iffy connections, I have found nothing in all the Klondike and Alaska archives. Nothing. A whole lifetime, most of it in twentieth-century Alaska, just plain gone. That's not as unusual as you may think. In a place always looking toward the future, the past often gets lost.

THERE ARE PEOPLE who come to Alaska to be alone. People who don't make relatives of their friends and who don't stay connected to their past — either immediate or distant. My great-grandfather didn't die alone in Alaska; he made it home, and he had a home to make it to. Some people aren't so lucky.

A while back, I wrote an obituary for a man who had been a familiar enough sight in Haines, yet he befriended so few people that he had been dead about four days, in an apartment near the post office, before a neighbor called and asked the police chief to check on him. Everyone in town saw him often because he walked miles most days, in all kinds of weather. He had a formal nod and was well dressed. A man in pressed slacks and clean walking shoes attracts a certain amount of attention in a place where most men, except schoolteachers, wear jeans or brown canvas workpants. A neighbor told me he was what she thought southern gentlemen must be like. My dog, Carl, and I greeted him on our morning beach walks. But we didn't really know him.

One couple did know him well enough to have him over on occasion for supper, but they couldn't shed any light on his past. "We knew him," said the wife, "but we didn't, you know?" She said that he sent them postcards when he left town, which he did often, in the dozen or so years he was in and out of Haines. Someone else said he was "a mystery." The last person we think he spoke with called him "a traveling man." It was impossible for me to find anyone who knew him well.

At the lumberyard, a handful of guys discussed the unnoticed passing. They tried to match the unfamiliar name with a face. After I described him—"You know, he's the guy who walks all the time; he had that van with the top sawed off"—a carpenter nodded his head, remembering. "He's the fella," he said, "who made the popemobile." Then they all knew who he was. About ten years ago, before the tour-ship dock was built and bus tours became the norm, he had cut the top off his van and fitted it with a homemade Plexiglas box so tourists could see the mountains and eagles without getting out or craning their necks. But the van was old, and the top leaked. He couldn't make a go of his tour business and left town.

One woman thought he might have gone to Texas, where she'd heard he had family. Someone else said Fairbanks. About a year later, he returned with a new idea. He hoped to manufacture small custom RVs here. All he needed was financing. "You could be talking about the space shuttle going to Mars," said one of the coffee drinkers, who the man had joined occasionally at the Bamboo Room for breakfast, "and he'd bring it around to his RV project."

At the post office, the staff felt bad when they heard the news. They thought they should have noticed sooner that he hadn't come in. When I told them he had been dead for about four days, one clerk did the math and tears welled up in her eyes. She said he had come in what must have been the day before he died, murmured something about seeing the light, and said good-bye. She said he had started crying, right at the counter, but she couldn't talk to him because there was a line out the door.

But maybe the people he knew in Alaska gave him what he wanted. Maybe he just wanted to be alone. Researching the man's life was a little like looking for clues about my great-grandfather. And if we can know so little about our contemporaries, it's no wonder I have had trouble tracking down stories from a hundred years ago.

My job was to write about a man's life, not investigate his death. Still, I couldn't help wondering how this current mystery would unfold, so I went to see the police chief. In the chief's office there's a photo of him as a young man, squinting into the sun with dog tags hanging on his bare chest. His hair was blond then, and he looked more like James Dean than Andy of Mayberry, as he does now. There is a beautiful woman on each arm. I had to ask. He told me it was taken in Vietnam during the war. He fought with the 173rd Airborne Brigade there. Right in the middle of that terrible time, a helicopter showed up and landed in their camp. Two Playboy bunnies, some publicity people, and a congressman boosting troop morale hopped out and quickly grabbed a few soldiers, took their pictures, and flew away as suddenly as they'd appeared. "It was surreal," the chief said now. I think he keeps the picture just to prove it happened. Had there been a photograph of Charlie Smith with Klondike Kate and one of her "girls" somewhere in that burn pile in my mother's childhood backyard—next to the cherry tree, the gladiolus, and my grandmother's clothesline?

I told the chief about what I had learned at the post office and asked if the dead man had been unhappy. The police chief, who'd spoken with him enough to know that "September eleventh was hard on him," said he had been "a little down lately" and that he'd had heart trouble. "He was sixty-one and died of a heart attack or maybe a stroke," the chief said. But no one knew for sure. He gave me the phone number of his family, which did, in fact, live in Texas. I spoke to a polite southern lady. She told me that her brother had loved Alaska so much that he'd walked from Fort Worth all the way to Haines. That is a really long walk. He'd taken a dog, named Brown, but had apparently left him with a family in Utah because traveling with the animal was hard. She also told me that a neighbor from Haines had called her after her brother died and wanted her to know that in the last conversation he'd had with him, her brother had said he was going to a place even prettier than Alaska. She said he must have had a premonition that his end was near. She felt better knowing that he had found God first.

I went back to the police chief and told him everything I had discovered. I asked if there was going to be an autopsy. That's when the chief sighed, took off his glasses, and leaned back in his chair. "What difference would it make?" he said. "He's dead, and that's enough for his family to bear. Why waste the state's money investigating something that isn't a crime and that we don't need to know?" It was not exactly a *To Kill a Mockingbird* moment; however, the chief had a point. My thoughts turned again to my great-grandfather. Maybe even if I had his papers, I wouldn't really know him. It could be that he'd left so few clues because he didn't want anyone to know. Maybe like this man, my great-grandfather just wanted to be left alone. There is also the possibility that he didn't do much that needed to be Duly Noted. What if he'd spent fifty years in some cabin by himself until he'd decided to head back home? The subject of this obituary may not be much different. My imagination had me dreaming up drama where perhaps none existed. I asked the chief if the paper should print that the cause of death was a heart attack. He thought a minute about the wanderer with big ideas, and said "unknown" was more accurate. "Just say unknown."

I wrote that he died of an apparent heart attack, which is what it says on the death certificate. But that was just the first line of the obituary. The last word went to a snowplow driver who sometimes had an early morning cup of coffee with him at Mountain Market. He didn't know anything about him at all, except what mattered: "I know he was a nice guy and I enjoyed his company."

My mother said from what she knew of him, my great-grandfather was a nice man, too. The iron bed that Charles Lawrence Smith slept in (and, I think, died in) at my grandparents' house is now tucked under the eaves in Eliza's room, looking out over the tidal flats and mountains of southeast Alaska, about as far from the oiled roads of western Pennsylvania as you can get and still be in this country.

When we first moved into our house, I wanted everything to be clean and new. I wanted it to look like the magazine clippings I'd saved. I had an old wingchair reupholstered and almost bought matching chairs for the dining room table, but decided that the funky assortment from our families' houses looked right at home around the table made by a Haines cabinetmaker. Underneath it is a worn Oriental rug from my mother-in-law's house.

My grandfather's old rolltop desk is in the kitchen, quickly filling with school papers, ferry schedules, and the manuals to new appliances. He'd climb out of his grave and organize the pigeonholes if only he knew what a mess it is. My other grandfather's cane leans against the wall in the hall by the piano. Across the room, a crystal pitcher with a heart etched in it catches sunlight on the windowsill. It came from Norway to North Dakota with the first Lendes to arrive in America. Chip's parents gave it to us as a wedding present. I imagine a farmer's wife arranging prairie flowers in it, and setting it on a handmade table in a sod hut. I can even see her stepping back to take in the room and smiling. Her new house, in a faraway place, is now a home. That's just what all these old things have done for mine.

DULY NOTED

A Japanese legend says that if you fold a thousand paper cranes, a wish will be granted. Well, we are all wishing high school freshman Rigel Falvey so much wellness as she battles Hodgkin's disease that our fingers hurt from folding cranes. Little children are learning how to make paper cranes in classrooms. High schoolers create hip cranes from teen magazines during lunchtime. Tanned summer guides fashion cranes from pretty patterned paper over espresso at Mountain Market. Friends gather at Friday night potlucks to make cranes. Library patrons fold them while they check their e-mail. If you still haven't made any cranes yet and would like to learn how, see Jeanne Kitayama for instructions. The cranes will be sent to Rigel in Children's Hospital in Seattle next week.

Paul Wheeler's Haines Brewing Company is celebrating five years in business and thirty thousand gallons of finely crafted brews. Paul has plenty of the two favorite seasonal beers on tap for summer solstice parties. Birch Boy Summer Ale is made with the birch syrup from the Humphreys' trees at 18 Mile. The Spruce Tip Ale is brewed using buds of local spruce trees. "Captain Cook came up with that idea," Paul said. "The spruce tips helped prevent his sailors from getting scurvy."

Colleen Harrier and Zach Taylor returned last week from an aborted ski tour to Mount Fairweather. They were forced to turn around near the halfway point after encountering difficulties with harsh weather and shuttling gear. A three-day storm had dumped four feet of snow. "Nothing went according to plan," Zach said. Although sunburned and rebuffed, the pair isn't discouraged. They intend to try again next year.

A Whole Lot of Love

MARY AND WARREN PRICE had eight children together, and Warren came to their marriage with three small children of his own. Father Jim, Sister Jill, and even some of the parishioners of the Sacred Heart Catholic Church call Mary Price "Mother Superior." Warren was more like the biblical Joseph—patient, hardworking, and always in the background. That was even more true lately. Since he'd come home from the hospital in Juneau, Warren hadn't been able to leave the house. I wasn't too surprised to learn, while I was taking the ferry home from a wedding in Juneau with my daughters J.J. and Stoli, that he had died.

The ferry schedule this winter and early spring has been difficult. Sometimes we don't have one for three or four days, and when they do come and go it is likely to be at three in the morning. The Sunday morning ferry up to Haines from Juneau was perfect; it left at ten and arrived at two-thirty. Getting down there had been another story. The last ferry of the week was Tuesday, and the wedding wasn't until Saturday, so we took our chances on the weather and flew—barely.

The rain was blowing sideways across the runway. The girls and I were in the biggest small plane in Haines. There were six of us, plus the pilot. He tried to take off and couldn't; the wind was too strong. As he motored back toward the terminal, I felt relieved. But then he decided to try it one more time. We raced down the tarmac, and instead of flying above the end of the runway, we were yanked off the side, jerking like a kite catching a lift. I swore. I thought we would die. I didn't reassure my frightened children. I cried. I was a really bad mother, and I knew it.

Luckily, the pilot was a really good pilot and *he* knew it. He got us level and moving forward (and up and down and a little sideways) all the way to Juneau. Thank God I had my rosary. I pulled it out of my coat pocket and held on tight. I shut my eyes and breathed deep, saying the prayers over and over as we bobbed through the waves of wind. Then I felt a kind of calm. I attributed it to prayer. Later, the bride's sister, Robyn, who is now in medical school, told me I was probably so scared I was in shock. That's why my hands were numb and I was tingly up to my elbows.

The first time I heard anyone say parts of the rosary was when my childhood friend Meg Dougherty, all red hair and freckles, shrieked, "Holy Mary, mother of God" as the small sailboat we were in capsized in Long Island Sound. It was more swear than prayer, but I liked the music in it. I'd repeated it myself many times since then without knowing it came from a longer rosary prayer, the Hail Mary: "Hail Mary, full of grace, the Lord is with you. Blessed art thou among women and blessed is the fruit of thy womb, Jesus. Holy Mary, mother of God, pray for us sinners now and at the hour of our death. Amen."

Then, a few years ago, I saw a Native woman take rosary beads out of her purse on a bumpy jet ride to Anchorage. As her fingers rolled the beads and her lips moved in silent Hail Marys—you say ten in a row five times as you make your way around the chain— her whole body changed from tight to loose. She was still jostled with every gust, but she looked comfortable, like the Queen of Sheba riding an elephant.

I have been wondering about the power and effectiveness of prayer for years. I pray often but in a random kind of way, and usually a little apologetically, as in "Dear God, I'm sorry to bother you, what with war, famine, and disease and all, but I'm worried about Sarah's math grades." Her grades did improve, but I wasn't sure why. I think it had more to do with extra help from the teacher than God. If you pray and then get help, does that mean God heard you? I wish I knew.

I was in the Presbyterian church once when a woman stood up and said she'd prayed for a bathtub and God had had Sears send one. She knew because it was yellow and extra long. Her husband was six foot two, and, she said, no one but God could have known this. Or that yellow was her favorite color. She said the original order had been for a standard-sized white one; they couldn't afford the custom length. She had prayed and prayed for a different tub, and then this one arrived. I had a lot of questions I never got to ask. Did God pay for it? Or even sign the purchase order? Did her mother send it but she credited God because her mother isn't usually that generous?

The one time I prayed harder than I ever had about anything— the time Becky and Don's son Olen was missing after his fishing boat sank—it didn't work. They never even found his body or the boat. After the funeral, when I talked about this with Jan, she said God was doing better things for people we love than we could ever know. She quoted the Second Song of Isaiah: "For my thoughts are not your thoughts, nor your ways my ways, says the Lord." She said I had to trust that God is good and great.

I understand that.

I just thought that this time God must have made a mistake; he must not have heard how much we loved that boy or realized how unfair it was for him to die at twenty when there were lots of really bad old people lurking around who no one would miss at all.

And there must have been at least one nice old man who would rather be in heaven than a nursing home. If Warren Price had been sick back then, a good God could have switched him with Olen. It would have been a win-win situation.

Warren had "been ready to go," Father Jim told all of us sitting around Mary Price's kitchen table a day after my return from Juneau. I was there collecting the information I needed to write Warren's obituary. We all knew that Father Jim was right. Warren had been housebound too long; he'd had a couple of strokes and had lost a leg to diabetes. Mary had been nursing him for years. This winter, just after Warren came home from the hospital in a wheelchair, Mary fell on the ice and broke her wrist and had to get it set in Juneau and arrange for one of her children to come and stay with Warren. But Mary rarely complained. Instead, she prayed. Mary goes to Mass almost every morning. Often Father Jim puts on all his vestments and says the service just for her. Hearing Father Jim and Mary talk made me want to have that kind of easy faith, the kind that is like breathing. Faith so clear you don't even think about it, you just feel it.

A few months earlier I had decided to learn how to really pray, the old-fashioned way, the way Christians have for over six hundred years—with a rosary, the string of prayers you can hold in your hand. I know rosaries are usually for Catholics, and I'm Episcopal, but I figure prayer is prayer. And the rosary prayers are directed to the Virgin Mary. I liked that. It would be easier to talk to a woman, a mother like me, than to God himself.

My rosary is made of blue glass, ivory, and light wooden beads with a silver crucifix hanging down the front. It looks like a necklace except I can't fit it over my head. Each bead and some spaces in between have a prayer to match them. A pamphlet came with the rosary explaining which bead is for what. It has the prayers printed on another page, and on the back are the Bible readings that tell the story of Jesus. After four or five tries, I thought I had the sequence of rosary prayers—the Our Fathers, Hail Marys, and Glory Bes—more or less figured out. But when I got to the bead for each new Bible verse—or aptly named mystery—I was lost. I had to open my eyes, flip over the pamphlet, and find it. It broke the spell. Maybe that's why the rosary didn't work so well on the flight to Juneau; maybe I wasn't doing it right. Sure, I felt better for saying my prayers, even if it was technically from shock, and yes, we didn't crash. But it didn't feel like God was holding me safely in the palm of his hand. Instead it felt as if I was hanging on to the hem of his robe while he flew through the air like Superman. I want to feel peaceful and secure during prayer. I want a reassuring answer. When I said the rosary on the plane, it was more like talking to myself than to Mary or God.

I told this to Kathy, who is Catholic, and she invited me to say a rosary with her small prayer group, so I could see how it was done. I needed help, and I had a lot of questions.

The church door was open and Kathy, Marie, and Dick, the banker, sat on two pews. Before I could ask them how to use the rosary properly, they started. The empty church was dim and plain and felt holy. I was nervous at first, but after the first few go-rounds, I fell into a rhythm of automatic responses with them. I did know how to pray. When Marie read the "mysteries," I understood them. I quit worrying if I was doing it right. With each repetition of the Hail Mary prayer, my cares receded.

When we were done, Dick read from a Thomas Merton essay about how God was in each one of us like a tiny, diamond-bright light. Prayer may not be a conversation with God at all. Maybe it is listening to that light inside you. Then Dick said we should close our eyes, breathe deeply, and say, "What is the question?" over and over again, blocking out all other thoughts. I had come looking for answers, and now he was telling me that prayer is a question?

Still, when they invited me to join them the next week, I said I would.

MARY PRICE COULD have used prayer to ask for real things over the years—with eleven children and Warren long-shoring and her working as a nurse at the clinic, I'm sure they would have appreciated the extra help. Maybe she did ask. But I have a feeling she got more answers from her daily rituals of Mass, lighting candles, and saying the rosary.

Watching Mary now, running her bustling household while making funeral arrangements for her husband, serving plates of food, answering the phone, and laughing with one of her grand-children, I am amazed at her strength. Warren is not the first loss for Mary. She has buried three sons. I'm not sure I could get up in the morning if that happened to me. Her boys were great kids. Steve died in a car wreck when he was still a teenager. Mary hoped Joe would be a priest, until he died diving for sea cucumbers a year out of high school. Warren's oldest son, Cookie, who Mary had raised as her own, died just this winter of a heart attack in middle age. Mary has practiced her faith so regularly, for so long, through so much tragedy, that she really believes Father Jim when he says of her sons, "God called them home early."

After Father Jim helped himself to coffee, he told everyone in Mary's kitchen how Warren had said he was looking forward to seeing "his boys again." The little house in the mostly Native neigh-borhood was packed with Mary and Warren's children and grand-children, cousins, nieces, and nephews. I had brought a box of doughnuts from the bakery, and I realized with a quick head count that I should have gotten two. I found a chair and moved some pa-per plates and took my notebook out to get down the details of Warren's life. He was a Tlingit, a Raven from the Frog House. He joined the navy before graduating high school and became a signal-

man in the South Pacific in World War II and later a Seabee in the
Korean conflict. He was proud of his service, and his children's. His
daughter was in the army for seven years, and his son Russell is cur-
rently a captain.

It wasn't very hard to talk with the Price family about Warren,
partly because of his age and illness and, I think, partly because
they all believed Warren was in heaven now. Before I left, Mary
invited me to a public rosary for Warren at the Catholic church
that evening. I don't think she knew I had been saying mine, and
I know she knew I wasn't Catholic. I wanted to go, I was curious
what praying the rosary with so many people would feel like, but
I just couldn't. I told her I was supposed to be at a school board
meeting.

Then Warren's cousin, an older Native woman with long gray
hair and bifocals, who hadn't said a word since I'd arrived, spoke in
a light Tlingit accent. "Warren is only going to be dead once. There
will be lots more meetings," she said. "You be there." She didn't look
at me, and she said it the way they call bingo numbers at the Alaska
Native Brotherhood Hall, emphasizing each word. Mary caught
my eyes and nodded her agreement. Father Jim said in his loud,
South Boston way, "Well, Heather, looks like we'll see you there.
Seven o'clock."

This time the Sacred Heart Catholic Church was full and the
lights were on. Dick was up front playing the guitar and singing
with Sister Jill from Juneau. I saw Kathy and Marie in the crowd,
as well as all the Price kids and family friends and relatives. Father
Jim passed out brightly colored plastic rosaries and the pamphlets
of prayers that come with them to the people who didn't have their
own. Sister Jill began by explaining what the rosary was.

"It is more of a meditation," she said. "The repeated Hail Mary
prayers are like a mantra. The words are not as important as the
thoughts attached to them. Tonight we will pray for Warren's soul

and for his family—we will think of them while we say the prayers to Mary. At each large bead I will share a mystery in the life of Christ; for this service we will use the joyous mysteries, the ones that focus on the Resurrection, to remind us that Christ died and rose again so that we—like him—and Warren will, too." And then we began, a hundred and fifty voices praying out loud in almost unison. I closed my eyes and jumped in with the rest. The words became one kind of sound and one kind of thought. They were like the wind off the water. About a half hour later, we were done, and everyone sat quietly, not sure if it was okay to leave.

Then Russell, the army captain in his uniform, stood up and thanked us for coming, on behalf of his mother and the rest of the family, and he echoed something he'd told me earlier at his mother's kitchen table. "My father, like me, was in the service, and like me, he saw most of the world. He always told us that he came back here because Haines—all these mountains, rivers, and lakes—is the most beautiful place he'd ever seen. And he'd seen it all. I have, too, and I believe that."

The Catholic church has very high windows that let in light, and stained glass on either side of the altar. We couldn't see out, but we knew what he was talking about. On the other side of the double doors, beyond the muddy parking lot, the boarded-up former grocery store, the Captain's Choice Motel, and the faded, flat-roofed, two-story buildings on Main Street, beyond the dirty piles of rotting April snow, the barking dog, the teenager jumping the curb on his skateboard, and the mother with a baby in her backpack, beyond the American and Alaskan flags on the pole at the library and the wood smoke rising from the chimneys of the big old homes on Officer's Row in Fort Seward, beyond the fishing boats in the harbor and the plane carrying the mail to Juneau, beyond all of it, holding us up and catching us when we fall down were the eternal deep blue sea and the mountains as old as the earth.

And then Russell said, "Seeing all your faces and hearing your voices together made me realize that the beauty in this community is not the scenery. It is right here, in the people. Thank you."

Maybe it was the rosary, or maybe it was magic, or maybe a little of both. All I know is that something big had happened. I left that church feeling light, brand-new, and filled with a whole lot of love.

And that is a way better answer to prayer than a bathtub.

DULY NOTED

Rain at a wedding brings good luck, and judging by the downpour Saturday evening, Kenny Waldo and Linda Smith should have overflowing good fortune the rest of their lives. More than three hundred friends and relatives packed the Sacred Heart Catholic Church for the brief formal service written by Linda. Her words were practical, personal, and at times funny, with references to Chinese proverbs, angels, and all "the great and petty perils of marriage."

About twenty well-wishers surprised honeymooning newlyweds Janet and Dan Harrington with a late-night serenade of chain saws, fireworks, and song Saturday at the couple's Lutak home. The group, led by ringleader Bill Darling, "almost caused a heart attack" with the chain saw, Janet said, but she invited them inside to carry on the day's celebration. The Harringtons were married earlier in the day at the Assembly of God Church.

Amy and Matt Goodman of Detroit, Michigan, spent ten days in Haines visiting their new niece, Madeline Jane Andriesen, and Amy's sister and brother-in-law, Lisa and Thom Andriesen. Besides playing with the baby, Thom says they did all the "usual things," including a Chilkat River raft trip and a day in Skagway. "The last night we had whales in front of our place," Thom said. "That capped it off."

Dave Long and Pam Hansen are engaged. The local guide proposed to the preschool administrator during a raft trip at the confluence of the Tatshenshini and Alsek Rivers. Nuptials are set for August 28 aboard the Haines-Skagway water taxi, on the water off Seduction Point. The boat's skipper, Leslie Ross, will officiate.

Mating for Life

STOLI AND I SKIED out on the river flats on a bright spring day —a day so warm that we didn't need jackets, hats, or gloves. The ski trail weaves around the clear, fast river channels. At one bend we stopped, hearing the familiar call of the trumpeter swans. They sound like Christian practicing his trumpet. We stood still watching a pair of swans glide across the water like model sailboats in a park. "I have seen old ships sail like swans asleep," I whispered to Stoli. It's the first line of a poem by James Flecker. I told Stoli that swans mate for life, just like people. They form pairs—or, as I said to her, they "marry"—when they are young.

Linnus didn't marry Steve until after they had built a house together and raised two daughters from her first marriage. The wedding was in their living room, with our friend Joanne officiating. In Alaska, anyone can be made judge for a day just for this purpose. Linnus wore a purple jacket and a black miniskirt. Steve had on a sport coat and tie. Joanne wore a man-tailored beige suit—pants and jacket. A handful of friends each said something from the heart about Steve and Linnus and marriage and love and friendship. Then Joanne said, "So, I guess you're married." And they kissed. We toasted them with champagne, ate gourmet appetizers that Debra had made, and then went over to our house for a turkey dinner. Leigh made the cake, and Becky Nash made two snails in wedding clothes for the top.

Leigh also baked the cake for another reception at our house, on a sadder occasion, following her father-in-law's memorial service. Leigh called and asked if she could borrow our big Suburban to drive her relatives to Chilkat State Park and sprinkle her father-in-law's ashes there. I said of course. Leigh's father-in-law had been living in Sitka when he died, so they had a memorial service there. He'd lived in Haines before that, and Greg, Leigh's husband, had grown up here. They wanted to scatter his father's ashes near his favorite place to kayak in the park.

I asked what they were doing afterward. When Leigh said they didn't know, she sounded brittle. She was overextended, with her own small children, plus houseguests, on top of planning this second service and her husband's grief. Greg's father was a big, booming man, a Methodist minister and an outdoorsman who had strong opinions on everything. Greg is a slightly built, shy artist. He doesn't go to church. His father's sudden death may have been harder because of what they hadn't been for each other. Greg and Leigh are my friends. So I volunteered our house for the reception afterward.

After putting fresh flowers on the table and dusting off the china cups and saucers my mother gave me when she moved to the country and decided she preferred ceramic Italian dishes, I drove to town and borrowed a thermal coffee pot from Mary Jean at Mountain Market and the arts council's cut-glass punch bowl from Mimi Gregg.

"Punch?" said Eliza, who was helping me. She raised her teenage eyebrows.

"Yes, punch," I said, a little defensively.

"Do you even know how to make punch?"

"Sure, just put some ginger ale and cranberry juice and ice in the bowl. It'll be fine."

It's easy to miss our driveway, so I told Eliza to tie some balloons to the wild roses next to the road. "Do you really think balloons are appropriate at a time like this?"

"Do you have a better idea?"

Eliza thought a minute and said, "Well, at least let's use blue ones."

Everyone found the house, and Leigh liked the balloons. We stood around quietly at first, offering simple condolences—we're so sorry and he was a good man and the heart attack was such a shock. Then Ted Gregg, in a madras sport coat, white bucks, and straw boater, shuffled in with his cane and announced loudly, "He was too young. I'm eighty-four and still have plenty left." He said it again: "He was too young, I say, too young." There was laughter and nods of approval. The widow smiled.

In the kitchen, Leigh told me that Greg and his brother from South Dakota had had a little trouble getting the lid off their father's ash canister. She said their aunt Eleanor, who had traveled all the way from Alabama for her younger brother's funeral, couldn't slide down the rocks to the cove they'd hoped to use for the ceremony. They hadn't realized she'd aged. The last time she'd visited Alaska, Greg was still at Haines High. Now he's a forty-something father of two. "But it was fine really," Leigh said. "I mean, the ashes fell out okay, we read a poem, the baby cried, and that was pretty much it."

It was hardest on Greg's mother. She and his father had been married fifty years. The preacher was not always easy to live with. But he was her mate for life, and now she was alone. I told Leigh what Budge McRae had said after his wife, Clara, a difficult woman if ever there was one, passed away: "Clara and I've been together sixty years," he said. "It may get a little lonely without her."

The party grew louder and more animated. Everyone protested when Leigh started to cut the cake; it was too pretty to eat. I found a camera, and Leigh posed, surrounded by admiring relatives and friends. The flash didn't go off, so we did it again. A baby crawled under the table. Someone let the dogs in, and Carl's wagging tail spilled a drink. Leigh talked with Greg's mother's friends and passed plates of cake. She helped their little daughter reach a cream puff and steered a pack of boys, including both our sons, outside to play on the beach. I was on my way to the kitchen to make more coffee when I saw Greg leaning against the doorway looking at Leigh with wonder and gratitude.

LINNUS SAYS NO one should get married until age thirty-five. She says if you marry any earlier than that, somebody has to give up too much. Linnus and I are sitting on my porch, our faces tilted toward the sun. Four trumpeter swans fly out over the river, on their way home to Chilkat Lake for the summer. I don't agree with Linnus. I tell her that sometimes young couples survive, and argue that Chip and I have been happily married for twenty years and that we were fresh out of college when we said our vows. She rolls her eyes and says, "You guys are like in the first percentile."

We both know the apparently happy couple who just split after twenty-eight years of marriage. They seemed a perfect pair. They matched. They looked more like brother and sister than husband and wife. They had a cool house, neat kids, and a good dog. They camped in exotic countries and hiked on local trails. I heard that the wife was the one who wanted a different life, in a warmer place. The children were grown, so she decided her job was done. Linnus heard that it was mutual, that they just decided not to be married anymore. We don't say more about it. Neither of us really wants to know the details. We are both a little rattled by the bad news on the small-town rumor network.

After my conversation with Linnus I can't sleep. Sure *I* am happy, but perhaps Chip is the one who feels he's had to sacrifice too much. That's why, when Chip looks up from the taxes a few days later and grumbles that he doesn't know where all the money goes, I burst into tears. Suddenly I see the pantry loaded with cans of corn, cereal, and dog food like a weight chained to his ankle. The next morning at breakfast we have an argument about nothing. I feel terrible. He looks confused. There is no time to talk; he's late for work, and I have to fix school lunches.

We're going to Whitehorse for the weekend. The girls have a swim meet there; Christian has an orthodontist appointment. Now I don't want to make the five-hour drive or spend the weekend away, and I say so on the phone to Chip at midmorning. He tells me it's too late; he's already arranged for Steve and Linnus to watch the animals and has booked the rooms. The rooms? Usually we all camp out in one. Now he says, "I got a room for the kids and a room for us."

I put on earrings, pack the cooler, and clean the kitchen. It is sunny and fifty-eight degrees, a great spring day, when we head out the road. The children settle in the back seats of the big Suburban. I think about our first car, a 1981 Chevy pickup as plain as a green rubber raincoat. We bought it just before our wedding, which took place in an Episcopal church in New York. During the vows Chip struggled with the old language of the Book of Common Prayer, saying, "I pledge thee my truck" instead of "troth." We drove that truck all the way to Alaska and it's still here—and so are we.

AT LAST COUNT, 171 swans returned to the Chilkat Valley this spring (including the cygnets, which stay with their parents for a year or two). Many migrate annually to nesting sites on the lake. My friend Debra finds their feathers floating near her dock, or lying on the lawn. She keeps a vase full of them on the piano in the same room at her Chilkat Lake lodge where she had us all for dinner the night before her wedding. The remote lodge is accessible only by boat or plane, so we all slept over to be sure we were on time for the morning nuptials. Debra, who is older than I am and had never been married, met her Greg (there are a lot of Gregs around here), who was alone when he came to Haines, at a community choir concert. Greg sang a solo, and Debra played the piano.

For their wedding service, a dozen of us sat on the lawn in front of the lodge, in chairs from the dining room. The ceremony began when the bride's sister—she's a massage therapist in California—stood on the grass in front of the lake and summoned "the powers of the universe" to bless the union. Behind her, steep mountains reflected in the lake and a cutthroat leaped just for the fun of it. The groom's brother—he's from Minnesota—solemnly read a Lutheran invocation. Joanne recited a long nature poem that I think was really about sex. Whenever any of us want to remember the wedding, we say a line or two that stayed with us. Like the one comparing the evening sky to "stretch marks on the black-skinned belly of the night" or "sucking stones."

Greg and Debra stood, holding hands. They looked right in each other's eyes and exchanged direct, personal vows. It was intimate and brave. They are adults who had seen young love come and go. They knew what the sacrifices and rewards of a shared life are, and wanted all of it, every day—forever. When they finished, Debra's old friend Mel, from Anchorage, pronounced them husband and wife, and the rest of us wiped our noses and blinked back tears. We cried because we were happy, and because people we loved were happy, and because we were all happy in love together. Only adults weep with joy. Children don't. They haven't learned how rare moments of true happiness are.

That night, the bride's parents, John and Erma Schnabel, hosted a reception in town at the Elks Club. Families, friends, and neighbors joined our small wedding party, dancing all night long to a

Cajun band from Juneau. I watched from behind the punch bowl as Chip twirled J.J. until her braids stuck straight out, and those good tears came back. Debra's brother Roger gave the couple a new pickup for a wedding present. There's a red stripe, four-wheel drive, and cup holders. It's a lot nicer than the truck we left our wedding reception in.

THE ONLY FANCY extras on that pickup were Chip's tape deck and stereo speakers. Chip still likes his road tunes. And now, as we drive past the turnoff for the Chilkat Lake boat landing on our way to Whitehorse, he puts in a CD. It's Little Feat. I hate Little Feat. But it's a gorgeous day and we are driving to the Yukon on the prettiest road in the world. And we have our own hotel room.

Chip has been watching the war and tells me about it. I think it is reality TV gone mad and say so. I see every American soldier as a son or daughter, and every Iraqi mother with a crying baby as a distant relative. Chip says, "I look at the troops and wonder how I'd do in the same situation, that's all." I think about the time when I was pregnant with Eliza and a car in front of us flipped off the road into a swamp. Chip stopped our car. One man was dead, another unconscious. Chip carried him out of the water and gave him CPR until an ambulance came. The injured man lived. I look at Chip now and know he would do just fine in a war. I tell him so, and he squeezes my hand.

Two hours later we stop at the only store in Haines Junction. I buy a Coke. I drink Coke only on road trips. This is because I want to stay alert but won't drink bad coffee. Chip will drink warm brown water with powdered creamer. While I sip the Coke, he tells the children with amazement, "Your mother has come a long way." When we were first married, I was a vegetarian. On the cross-country drive to Alaska, I wouldn't touch bacon or eggs, and certainly never soda. "She asked for fruit and granola at every truck stop in America," Chip says.

It's Chip's turn to drive and I pick the music, someone we both like — Lyle Lovett. We saw him in concert in Seattle when I was pregnant with baby number four and Chip was running a marathon. He felt like a gazelle and I felt like a hippo and he wanted to cheer me up.

In Whitehorse that night, the kids order in a pizza and watch TV in the hotel. Chip takes me to a fancy Greek restaurant. We eat pasta and drink wine and, after checking on the sleeping children, head to our own room and behave like newlyweds.

In the morning, we get breakfast out of the cooler in the kids' room. I tell the children that this is how movie stars and famous athletes eat on the road. "It's called room service." They are in junior high and don't believe me. Chip says I'm crazy, but I know it's the good kind of crazy, not the after-twenty-years-of-marriage-I-can't-take-it-anymore kind of crazy.

The swim meet is not too long; the orthodontist visit, painless. The children go shopping, and we go for a run next to the Yukon River. I am able to match Chip stride for stride. "Not bad for an old lady," he teases.

"Not bad for a bald guy," I shoot back.

We all go out for pizza and a stupid Adam Sandler movie because it's rated PG-13. There's no movie theater in Haines, so we take one in when we can — even when it's really dumb.

On the way back, Chip drives first. I want to hear Canadian Broadcasting's Sunday morning radio show. He wants to listen to a country station. Instead of arguing, I look for a CD, and Chip says he already has one, and turns up my favorite love song sung by one of his favorite singers. Merle Haggard leads and I sing along, in my out-of-tune way. Chip doesn't mind, because he likes the words as much as I do. "That's the way love goes, babe . . ."

WHEN WE GOT home from Whitehorse, I had an obituary to write and a wedding to go to. Debra's uncle Marty Cordes had died. When I asked her about Marty, the first thing she talked about was his marriage. She said, "It was never just Marty. It was always Marty and Allie." Debra's uncle Marty kept that special look in his eyes for his wife, Allie, almost until the day he died. His last year was difficult, and he slipped into the fog of dementia. For more than fifty years, though, they'd remained a starry-eyed duo. And they'd looked great together—like Lombard and Gable or Bogie and Bacall. Marty was handsome and witty. Allie was trim and stylish in her scarf and sunglasses. Writing his obituary, I learned that Marty was the first man in this working-class town to wear Bermuda shorts. "I like to think of Allie and Marty as bohemian," Debra told me. "They had *Scientific American* and *Playboy* at their house, which when I was growing up in Haines made them very different." It still does.

Marty named his only son, now a banker in London, Omar, after his and Allie's favorite poet, Omar Khayyám. At the memorial service, Omar quoted the famous lines that summed up his parents' marriage:

> A Book of Verses underneath the Bough,
> A Jug of Wine, a Loaf of Bread—and Thou
> Beside me singing in the Wilderness—
> Oh, Wilderness were Paradise enow!

At Saturday's wedding, the bride was twenty-one, the groom perhaps a year older. Not much younger than Chip and I were when we got married. They said their vows with clear, honest voices full of hope and love. The groom gazed at his high school sweetheart as though this was the moment he'd been preparing for his whole young life. He looked, one friend said afterward, as though "there was no place he'd rather be."

At the reception I sit at one of the tables in the park and look at the big red-and-white striped circus tent swelling and contracting in the breeze off the water, and think it looks as if it's breathing, or maybe it's a heart pumping. I think about how I went from my parents' house to living with Chip, without much of a gap in between. I wonder how different my life would have been if I hadn't done that, if I would even be the same person. Was Linnus right about waiting until thirty-five?

There are days when I can't get into the bathroom, the music blasting from my children's bedrooms sounds like a battle of the bands, the dog pukes fish guts on the rug, and the washing machine makes an alarming clunk before a cloud of smoke belches out of the laundry room—days when I question if this is the life God planned for me. And there are nights when I've cooked another meal for seven and am doing the dishes while Chip is going out the door to work on the sailboat he is fixing up or to an assembly meeting, and I resent the division of labor at our house. Then I feel as if I'm stuck in an old *Donna Reed Show* rerun. Only instead of salon-groomed hair and an ironed dress, I've got on a baseball hat and sweaty running clothes.

But right now, on this beautiful afternoon, I wouldn't change a thing. The praise band from the Haines Cornerstone Foursquare Gospel Church is playing one of Anne Murray's old country-and-western hits. I hum the words: "Could I have this dance for the rest of my life?" Little Leaguers, back from the game and looking for their parents, run through in uniforms, grabbing plates of fruit salad, sandwiches, and paper cups of lemonade. Christian checks in, flushed from his team's victory. Eliza and Sarah coax J.J. and Stoli into a line dance. The groom grew up twenty miles up the Chilkat River in the Tlingit Indian village of Klukwan, so there are also plenty of Alaska Natives here, too, both as guests and in the wedding party. Outside the tent, little children run in circles and nursing moms sit on chairs, chatting. After the ceremony, we'd all blown bubbles instead of throwing rice, and now a dad blows more for a delighted toddler.

Then Chip comes up behind me and asks if I'd like to dance. He looks at me the same way he did when we got married. The same way Steve looked at Linnus in their less than conventional wedding, the same way Greg looked at Debra, and the same way the groom looked at the bride in the church today. It's also the same way Leigh's husband looked at her when she cut the cake after his father's ashes were scattered, and the way Marty looked, I'm sure, when he read Allie poetry. I bet it's the way swans look at each other when they are about to take flight. It's what Bonnie Raitt wants us to hear when she sings, "Your sweet and shiny eyes are . . . like meat and potatoes to me."

There is no secret to being, as Linnus says, in that "first percentile," that minority of young couples who stay together for life. It's as simple, and as complicated, as keeping that look in your eyes.

DULY NOTED

A foot of light, fluffy snow fell Monday night. Tuesday afternoon the temperature rose fifteen degrees and the wind shifted to the south, creating perfect conditions for surreal, tumbleweed-like snowballs on the school fields and the wide beaches at the bottom of Cemetery Hill. The white balls also rolled down Main Street as if being pushed by unseen hands, prompting one onlooker to suggest that the angels were bowling. Some grew to the size of basketballs before they became too heavy to move.

Friday night singer-songwriter Livingston Taylor made fans at the Chilkat Center laugh and cry with his sentimental tunes. Livingston tries to come to Haines every year to visit friends Bart and Lenise Henderson. He opened the show with a story that's well known to locals. At the airport, a van driver offered him a lift to town. He asked where he was going. Livingston said, "To Bart and Lenise's." That was all the direction needed. Livingston told the audience, "That just doesn't happen anywhere else. This is a very special place." Later in the show he said Haines was "quite simply the loveliest place on earth."

Haines has been chosen by *Outside* magazine as one of the top ten towns in America to live in if you are a millionaire. The editors of *Outside* said Haines is paradise if you don't have to make a living here.

Prom night was a success for the Haines High senior class. Prom king and queen Ben Egolf and Liz Scott reigned over a court that included prince and princess Wes Hoffman and Eliza Lende, duke and duchess Joey Jacobson and Amy Gross, and butler and maid Nik Hura and Sarah Lende. "What Dreams May Come" was the theme of the Saturday night ball. The school gym was "dreamily" decorated in blue and silver with an artificial pond and waterfall and a dramatic castle-gate-style entrance.

If I Saw You in Heaven

LEE HEINMILLER, TONY TENGS, and I were all having coffee at the Bamboo Room. Tony's father, Marty Tengs, had owned the grill and adjacent Pioneer Bar for years. Now Tony's sister, Christy, and her husband run the place. Tony and Lee had just finished setting up the sound system at the Alaska Native Brotherhood Hall for Matt Bell's funeral that afternoon. "At least you'll be able to hear what people are saying," Lee said, taking a bite of his cinnamon roll. Matt was twenty, and had drowned three days earlier in a popular swimming hole. These guys were helping because they grew up with Matt's parents. Lee's mom and dad were one of the original families who bought the old army fort after World War II, along with Marty and Allie Cordes and Ted and Mimi Gregg. Tony helped choose the music for the service. Another friend was going to play the piano, but there would be taped songs too. "They're going to use 'Tears in Heaven,'" Lee said.

When I heard that, I thought maybe I shouldn't go. If I do, I thought, they better have a stretcher and the ambulance crew standing by to pick me up off the floor and carry me out when it's over. Eric Clapton's anthem to his four-year-old son who fell from an apartment window to his death makes me cry when I hear it on the radio. Hearing it in a packed community hall, looking at a casket, will unglue me.

Earlier that morning I had gone up to the Bells' house to get some background for the obituary. Matt's mother had a new puppy sleeping at her feet. It was born with three legs. She said Matt had brought the dog home recently and talked her into keeping it. At the time, she didn't know why. They were a family of four—two parents and two sons—and now there were just three. She thought Matt wanted her to know that, like this three-legged little dog, they'd be okay. She thought he may have known that his life would be cut short.

I told the guys about that, and Tony said, "Did they tell you about the visitation? About seeing Matt—I mean, his ghost?" They had. Apparently, the day after he died Matt's ghost stood right in his parents' living room and talked to his father, reassuring him that he was at peace. I told Tony and Lee that I believed it.

Tony said he thought it was true, too. The night before he had been with the Bells at the fire hall saying their last good-byes to Matt, whose body lay in the casket. "His face had this bloom," Tony said, "like you could see his soul."

I've worked on other obituaries during which the family told me of signs they'd gotten from another world. Once, a long-dead brother came to see his ill sister the night she died. I think he encouraged her to come with him wherever he spent eternity. The brother's ghost even stayed in the kitchen with her spirit after his sister died. They banged pots and pans and made all kinds of noise, until the widower told them both it was time to go. The thing that spooked me most was that the brother had died at nineteen from a brain tumor and a stroke had felled his younger sister when she was eighty-three. I asked Tony and Lee if they thought that answered Eric Clapton's question: "Would you know my name if I saw you in heaven?"

"Sure, it does," Lee said, and launched into several tales of his own paranormal experiences.

Rather than fearing the unexplainable, people in Haines tend to embrace it. We want to believe there's more going on than meets the eye. Take last winter's close encounter with the great beyond. It happened one early morning in January, during my annual low point, when I was wondering if I had clinical depression or the light-deficit illness common in northern regions, seasonal affective disorder. Or was I just in a really bad mood? Then something incredible happened. A brilliant flash lit up the yard brighter than summer sunshine. It was like lightning, except there was no thunder. No bang, no smoke, no crash or burn. The whole family froze, and before we could even duck, it happened again: A second flash made a positive, then negative image out of the basketball hoop and spruce trees in our snowy yard.

"Whoa!" yelled one of the kids from the mudroom. "What was that?" We ran to the windows but couldn't see any flames or smoke. On the back porch, there was no remnant of that flashbulb-bright light. The only glow at all was the midwinter sun slowly rising. Chip guessed that a transformer out on the road had exploded. I thought a jet had fallen from twenty thousand feet up on its way between Juneau and Anchorage. But why was it so quiet? The teenagers put a colander on their little brother's head, made space-alien noises, and sang, "It's the end of the world as we know it." The announcer on KHNS said no one knew what the mysterious flash was, but callers confirmed that it had lit up the sky from Mud Bay Road all the way out to Mosquito Lake. They saw it over Main Street in Haines and fourteen miles up Lynn Canal on Broadway in Skagway. It was weird and sort of thrilling.

Space-alien invasion or not, the kids had to go to school. On the way back from dropping them off, I stopped in at Mountain Market. Everyone was talking about the flash as well as the accompanying boom some folks had heard. A few people recalled the series of UFOs that normally skeptical people swear they saw some winters back. I thought about the night I was nursing J.J. and watched one of those flashing green lights travel over Lynn Canal through a starry sky. It sure looked like a spaceship to me, too. We never did find out for certain what it was.

Then there's electrician Erwin Hertz's story. When he was fifteen, back on the family farm in Montana, he saw a flying saucer. He was getting the cows in from a lower pasture when he felt as if someone was watching him. He turned around and saw a giant spaceship with lights all around the top. "I froze, looking at that thing, and it was looking at me," he recalled to the group at Mountain Market. Before he stepped out into the snowy parking lot with his coffee and muffin to go he said, "I can still see it right now." He had no doubt that the bright light everyone was talking about could have been a visitor from another world. He's even almost been to one. When Hertz (everyone calls him by his last name, even his wife) was a newlywed he was working as a logger and was hit by a falling tree and transported to another dimension. "I learned that I could go anywhere in the universe on a thought," he said. It felt so good to be floating out there above his body and the friends who were trying to revive him that even though he had just married and was very much in love, he lost all desire to be on earth. Maybe that's why Hertz seemed to handle his son's death so well. Jesse was just twenty-eight when he died in a car wreck out at 18 Mile on the Haines Highway.

One Mountain Market color commentator, who didn't share Hertz's hope that the unexplained phenomenon might be friendly Martians or a visit from angels, said the whatever-it-is was "definitely man-made on this planet." He knew because he'd heard it from a friend who worked at a remote radar site above the Arctic Circle. Someone else said it was a stray missile from Russian tests scheduled for later in the week on an island in the Pacific. "Think about it," he whispered, leaning in close. "Why would they tell us what they're doing out there? Like we'd ever tell the Russkies just when and where we're going to test top secret weapons?"

"There's nothing in Haines," one of the fuel-truck drivers announced, helping himself to a refill of coffee. "Fred saw it up on the pass. It probably hit near Whitehorse." At noon, the radio news reporter chasing the flash and bang announced that "it" might have crashed outside the tiny town of Carcross (short for Caribou Crossing) up on the White Pass, over the mountains between Skagway and Whitehorse. Still, no one knew for sure what "it" was.

Thinking back now on all of this makes me realize that there are some surprises still left in this world. We don't know something about everything. Big Brother might be watching most places, but not Haines. He hadn't caught this flaming fireball from outer space that broke through our sky and careened over the mountains of southeast Alaska and the Yukon. No one knew about it all. Except us. It had taken the better part of a whole week to convince people Outside that we had actually seen what we'd seen.

When I asked my editor at NPR if I could do a commentary on it, she said no, because they couldn't confirm that it had happened. I think she thought I was making it up. Luckily, there were pictures. One Canadian real estate agent posted them on the Internet, so I was able to write about it in my *Anchorage Daily News* column and for the *Christian Science Monitor*.

Turns out, after checking reports from Haines, Skagway, and the Yukon, scientists all over Canada agreed: "It" was a meteorite. A falling star. It could have smashed into Haines, eliminating all of us, just like the dinosaurs. Instead, it blew up in the sky and scattered charcoaly bits of the heavens on a frozen lake, miles from anyone. After we'd had a day or two to get used to the idea that we had seen—and survived—something rarer than a total eclipse of the sun and more unpredictable than a tornado, people were calling it a miracle, and smiling when they said it. A good mood prevailed. Rather than be terrified about our near miss, we were thrilled. All eyes and hearts tilted toward the sky and the beautiful, mysterious, and very good universe.

MAYBE MATT BELL was flying around out there above Haines, too, and nobody knew it. Thinking about what Matt's father and Tony had said about that possibility made being at Matt's funeral a little easier. The Alaska Native Brotherhood Hall was so full that latecomers had to stand outside. A borough assemblyman gave a eulogy that took us back to the days just before Matt's birth when his own brother and a friend—they were not much older than Matt was when he died—were missing and presumed dead in a plane crash. They had been on their way to a moose hunt. The wrecked plane wasn't found until years later, hidden in the woods within sight of the airport. "In those dark days," the assemblyman said, "Matt's birth was the only good news in town." Then, one by one, people stood and shared their memories of Matt. His grandmother talked about giving him a red fire truck for Christmas when he was four: "His face just lit up, he was so happy." An aunt said how much she would miss hiking with Matt: "He protected me from the bears." An elderly neighbor talked about how he always came to shovel her out of the snow or fix her car: "He never said much except 'Yes ma'am.'" Clearly it was Matt's actions that spoke louder than his words, and endeared him to her.

When anyone dies, it sends out ripples of grief in a community. When a young person dies, it's more of a storm surge or even a tsunami. I looked around the Alaska Native Brotherhood Hall and counted more than a dozen parents who had survived the death of a child. In public, they appear to be an exclusive club of brave, wise, and compassionate people that nobody wants to join. Privately they must have moments of despair and anger. I know Hertz's wife didn't accept their son's death the same way he did.

I caught the banker's eye and wondered what he was thinking. Dick wears Hawaiian shirts to work, and his glass-walled office overlooking the harbor is full of large tropical plants, cacti, brain-teaser toys, and moving liquid tubes that must be related to the old Lava lamps. He also ruminates often about the meaning of life. For Christmas he gave me a subscription to the *Noetic Science Journal*. The last time I saw him, he told me of an out-of-body experience that he'd had when he was a little boy. He was playing with friends, one of those hyperventilating games where you breathe very fast and then someone comes up behind you and squeezes the air out of your lungs and you pass out. Your mother told you never to do that, and this is why. It almost killed Dick. He floated up in the sky and could see himself lying on the ground, while the other boys tried to revive him. He remembered looking down at a red ball on a flat roof. After Dick came to, he found a tall ladder and checked. The ball was there. "There was no way I could have seen it," he explained, "if I hadn't really left my body and soared above the neighborhood."

Looking at all the people at Matt's funeral was close to an out-of-body experience for me. I remained in my seat, but I felt as if I were high on the wall. I could see everyone clearly that way, and how we all fit together and how tightly we were all holding on to one another with otherwise invisible ropes. In school the children learn drownproofing skills at the swimming pool. Matt couldn't take advantage of that training because he had hit his head. He never had a chance. The children learn that the best way to survive if your skiff capsizes and sinks is to link arms in a circle and hold on tight. That's what we were doing for the Bells that day. When my body returned to my seat, I realized that Hertz had been speaking, and I heard him say that two years ago Matt's parents had consoled him on the loss of his son; now it was his turn to help them. Many people put their heads down. It was hard to listen to that. It was hard to be reminded of so much loss. Then Hertz threw us a lifeline. He started talking about a TV show. He said he had recently bought a satellite television dish and had been watching *Who Wants to Be a Millionaire?* He recalled that on one episode the question for $125,000 was, "Who was the most powerful prophet?" The guy on TV had missed it, but Hertz hadn't. "It was Elisha, an apprentice to Elijah," he told us. "Elisha gained twice as much power as his master because he saw Elijah's spirit ride up to heaven in a fiery chariot."

Chattering on that way about something that didn't make a whole lot of sense—or make anyone cry—worked as well as a life preserver to buoy our spirits. I understood why Hertz liked that image so much. He had actually seen a fiery chariot or two. Thinking about that made me—and, I suspect, other mourners—smile. Chip leaned over and whispered, "God bless Hertz," and Hertz kept on going, now talking about another question on the TV show. "This one was for sixty-four thousand dollars," he said. "How about that, a real sixty-four-thousand-dollar question."

While he talked, I looked through the open door at two eagles circling in the warm breeze high above the water. Although I've seen thousands, the sight of an eagle in flight still moves me in a way I can't explain. It's like a prayer. In Tlingit legend, all animals, rivers, and even places have spirits, just like people. Tlingits believe that human and natural spirits are not separate but intertwined, and that those spirits move throughout time and space. A child who is named for a grandmother is so closely linked to the elder's soul that she is even called "Grandma" by her parents. In the same way, an old man's "uncle" can be an infant.

I fanned myself with the funeral program and wondered if eagles and spirits and mountains and maybe even strange lights and meteors are God's way of getting our attention. Do we feel God's presence because we are looking for him, or do we feel it because he is looking for us?

Then Tony hit the play button on the stereo and Lee fiddled with the dials on the amp and we all listened as Eric Clapton wondered out loud if his dead young son would recognize him if they met in heaven. Grown men had tears running down their faces.

When I got back from the service, the house was quiet. Christian was the only one home. I hugged him and told him I loved him and said he could have anything he wanted. "You name it," I said. "Anything at all." Just please, I didn't say, don't die before I do. Please don't let me talk to your ghost. I don't want to watch you leave me on a fiery chariot or eagle wings. I don't want to know if I would be as brave as Hertz. Even if you would know me if you saw me in heaven, I'd rather just believe it's true than have my own story as proof. I never, ever, want to join the club of parents who have lost children.

Right then I would have given Christian a trip to Seattle to see the Mariners play, a thousand dollars, *and* a puppy. His eyes lit up at the possibilities. He knew I was serious. He could also tell that I was little crazy with real and imagined grief. He smiled and said, "How about a bacon cheeseburger, fries, and a milkshake at the Bamboo Room?"

The exterior wall of the Bamboo Room and Pioneer Bar has a photomural from the old days on it. In the picture, Tony's father is the smiling, black-haired bartender. Larger-than-life-size young men and women turn around and smile for the camera from their stools. I recognize most of them. I wrote their obituaries. Like Tony's dad, they are gone—but not very far. I couldn't help feeling that someone I couldn't see—maybe a whole bar full of someones I couldn't see—was watching with approval as Christian and I slid into the red vinyl booth and picked up our menus.

DULY NOTED

Haines's own Dixieland-style swing band, Lunchmeat and the Pimentos, traveled to New Orleans for the Crescent City's world-famous jazz festival. While there, Beth MacCready's father, Douglas MacCready, married Carrie Bradley in an eclectic service in Jackson Square on May 2. The French Quarter wedding was held next to a statue of Andrew Jackson inscribed THIS UNION MUST AND SHALL BE PRESERVED. "We passed around champagne to everyone in the square," said Beth. "It was great."

This month's *Alaska* magazine features a photo of Sharon Miller in her sightseeing buggy pulled by a llama. She described the enclosed red wooden carriage as a "colorful phone booth on wheels." Sharon told the magazine that a wolf killed one llama this winter, but the five remaining llamas are "thriving." She also said llamas are smarter than they look.

Monday's ferry was filled with the first tourists of the year, a group of Elderhostelers from New Zealand and the U.K., as well as a host of musicians returning to Haines from the Alaska Folk Festival in Juneau. Dr. Feldman played the concertina while a pickup chorus sang sea chanteys. The informal concert took place in the ferry's forward lounge.

Three Haines grandfathers are resting up after a seventeen-day float trip down the Mackenzie River. Tom Jackson, Bob Budke, and Wayne Walter undertook the trip in a flat-bottomed riverboat, a Lund skiff, and a Zodiac. They started on the Muskwa River in Fort Nelson B.C., and then joined the Mackenzie via the Fort Nelson and Liard Rivers. "It was a nice trip, challenging; it was not your Disney World trip," said Tom, who also mentioned that the biggest problem was finding level, mud-free campsites.

When Death Didn't Stop for Angie

WHEN CHIP'S GRANDMOTHER Angie had a heart attack a few weeks into the new year, we flew to Virginia to say we loved her, but we packed dark clothes. Angie is almost ninety-four. She looks a hearty eighty. She walks with a cane but stands up tall and has plenty of wavy white hair. She watches C-SPAN so she can yell at the Democrats, and she usually wins at rummy because she cheats.

If someone reads this to her, she will say, in her New Hampshire accent, "That's a damn lie." Then laugh, because she knows it's true. Angie has lived near her daughter, Chip's mother, Joanne, her whole life—and the last thirty-nine years in the same home. Angie baked the pies, birthday cakes, and chocolate-chip cookies of Chip's youth. She knit him mittens when he was small and told him to cut his hair when he got older. It's almost as if he had three parents.

That's why we left Haines for Virginia at noon—about two hours after Chip's cousin called saying, "If you want to see Angie alive, you better be here in forty-eight hours." Eliza was still home for her winter break from college, so she promised to take care of everyone. We managed to fly out at a clear hour between snow-storms. Planes hadn't flown in or out of Haines for a week, so we were lucky. The ferry wasn't an option because one had just left and there wouldn't be another for two days. We got the plane tickets on free miles I didn't we know we had. Chip took all of this as some sort of sign we were meant to get there. But as the Alaska Airlines jet took off in Juneau, I thought, a little wistfully, that we could have gone to Mexico.

We flew all night and drove right to the hospital from Dulles Airport with Chip's father, Phil, who chatted with every tollbooth worker on the way. Angie was in the intensive care unit. It was a shock, seeing her in a hospital bed, with all the monitors, tubing, and blankets tucked mummy-style up to her chin. Chip kissed her on the cheek and said how well she looked. He also whispered, "I love you," something he doesn't say easily. Angie was so happy to see him she glowed.

I want to be like Angie when I die, old and in bed. In my day-dream I'm under my own quilts, with a dog on the bed and the familiar view out our bedroom window. Chip is there—I have already decided I have to go first. I don't think I can live without him. Then, still in my little dream, I think, Wait, if I'm that old I probably can't get upstairs; so I adjust the scene and move our bed down to the sunroom. And this way there's more space for everyone to gather in the living room. Then I think, Hold it, what are you doing? Come back to Angie and Chip. This is a real end-of-life moment. Pay attention. Be present. Maybe it's the long trip, or the Dramamine, but when I try to focus on Chip and Angie again, everything is blurry.

Angie has a black eye, the result of a tussle when her heart stopped in the middle of the night. "You should see the other guy," she tells Chip. We stayed at the hospital all day with Chip's sister, parents, four cousins from New Hampshire, and Uncle Pete, taking turns sitting with Angie in pairs. (The ICU rules allow only two visitors at a time.) I was with Chip's mother when we noticed Angie dozing off. I could feel Joanne tense up when Angie's eyes shut. We both watched the monitors blip and flash heartbeats and respiration. I thought, What if they stop, what if she dies while we are sitting here?

Joanne must have been thinking the same thing, because after three or four long minutes of staring at the machines in silence, she said, "Let's go get some lunch."

In the cafeteria, Chip's cousin Cheryl, who manages a nursing home in New Hampshire, where everyone in the family lived until Chip's parents, with Angie, retired to Virginia to be closer to Chip's sister, Karen, said that when her clients are near death they often see a white bird on the windowsill. Sometimes they talk to long-dead children or spouses. She said one man asked her when his wife was coming back and when she reminded him that she had passed away nine years ago, he said, "That's right, I forgot—you can't see her, can you?" Cheryl believes dying is walking through a door into another world—and that it doesn't always lock behind you.

"Sometimes," she said, "people even die and then come back to life." A while ago, she had declared a woman dead—"I mean she was dead. No vitals, gray skin. Dead." About half an hour later Cheryl was tying an ID tag on the dead woman's toe. "She sat right up and asked what the hell was I doing?" Cheryl said. "I know she was dead, so I nearly had a heart attack myself."

I said she must not have really been dead and Chip's sister, Karen, agreed. "There is no mistaking death," Karen said. But she also thought there was something to Cheryl's death-as-transition theory. Her favorite horse had died recently, while she was competing in a horse trial with him. He was running at thirty miles an hour when his aorta ruptured. "It was like pulling the fuel hose off an engine," Karen said. "He dropped like a ton of bricks." What she couldn't explain was how, at the moment of death, he managed to fall skidding sideways, keeping her safe, rather than tumbling headfirst and killing her. "I had a real bond with Scotty," she said. "He felt the same way. He loved me even after he was technically dead." Cheryl nodded. Then someone else got out a deck of cards and a noisy game began.

By midafternoon Angie's health and spirits were much better. She urged me to rest, saying I looked tired. The doctors couldn't believe it. They had originally said she had a 20 percent chance of surviving a day; this morning they'd given her fifty-fifty odds, and by the afternoon they were saying it looked even better than that.

My brother-in-law arrived around four and in a bad mood. Steven had forgotten to bring his wallet to the airport, so he'd missed his first flight from Manchester, New Hampshire, to Baltimore. From there, he'd taken a train to Washington, D.C., but he'd had to wait an hour while Phil and Chip got lost trying to find Union Station. When he'd finally gotten to Virginia, he'd called his girlfriend and learned that she had wrecked his car.

All that—and now Angie might not even be dying.

Steven gave his deathbed speech anyway, telling Angie he loved her and thanking her for saving his life when he almost burned the house down. Then he said that at this rate she'd live as long as her father, Great-grandpa Tom, had. Angie reminded him that she was already older. Tom had been ninety-one when he'd passed away. "Yeah, but he drank and smoked a lot," Steven argued. Which didn't help, but Angie let it go and did something no one else had been able to do: She took the fight right out of her grandson by saying that she loved him.

Chip's family was the loudest and largest in the visitors' room of the ICU, where everyone else spoke in whispers and cried a lot. They were reprimanded by a nurse and a social worker for playing cards so irreverently. When I commented to one cousin on how well Angie was doing, she said, "She's almost a hundred; she can't go on forever." Another chimed in, "Want to bet?" and they both laughed.

By her dinnertime, Angie was playing cards, too—with all her monitors flashing. She was still cheating. "If she didn't, then I'd really be worried," Karen said. "Then she might be getting ready to meet her maker."

We didn't get back to Chip's parents' house until after nine. We lit the fireplaces, poured drinks, and turned on the Patriots play-off game. Friends came over and joined us for tacos, which the cousins made. The neighbors brought over more shredded beef and tortillas. The terriers took turns sitting on Joanne's lap, and Phil's kitten rubbed his ankles while he put on Christmas music. "I know it's January," he said, "but I do enjoy it, especially with all the family here." The party went well past midnight.

Angie was even better the next day, eating canned pears and cottage cheese and wondering why she couldn't have "just a little" coffee. By that afternoon she was scheduled to move out of intensive care and asking Phil to bring his electric razor to trim the fuzz on her chin. Because Angie was doing so well, the cousins were concerned. If Angie came home soon, they worried, she might require more care than Joanne could handle. They urged Joanne to consider the possibility of a nursing home.

They weren't just talking about Angie's future. What they were really saying was how much they appreciated all Joanne does, and did, not just for Angie but also for all of them. They missed living near her. My mother-in-law was not expecting this. She said thank you and looked away. The tender moment didn't last long. There was a lot to talk about. This is a family of optimists; they've never thought about worst-case scenarios, like death. Now they wondered: Did Angie have a will? Where was it? Who had power of attorney? What about a living will? Did she want to be kept alive by heroic measures, be on life support, or be allowed to go peacefully next time? Who would be strong enough to decide? Angie's near miss provided an opportunity to get these questions answered while she was still able to help. Attorneys were called from cell phones in the parking lot, the will found, and systems put in place for the next time.

Everyone in my family is a pessimist. We think every freckle is melanoma. My grandfather built a large wheelchair-accessible home when he was in his sixties, because he was sure he would be an invalid any day. He died of a stroke in his mid-eighties and never needed more assistance than his cane. Still, when my father insisted that Chip and I draw up a will as soon as we had children, even I thought it was weird. Chip thought my family was nuts. Now it makes us both feel better, especially at times such as these, when we are far from the children.

The biggest question for Angie was about something called a DNR order. It means do not resuscitate. If Angie has another heart attack, the doctors are now instructed *not* to use everything in the hospital's power to bring her back to life and keep her heart beating artificially. Angie wanted it this way, and so did everyone else. It was an easy decision. Angie said she bet you couldn't find anyone she knew who would say, "Keep me alive no matter what" or "I want to live hooked up to feeding and breathing tubes."

In Haines, that's how most people feel, too. If we didn't, we'd live closer than a boat or plane ride to the nearest hospital. My neighbor has had a serious heart attack, and survived a Coast Guard helicopter medevac in a snowstorm. But when a doctor in Seattle suggested that he and his wife move there because next time he might not be as fortunate, they declined. Were they supposed to sit in a new condo in an unfamiliar city waiting to call the ambulance? This winter they are busy building a boat in their shop. If Angie's heart had quit at our house on a snowy January night, she probably would have died. At the funeral we would have said she'd led a good life and had a good death.

BEFORE WE LEFT for Virginia, on New Year's Day, we had friends over for dinner. Richard told a story about his college roommate's father, who was, he said, "the real thing, an honest-to-God cowboy." He was in his sixties when he learned he had potentially fatal cancer. "Now that I think about, he was probably about my age," Richard said, a little startled that time was passing so quickly. The "old" cowboy rode out into the desert and shot his horse and then himself. Chip reminded everyone of the white-haired carpenter who'd made our children's dressers and toy chest. Clarence took his life for the same reason the cowboy did. He had cancer and didn't want to go the hospital, or be dependent on anyone. He had lived by himself a long time. Well, almost by himself: "I think he shot his dog, too," Chip said.

I thought about that conversation, and the new DNR order, while I watched Angie laugh and play cards with her adoring family in the hospital. I don't know—when it's possible to prolong the life of someone you love, even a very old someone, at that moment, for me it would be almost impossible to choose not to. There was no DNR order in place when Angie was rushed to the hospital. The doctors and nurses did everything they could to keep her alive. While she was in their care, her heart stopped beating—twice—and they got it going again with machines, chemicals, and enough muscle to accidentally give her a black eye. No one said, She's almost ninety-four, what's the point? Even in this wisecracking family, there was no joking around when Cheryl called us to come say good-bye. I prayed that Angie would live long enough for Chip to see her one more time. It's easy to applaud the old cowboy, because he's not your father or husband or son. The truth is, there aren't many real cowboys left.

With Angie scheduled to come back home after a few more tests, the cousins, Uncle Pete, and Chip's brother decided it was safe to leave. Angie wasn't dying this week after all. Karen had meetings in Los Angeles to get to. Chip drove her to the airport early the next morning. After they left, Joanne and Phil shuffled back to bed in their slippers. It had been a long week. I rinsed the coffee cups and put them in the dishwasher. Then I let in a cat and lingered at the door, watching the sun rise over the brown Virginia fields.

DULY NOTED

A big crowd of local musher Dan Turner's supporters turned out for the start of the Yukon Quest sled-dog race in Whitehorse last weekend. Many mushers say the Quest is tougher than the more famous Iditarod because mushers aren't allowed as much outside support. Nearly twenty well-wishers sent Dan and his dogs down the trail to Fairbanks.

In the middle of Friday night's blizzard Dick Aukerman dislocated his hip at his Mud Bay Road home. "When that hip pops out," Dick said, "you can't do nothing." Deep snowdrifts kept the ambulance from getting up the Aukermans' driveway. Fortunately, neighbor Russ Walton arrived in his front-end loader and cleared the way. Dick says he can't thank everyone enough. "Russ, the EMTs—they really are something special."

Friends thumbing through Bailey's Woodsman Supply Company sale catalog were surprised to see a color photograph of Albert "Whoopee Sam" Sampson demonstrating a small sawmill at the fair last August. The caption tells of the company's Haines visit with Albert and his wife, Georgia, and thanks them for the generous hospitality. Bailey's spelled Albert's nickname "Whoopy," but Georgia said it probably should read "Whoopee," although "it's not like he ever signs his name that way."

Haines's first baby of the New Year was born in Bartlett Memorial Hospital in Juneau. Grandma Irene Stigen said the brand-new girl got the honors because the second baby of the New Year was a born gentleman: "He let the lady go first." She should know, because she's his grandmother, too. They're twins. Jordan Kaye Stigen arrived early Sunday morning, beating her brother Jacob Ray by a couple of minutes and a few ounces.

Alaskans Dear

WHEN TOM WARD SR. collapsed and died while loading fire-wood into his pickup, I heard about it within the hour. Tom was seventy-two, the patriarch of a large family. He had four children with his first wife, Marge, and inherited about a dozen stepchildren and stepgrandchildren from his second wife, Irene. It seems as though he was related in one way or another to half the people in town. His nephew owns Howser's, the big grocery store on Main Street, his son runs the freight transport company, and his two daughters-in-law teach and coach at the school. By all accounts, Tom was the first non-Tlingit native son of Haines to live his entire life here. Speaking at the funeral, another lifelong resident, Debra Schnabel, now in her forties, called his passing a "coming of age" for our little town.

I waited a day before calling Irene to get the information for the obituary. Her daughter Barbara answered the phone. Barbara teaches kindergarten, and my children have been in her class. Her husband is an ultraconservative school board member with whom I often tangle. Barbara invited me up to the Ward house for lunch. I drove out to the edge of town where Tom had built their sun-filled home on a bluff overlooking the river. Inside, Marge led me to the big dining room table, where Tom's children and their spouses were eating, along with Barbara's teenage daughters and Tom's widow, Irene.

That's right—both wives and their families, together, planning the funeral and comforting their shared grandchildren. The house was filled with people. Tom's daughter offered me a plate of turkey and mashed potatoes; his son handed me a cup of coffee. Many of Tom's twenty-one grandchildren were home from school. The older ones helped greet visitors; the little ones were roughhousing in the back bedrooms. One walked through carrying the puppy Tom had given Irene for Christmas. A next-door neighbor came in with a pie, mumbling condolences. She is twenty years older than Tom was. Ever since her husband died, she'd depended on Tom to cut her firewood and plow the driveway. She also liked his company, and made sure there was fresh coffee and something sweet for him to eat every time he came over.

As I drove home, I passed Leo Smith out in his yard. Leo and Tom had been good friends; I'd seen them heading out on moose hunts together or pulling their pickups into the Elks Lodge for a beer after a day of tree cutting. Leo had cleared the land behind our cabin when we'd decided we needed a field in which to play softball. We had worked kind of like a pitcher and catcher, me signaling which trees should go and which ones should stay, and Leo nodding yes or no over the noise of his skidder. One morning as we were working, Leo cut the engine and climbed down from the tractorlike machine with giant pincers, for grabbing logs. Leo wanted to talk about a large, table-shaped boulder. I had signaled him to move it. It was right in the middle of the outfield. Leo wasn't so sure. So we walked around the boulder and then Leo, tipping his cap back and choosing his words carefully said, "It's a pretty nice rock, really, and a good place to sit." He looked up at the view. "A person could do worse than sitting on a rock like that and looking out at the mountains. Meditating, isn't that what you call it?"

The rock stayed.

Leo Smith Logging Company, or what's left of it, occupies the lot next to our lumberyard. In the yard there are parts of front-end loaders, an old crane, fuel tanks, boat and equipment trailers, choker cables, and a rusted yellow bulldozer. These days Leo's logging is pretty much confined to firewood and new home sites. After the last sawmill closed, the city built a cruise-ship dock right across the street. Now this little block of old Haines is surrounded by new Haines: bike, kayak, and rafting guides, gift shops, even an espresso stand. Leo has turned down offers from tour companies wanting to buy his doublewide trailer home. He likes the view of the harbor and gets a kick out of meeting revelers returning to the cruise ships to go to bed just as he and George Anne begin their morning walk—Leo still keeps logger's hours.

When I asked Leo if he had something to share about Tom, for the obituary, he got very still. "Let me think about it," he said. A little while later he knocked on my door. He knew what he wanted to say now. I invited him in and gave him some coffee. He sat at the kitchen table, with his cap in his hands, and started to tell me about his last moose hunt with Tom, but he stopped in midsentence. Then Leo, this tough, gentle old logger, started to cry. I didn't know what to do. Leo stood up, wiping his wet face with a bare hand, and said, "Tom was a good friend, you can print that in your paper. He was a darn good friend." And he walked out the door.

OVER THREE HUNDRED people packed the Chilkat Center for the Arts for Tom Ward's funeral, a formal, dignified service conducted by Tom's brothers from the Benevolent and Protective Order of Elks. Tom was remembered as a hardworking, happy man. His sister said, "Tom's probably cut a load of wood for the Lord by now—he'll be keeping heaven warm." His oldest granddaughter read an essay she wrote, "Grandpa's Garden." The

Presbyterian pastor's wife sang the state song, "Alaska's Flag." It fit Tom well.

> *Eight stars of gold on a field of blue—*
> *Alaska's flag. May it mean to you*
> *The blue of the sea, the evening sky,*
> *The mountain lakes, and the flow'rs nearby;*
> *The gold of the early sourdough's dreams,*
> *The precious gold of the hills and streams;*
> *The brilliant stars in the northern sky,*
> *The "Bear"—the "Dipper"—and, shining high,*
> *The great North Star with its steady light,*
> *Over land and sea a beacon bright.*
> *Alaska's flag—to Alaskans dear,*
> *The simple flag of a last frontier.*

Marie Drake of Juneau originally wrote the words as a poem. But the tune was composed by a woman from Haines. One story claims that Elinor Dusenbury, whose husband was the commanding officer of the old army fort here, wrote it several years after she left, because she was homesick. I like the other version better: that Elinor composed it from the ship taking her back East after her husband's years of service here. It's nice to imagine her humming the simple, proud, and a little bit sad tune as she watched our town fade into the distance.

A SWEDISH HIGH school exchange student came to Haines one fall and, after driving in from the airport, was given the town tour. When asked what she thought of it, she said she liked what little she'd seen. When she was told there wasn't any more to see, she wept and begged to be taken to a real American town.

Tom Ward would have told her, This *is* a real American town. Right out of Haines High School, Tom was sent to the jungles of

Asia to defend America. He spent the Second World War building the famed Burma Road. Back home, he put his wartime skills to use maintaining dirt roads for the territorial government. Alaska didn't become a state until 1959, when he was thirty-four. After Tom retired from the Alaska Department of Transportation, he kept busy plowing driveways; cutting, splitting, and selling firewood; running a small sawmill; and gardening. He fished commercially for salmon, and at one time owned a gillnetter. Like most people here, even now, Tom didn't have a "career." He had jobs. For a while he skippered the mail boat. Today the mail flies in on small commercial planes or is hauled on the ferry. And the big sawmills of Tom's younger days have closed. Haines has evolved into a seasonal tourist and fishing town. We still don't have a traffic light, not even a yellow flasher, but the streets are almost all paved now.

I learned a lot about Haines from Tom's friends. But by the way his family spoke of him and the way they treated one another, I also learned a lot about Tom's character. The feeling around the table that afternoon when they helped me write his obituary was more like a family reunion than a wake. With old family and new family, the room was full of noisy love. In many ways, Haines itself is like the Wards. There have been bitter splits, but we still live together in relative harmony. There are times when we are angry with each other for years, but we nod hello, time young runners at school track meets, and sit near each other in the bleachers at basketball games. Tom's son-in-law the conservative school board member and I have ongoing battles about school prayer, teaching tolerance, and what is patriotism—he's a Republican "America right or wrong" Vietnam vet; I'm a liberal Democrat. But we still work together. He has read eulogies I've written at veterans' funerals. I've often quoted him in an old soldier's obituary.

Our former city mayor made a big mistake when he told a

reporter down at the *Juneau Empire* that Haines was a "gripey community" full of whiners. He lost his seat on the council in an election a week later. By a lot. Then he moved away. As my farm-bred Pennsylvania grandmother would say, he shouldn't have "aired our dirty linen." What the mayor should have said was that Haines was prone to disagreement. We don't whine; we argue. Haines is the easiest town in Alaska to represent in the legislature: No matter how our delegation votes, they'll please half of us. What the mayor didn't say was *why* we fight so much. It's because we care about this place and what happens to it. We care about mines, roads, and land-use issues of all shapes and sizes. Not to mention the school, health clinic, helicopters, tourists, high school basketball, and salmon.

When my sister first visited Haines from Brooklyn, she couldn't believe how worked up we got over zoning and the decline of the public radio station. Back home she has to park her car on alternate sides of the street Monday, Wednesday, and Friday, and doesn't know why. She thinks it has something to do with snow removal. I asked why she still did it in June, and she shrugged; she's a big-city gal with better things to worry about. In Haines, such regulation would cause public outcry, and if that didn't fix it, we'd start another petition to recall the city council. The latest census figures put our population at just over twenty-four hundred. That means we're big enough to avoid people we don't like, but small enough to have to be careful about what we say in public. The longer I live here, the more I understand how important it is to choose my words—and battles—cautiously.

Twelve of us had dinner together the other night at Debra's house. We argued loudly about a close borough assembly race between an old sage and the new millionaire. The old-timers among us (several were born and raised in Haines or Juneau) confirmed that the issue wasn't a vote for the new money but, rather, a vote against the other candidate. It was pointed out that money didn't get votes; if anything, it lost them. The old sage was challenged because of his history here: The better you're known, the less chance you have at holding public office. Tom announced that he wouldn't speak to anyone who voted for the millionaire. We knew he'd never be able to keep his word, because it was clear that our dinner party was as divided as the rest of Haines. Absentee ballots would decide the winner.

With that, the debate switched from local politics to music. This is one area where we have a broader view, especially when Mick Jagger is as close as Seattle. The new question was, Should we cash in our latest Alaska Permanent Fund dividend checks to fly down and see the Rolling Stones in concert? If you had taken a poll right then our party would have been evenly divided. Steve and Linnus were going, but Joanne thought it was crazy. That former mayor would take it as proof that we just can't get no satisfaction.

PERHAPS SATISFACTION COMES in other ways. I'm thinking of a fund-raiser a few years ago when Chip paid five hundred dollars for a dozen cream puffs. I had spent the night in Juneau. I barely was off the ferry when a friend out in the parking lot asked, "How 'bout those cream puffs?" At the post office, I got knowing glances. Everyone I saw smiled broadly and noted that Chip must have *some* sweet tooth.

The whole story is more complicated. Chip bought the cream puffs at an auction at the American Legion. The proceeds went to help the parents of a child with cancer of the optical nerve. They needed help paying for treatments and the associated expenses of staying in California, where their daughter must go to get them. Nikki is blind, a result of the tumor she's had since she was a baby. She is the only child of a couple who adopted her after being childless for years; a few months later she was struck with this debilitating illness. Since we've known her, Nikki has been fighting cancer. She lost her eyesight early on but she's cheerful, funny, and as my mom, who when visiting us has spent time with Nikki, says, "She's sharp as a tack."

My daughter J.J. and Nikki are playmates. J.J. talks all the time. Nikki enjoys a good conversation. Together they never run out of things to say. Nikki's dad is Haines's emergency coordinator—the man in charge of preparing for an earthquake, oil spill, or enemy attack. He works most days on Haines's emergency response plan. He also sells houses to supplement his income. Once, when we were all having coffee and cocoa at Mountain Market, Nikki felt her way over to our table. She has a stick she waves back and forth, tapping the ground and obstacles. She sat down and asked what we wanted to talk about. No one answered right away, so she said, "How about real estate?" Everybody laughed at the little redhead talking just like her dad.

Her dad is why Chip bought the cream puffs for five hundred dollars. Jim is not the kind of guy to ask for help. His picture is under the glass counter at the Alaska Sports Shop, with all the other pictures of local hunters and their dead animals. He's holding up the head of a trophy bison he and Dr. Jones shot near Delta Junction. He's a volunteer fireman and a good Catholic. He takes care of his family. They have insurance, but it's not enough. Nikki's cancer came out of left field. Chip said, "I don't know what I'd do if it was one of our kids."

When close friends reported that the cost of Nikki's treatment was off the map, it was time to help. Friends, neighbors, churches, Elks, and Nikki's teachers got busy. With barely a week's notice they gathered donations and arranged for a fund-raising dinner and auction. An award-winning chef donated her salmon-in-phyllo-dough dish that was a semifinalist in *Sunset* magazine's annual cooking contest. A commercial fisherman made a small salmon net for family use. Businesses donated practical and pretty things, from metal roofing and a side of beef to handmade jewelry and original paintings. The new millionaire, the same one running for office, offered a ride in his helicopter. Dr. Feldman donated a vasectomy. My friend Leigh wanted to do something special. She's the one who baked the cream puffs. Everyone loves Leigh's cream puffs.

Chip is not a big spender. He enjoys simple things, like family dinners at the end of the day. We have them nearly every night. His favorite holiday is Thanksgiving because, he says, it's just like Christmas but without the presents. New shirts stay in the wrappers in his closet until his old ones wear out. He has four pairs of pants and a Timex watch. His favorite jacket is a black-and-white wool one he's had since college. He owns a building supply store and doesn't have any expensive tools. An avid reader, he rarely buys books; he uses the library. And his trucks have to break down completely before he'll buy a new one.

Yet after he splurged on the cream puffs, he was happy for a week. He said that he'd planned on spending five hundred dollars at the fund-raiser. It was a lot more fun to bid on cream puffs than the higher-end items I was hoping for—the load of gravel for the driveway or some round-trip plane tickets to Juneau. We were talking about it over a beer before dinner, while watching the kids play on the beach. They are all healthy and happy. "We don't really need anything, anyway," he said.

Everyone had a great time at the fund-raiser. People who hadn't been together at a social event in years cheerfully bid against each other, paying too much for things they didn't need. There were environmentalists and developers, Catholics and hippies, newcomers and old-timers, Natives and whites. Everyone spent more than they had, and loved every minute of it. A carpenter paid over three hundred dollars for a drill Chip donated. He could have bought it for half the price in our store.

Lib Hakkinen, our town historian, says that sometimes things have gotten so bad here that people have wondered if they would be able to make enough money to stay. Like Tom Ward, though, they figured out a way. With Nikki's health, I'm sure that her parents have thought about moving to a city with a hospital. But they haven't. Haines is their home.

TOM WARD'S FLAG-DRAPED coffin rests on a mat of wood chips at the cemetery. The pallbearers, all workingmen like Tom, look uncomfortable in their rarely used suits and ties. Some don't fit as well as they did the last time they were worn. It may have been years. The men don't have overcoats on. It is four below and feels even colder this close to the river. On the way out, straggling mourners stop briefly to brush snow off headstones. One cuts through the knee-high drifts to pray over his daughter's grave. She was killed in car wreck not too long after she graduated from high school. At the reception at the Elks Lodge, the bar is open and the tables loaded with potluck dishes. The party lasts late into the night.

When I turn in the two-page obituary, my editor, Tom, roars, "Jesus, Heather, the guy was a woodcutter, not the governor." Then he puts it on the front page.

DULY NOTED

The ice at Chilkoot Lake hardened up for skating this week, and with no snow on the ground you can drive to the landing. Sue Libenson and friends skated in the moonlight at her birthday party Saturday night. Sunday afternoon the Port Chilkoot Bible Church held a skating party.

Candlelight, a warm fire, pasta, Caesar salad, garlic bread, and Leigh Horner's famous cream puffs contributed to a fun night out and a good cause Saturday evening at the Senior Center as the Haines Hockey Association hosted their first fund-raiser to pay for Mary Jean Sebens's dental work after injuries sustained in the Haines Olympiad Hockey Tournament. Funds will also be used to purchase mouth guards and helmets. Organizers and chefs Tom Morphet and Steve Williams are already planning the next dinner. "I feel real fortunate," Mary Jean said. "I just felt so much love from everyone." Her competitive spirit hasn't dulled. "If I had stayed in the game our team would have been in the championship," she said.

While most residents have been enjoying the ice on Chilkoot Lake, Teresa Hura says Chilkat Lake is also close to perfect. She says the ride in on the snow machine to get there was well worth it. Teresa spent an enjoyable day last weekend skating from her cabin to neighboring camps. Night skating has benefited from the impressive aurora borealis displays and the howls of wolves. Teresa says as many as fifteen wolves have been spotted on the lake ice.

Registration for the fourteenth Buckwheat Ski Classic is now open. The annual cross-country ski race is set for Saturday, March 25 in the White Pass above Skagway. Competitors will race in ten-kilometer, twenty-five-kilometer, and fifty-kilometer heats. Entry fees cover the cost of a prerace breakfast at the Presbyterian church, a postrace dance and banquet at the Eagles Hall, and, says organizer Buckwheat Donahue, "a really cool T-shirt." Entry forms are available at Lutak Lumber.

Fire and Ice

AFTER THE LAST fisherman's funeral, I decided water around here is best when it's frozen. As I help my youngest daughters into their ice skates, I hum the old carol "In the Bleak Midwinter": "Earth stood hard as iron, / Water like a stone." The afternoon is so perfect; it's like a big exhalation, throwing off all that crummy winter-weather tension. The bowl that Chilkoot Lake sits in is protected by a rim of high mountains and tucked back into a valley. Although a north wind blows forty knots across Lynn Canal, icing boats in the harbor at the foot of Main Street, here on the lake it's calm. Dark spruce trees and white mountains reflect on ice as hard and shiny as a marble floor. Chilkoot Lake is so big that, although I recognized the handful of Subarus and pickups parked on the road, their owners are out of sight. Looking across the ice, I can't see a soul.

I learned to skate on an artificial rink on Long Island, the kind filled with organ music and people in rented skates all circling around and around in one direction. I still can do crossover turns only to the left. Skating at Chilkoot is as different from skating at a rink as swimming laps in a pool is from snorkeling in the tropical ocean. Instead of weaving in and out of other skaters, the girls and I quietly glide about a mile out, to where the rest of the family is already playing hockey. Chip and the three older children are crazy about the game. It's only a matter of time before the two younger girls join them. The games are so fast and rough that it's no place for cruisers like me. Every time I think about playing hockey, too, I'm reminded of the mother in *A Prayer for Owen Meany*. Instead of being killed by a Little Leaguer's foul ball, I'm sure a stray hockey puck will catch me right in the temple.

A safe distance from the game, a group of children my girls' age are learning to make figure eights. Leaving J.J. and Stoli there, I venture beyond the sounds of the game, beyond the voices and scraping of blades on ice. I am so far out I can't even hear a dog bark. The ice is absolutely smooth and clear and the air so cold that my breath makes frost on my eyelashes, scarf, and on the edges of my wool hat. I skate with my arms wide open, singing out loud: "I could have danced all night . . ."

Near the middle on the western side, I can see open water and an orange buoy ball floating way out in the distance, marking the danger. The best skaters, the oldest and wisest, have assured everyone that the rest of the ice is thick enough to hold a dump truck. Now I wish there were a dump truck here so I could see for myself. In places, the ice does look new, similar to the thin layer that appears overnight on puddles in September. The kind of ice that breaks like glass when children stomp on it. I slow down but keep moving across the stillness, hearing nothing but the *scritch* of my blades and the occasional muffled thud of a pressure crack underfoot. That sound makes my heart beat faster. What if the ice won't hold? Can I make it to the shallow end in time? I am about to turn around and go back when I see the tracks of a lone skater. Two graceful curves of white on the dark green ice, repeating in a simple pattern over the lake.

I catch up with Linnus and feel much better skating with a friend. We push and glide fast for fifty minutes in one direction, then slowly circle back to check on the children, Chip, and Linnus's husband, Steve, who is also playing hockey. Everyone is happy, so we leave them again and zigzag silently along the shore, back to the landing, looking for wolves in the woods.

ON THE WAY HOME, Chip and I take the kids to the museum in town to look at a traveling exhibit of blown-glass bowls, vases, and balls by world-renowned artist Dale Chihuly. They are beautiful, but they can't compete with the swirling patterns of frost and bubbles suspended in the clear green ice at Chilkoot Lake. I think I love those much more than the fancy glass because I know they won't last as long.

As if Mother Nature wants to prove the point, the day after our perfect skate we wake up to whirling snow. Across town Tom Heywood looks out the window, too, and knows he doesn't have much time to enjoy the lake. Soon snow will cover the ice. Tom hasn't been skating yet this season and is in a seize-the-day mood. But the rest of his family isn't. His wife, Liz, has a cold, and the kids don't want to go. When his ten-year-old says he prefers his computer game, Tom leaves, alone.

Steve and Linnus, who also decided to get in one more skate before the heavy weather, come ashore as Tom starts out. They tell him the skating is great. Tom follows their tracks in the thin coat of dry snow out into the white winter wonderland. He is alone, so alone, in such a beautiful place that he thinks, *This is unbelievable.* He is happy; skating makes him feel light and carefree. The same way it does for me.

Tom is a mild-mannered former midwesterner. A pilot, he has his own small plane. At forty-six, after teaching first and second graders for twenty years, he's retired and with Liz owns the Haines bookstore. He had children relatively late in life—two adopted Korean sons and a biological daughter. When he taught my kids,

their favorite time of the day was when he'd play the guitar and sing
with them.

Since no one is watching and he's in such a good mood, he dances.
A few fancy moves, some curlicues, a swirl, and a loop on the white
surface. He's left behind the other tracks now and skates toward a
buoy ball. He wonders what it's doing out on the ice. He decides to
go beyond it all the way to the end of the lake, something he can't
do with the kids. It's a long way down and back, nearly ten miles.
He's thinking that there is no place he'd rather be when suddenly,
completely without warning, the ice gives out. One second he's
skating, the next he's in the water. *This can't be happening.* Tom is
incredulous. *I can't believe this.*

Hanging on to the edge of the ice, up to his neck in frigid water,
Tom Heywood doesn't watch his life move before his eyes like a
movie. Instead, he sees one still image of his wife and three children. *I am not ready to leave them,* he thinks, kicking to keep his
head above water and gripping the ice with his left hand. He knows
he can climb out, and he says so, out loud, to the fish below and the
mountains above. "I can do this," he repeats, echoing the Little Engine in the story he's read so many times to so many different children. "I can do this, I can do this." Like an icebreaker, he moves
toward his tracks, hoping he'll find the solid section that held him
just moments ago.

It's so clear what he has to do; the challenge is so immediate that
he acts without hesitating—almost. *This,* Tom thinks for just a
second, *is how people disappear and are never found.* The snow keeps
his hands from slipping; he has a good grip, but the thin ice caves
in with each attempt to climb out. His long johns, jeans, sweatshirt,
and down coat are heavy. He's working so hard he doesn't feel the
cold. He almost gets his right knee up but the ice breaks, again and
again. He's not a churchgoer and knows he shouldn't expect a hand
now, but he prays for help.

Finally, after almost getting up and crashing back in the water six or seven times, he pulls himself out and crab-scoots on all fours until he's sure he's on safe ice. With a shout he thanks the angels of Chilkoot Lake and skates back faster than he ever has. He sails by the patterns he made earlier and knows that *that was a different life.* He hears a cracking sound and his heart beats harder until he realizes it's the ice chipping off his coat, jeans, and ice-crusted skates. On the shore, arriving skaters help get him to his truck and take his skates off, but he waves them off and drives himself home. All he wants to do is get there. His family is at the kitchen table when he walks into the house. There's so much Tom wants to say, he is so grateful and loves them so very much, but all he can manage is "I had a bad experience." Later, he makes a sign warning of thin ice and drives back to the lake with it.

At the bookstore Monday morning Tom greets well-wishers, who all want to hear his story. We think it's a miracle he got out alive, especially with none of us there to help him. Tom says that isn't necessarily so. "I know people say you shouldn't go out alone," he tells us, "but I'm really glad no one else was there. If Liz was with me, we both would have fallen through, and I can't even imagine what would have happened if I had the kids." Then he says, quietly, "I'm certain that somebody else would have gone in, so if it had to happen, I'm glad it was me." I ask him if he'd skate again. "When I know it's totally safe," he says. "And I'll be real cautious if there's any kind of snow."

WHICH IS ALL there was for the next two weeks. As the third line of "In the Bleak Midwinter" goes, "Snow had fallen, snow on snow, snow on snow." It could have been making me temporarily insane. Although I don't think that excuses me from thinking vengeful thoughts or almost committing a crime. Maybe I was just so cold I wanted to heat things up. I had been having trouble coping after close friends of mine split. He'd left her for a woman twenty years younger. I'll tell you the story, but I won't use names; this is too small a town for that. The whole episode had left me feeling as if my heart was under a glacier. It was just enough pressure to cause permanent damage, but not enough for people to notice unless they looked closely.

When my friend who was left home alone asked me and another friend to help her switch around the bedrooms in her house, of course we said yes. We would do anything for her. How we got from simply moving her old bed to almost cutting it up with a chain saw, tossing it out the window, and burning the mattress in the new girlfriend's driveway at midnight, I'm still not sure. The three of us were playing a card game in my kitchen on a Saturday night when the question of what to do with the old bed made a spark that caught fire. Before we knew it, we were all excited and talking at once.

Chip has a dump truck. We could put the mattress in it, tip it off the back under cover of darkness, and light it before speeding away. We'd never have to get out of the cab. No one would know who did it, unless we passed Fireman Al on the way home. When Al was in college he burned his folk's cabin near Chilkoot Lake down to the foundation. It was an accident, and no one was hurt, but he decided to become a fireman instead of a biologist after that, so he could help prevent such a catastrophe from happening to anyone else. We agreed that Al would recognize us for sure.

"Then we'll wear ski masks," one of us said. "And dress in black," another said. "And light it with a Molotov cocktail," added the third, a librarian, who also mentioned that "you can learn how to make them on the Internet." I thought we were doing some heavy housecleaning, not starting a riot. Luckily, our friend with the bed said that we couldn't toss a bottle with fuel in it. The leftover shards of glass might cut a dog's paw.

As I served up warm apple pie and ice cream, I recalled the song "Alice's Restaurant" and all those eight-by-ten glossy photos at the trial, and I knew that while burning your own property in someone else's yard might not be arson, it would, at the very least, be littering. We could all end up in jail, as Arlo Guthrie had. When I said so, one of my friends reminded me that Guthrie's story did have a silver lining: "I mean, he didn't have to go to Vietnam, right?"

But she knew what I meant. It wasn't the law or government we were worried about, it was a higher authority. "If we burn your mattress this way now," she said to our friend, "the smoke will only soil your soul—and ours." We all agreed to a private bonfire on the beach, with just the three of us, the next day.

Still, I worried that the black smoke from all that foam rubber would attract Fireman Al and the volunteers. Chip came into the kitchen and put his pie plate in the sink with the others. "When they see who it is and what you're burning," he said, "they'll run."

Before we went to sleep, I asked Chip if he thought I was crazy. "Yes," he said, "but you were when I married you." I thought about our wedding, how happy we were, and then my friend's wedding, which had been such a fun day, too. I was suddenly dizzy with a grief that was worse in some way than the dying kind. I was so afraid it might happen to us, too, that I turned out the light and kissed Chip hard.

In the morning my friend canceled the burn. She'd heard that the wind had blown most of the snow off Chilkoot Lake and said she'd rather go skating. So instead of standing by a bonfire watching her old life go up in smoke, we started her new one gliding over thick ice.

A few weeks later, I went to see Father Jim. I was writing a story for the paper on his Catholic mission boat, the *Mater Dei*. We met over coffee in the rectory. When the interview was done, I told him I'd been having some trouble lately with forgiveness. I didn't tell him how we'd almost burned a man's marriage bed in his new girl-friend's driveway, but I did ask if you could still be a good Christian if you were thinking really bad thoughts. "Heather," Father Jim said loudly in his South Boston accent. (I think he used to work in big cathedrals.) "Heather," he said, warming up for the punch line the way he does. "Heather, when God taps you on the shoulder and says it's time to go, he'll ask you one question: *Have you been good to my people?* If you can answer yes, then you've got it made."

On the way home, I ran into Christy Tengs Fowler, a close friend of the Stuart family's, at the library. She asked me if I'd be writing Gene Stuart's obituary. I told her I would be, as soon as I finished Father Jim's story . . . and I needed to record an essay for the radio . . . and I had to write my column, too. I didn't have time to visit with anyone about anything right now, especially that obituary. It was terrible and sad and could wait—the weekly paper wouldn't be printed for six more days. But Christy needed to talk and I'm her friend, so I slowed down and we moved out of the doorway to a quiet corner. Gene had died that morning in Seattle from the burns he'd suffered in a fire at his remote cabin the afternoon before. He had been lighting a woodstove with diesel fuel and the fumes had built up and it had exploded. He was on fire when the friends who were out there with him pulled him through the window and then "dropped and rolled" with him on the ground to put the flames out, the way Fireman Al has instructed us all to do. A helicopter that usually transports extreme snowboarders and skiers saw the cabin in flames and radioed town. They flew Fireman Al and an emergency medical technician in to help Gene just as it was getting dark. Then a Coast Guard chopper flew him out of town from the airport. Doctors at the Juneau hospital decided to send him on to a burn center in Seattle, but there was not much that could be done. If that wasn't bad enough, Gene's dog, Willow, died in the fire, too.

Gene was a sawyer in the old mills; he ran the huge blades that cut logs into boards. When the mills were shut down, he became a fisherman out of necessity, naming his boat *Reluctant*. Mostly, Geno, as his friends called him, was a practical joker. He came up with electrician Erwin Hertz's slogan: "Hertz Electric—We'll Fix Your Shorts." Gene was a good man, and he was good to God's people. I told Christy what the priest had said about that, and I decided to take his words to heart. I promised Christy I'd start Gene's obituary whenever the family was ready, and asked her to let me know when they wanted to talk with me. My other projects would have to wait. Christy told me she felt awful for Gene's widow, all alone in her house. "She doesn't even have her dog," Christy said. She also couldn't help thinking about how quickly life can change.

When I got home, Chip's big old boat with the blue tarp flapping on the deck looked as pretty as a white-sailed sloop in the harbor. The skates and boots all over the floor in the mudroom, the dishes in the sink, and my good old dog sleeping on the couch all seemed to shout, *A family lives here; they are busy and happy and a little messy but someday that won't be so and you'll be sorry.* A little joy has come from all this winter's sadness. After Tom fell into the lake and lived to tell about it, his wife, Liz, said she didn't care anymore what he bought her for her upcoming birthday; he'd already given her the best present ever—himself. My friend's divorce has given me a new appreciation for my own marriage. That doesn't mean I would want the bad in order to have the good, but I know that love and life are all mixed up with loss and death, just like beautiful bubbles frozen in the lake.

Robert Frost wrote that the world may end in fire or ice. Well, from what I've seen, heard, and imagined of both this winter, all I can conclude is that the world could end in any number of ways, and there's nothing anyone can do about it. The only choice any of us has is what to do if we're still here after it happens. Do we die a little death every day ourselves or do we reach for someone's hand and dance again?

DULY NOTED

The Lynn Canal Community Players "King of Fools" float took first prize in Saturday's first ever "Mardi Gras in July" Parade. The Harbor Bar's "Pirate Ship" float took second. Having a parade on the Fort Seward Parade Grounds may seem obvious, but according to Officers' Row resident Annette Smith, it took two seasonal workers from the Hotel Halsingland to suggest it. "They were sitting up on the hotel porch roof one night having a few beers and looking out over the parade grounds and they said, 'Gee, someone really ought to have a parade here.' At least that's how it was told to me," Annette said.

The Sheldon Museum held its annual volunteer luncheon last Tuesday. For this year's tropical theme, volunteer Jane Bell said, "Most everybody wore flowered shirts." Milestones for the museum this year included Joan Snyder receiving the First Lady's Volunteer Award from Susan Knowles and the museum's first all-male, all-ex-marine volunteer staff day with Alan Traut, Roy Lawrence, and Frank Draeger. Another gender barrier fell when the Doll's Fair was organized by a mostly male crew, which included George Mark, Mark Klevons, Paul Morgan, Matt Turner, and Alan Traut.

Byrne Power, the KHNS program director, has opened Imago Video in his Quonset hut in Fort Seward. Hours are Thursday, Friday, and Saturday from six to nine P.M., or by appointment. Byrne specializes in foreign, independent, old Hollywood, and art films the other video stores don't have.

Tim June spent the summer solstice sailing his wooden ketch *Keku* in the Juneau Yacht Club's annual Around Admiralty Island race. Tim said he and two crew members planned on taking turns at the helm, but they all ended up staying awake most of the time. "It was still light enough at midnight to not need a headlamp to read the chart," he said, "and by two-thirty or so the sun was shining."

Curtain Call

I WAS TWENTY-FOUR years old with a husband steering, a baby in the car seat, and two huskies in the back of the truck when, in the spring of 1984, I arrived in Haines from Anchorage, where we had been living for about a year. Driving down from Alaska's frozen, flat interior into the Chilkat Valley in April was a lot like going from black-and-white Kansas to the colorful Land of Oz. The mountains were huge and jagged. Everything else was wet and green or blue and bright. I called my mother in New York, from a phone booth on Main Street. I could see down over the Harbor Bar to the bay and mountains beyond. It was hot and sunny. I was wearing shorts. I told her that Haines looked like Switzerland, only on the ocean. Chip was already fishing. This was spring—king salmon, daffodils, and green grass. Chip had been here earlier and had found us an apartment in one of the big houses on Officers' Row, in old Fort Seward.

Ted and Mimi Gregg, who lived in their own home next door, owned it. During World War II, Fort Seward was the U.S. Army base in Haines. After World War II, when the army left, it sold the fort as surplus; the Greggs and four other families bought the decommissioned turn-of-the-century army base, sight unseen, with the hopes of turning it into an artists' colony, and moved to Haines from the East Coast. They've lived here ever since.

Today, the most popular postcards of Haines are the ones of the classic white buildings surrounding the parade grounds at Fort Seward. The best pictures are taken from across the cove, with the dramatic backdrop of five-thousand-foot snowcapped mountains.

There was (and still is) a bar in the Greggs' front hall. Ted painted the portrait of a naked lady that hangs in a gilt frame over it. There's also a baby grand piano in the living room. It belonged to Mimi's mother, an opera singer.

I met Ted while he was mowing the lawn. Chip had started his new job and was out at the sawmill. Baby Eliza was in the backpack. Ted wore faded pink canvas pants, a white button-down shirt, and a tall straw hat that looked like a potato ricer with a beak. He stopped mowing. "Just like Madeira!" he said, in a slightly patrician accent. We silently admired the view. Then Ted said it again, wagging his hand at me to make the point. "Just like Madeira, Haines is just like Madeira." I have never been to Madeira, but I believed him, because he told me that's where he'd bought his hat. The whole scene was like something from a movie or a play.

The next morning I woke up to the sound of a chain saw and looked out the window to see Ted, in safety goggles, carving a woman's torso from a stump. Wood chips flew everywhere. When a small cruise ship docked at the old army pier at the bottom of the hill, the Greggs invited us to a party for the captain and crew. Ted grilled salmon, and his daughter-in-law Gail wore a cancan outfit and baked two cheesecakes for dessert. The sun slanted across the parade grounds and, across the inlet, mountains reflected the evening colors. Ted handed me a glass of wine. "Just like Madeira," he said.

Almost twenty years later, when I was writing Ted's obituary, a friend of the Greggs' recalled, "Ted was the ultimate host. You walked through the door and he had your coat on his arm and a drink in your hand." By then, I knew Ted well. So did everyone else in town. Writing his life story for the *Chilkat Valley News* would be a challenge. Not so much to get the details—he led a well-documented life—but to capture his character. I took a break from my drafting to get the mail. The post office was crowded. One of the clerks had had to leave town suddenly with a sick child, another was out with an injury, and the postmaster was away on his winter vacation, so there were just two guys left to handle all the packages and letters for the whole town. I ended up in the long line between Helen and Joan, two of Ted's contemporaries. We talked about him.

"Ted always had a good time," Helen said. Then she thought a minute and added, "All the men had a good time, didn't they?"

Joan, who, like Helen, is a widow, said, "Yes, but we're still here, aren't we?"

When old people die, friends and family are, for the most part, prepared. As Mimi said, "Ted lived a wonderful life, but he wasn't having much fun lately." He'd had several strokes and had spent the last few months in a nursing home in Ketchikan, where a daughter of his lives. Mimi had decided not to have a funeral. At least not right away. She had Ted cremated and was planning a concert and picnic on the parade grounds in the spring. Ted had never liked funerals anyway. He'd liked parades, parties, and plays.

The Greggs had founded the Lynn Canal Community Players, and for fifty years Mimi and Ted had tried to make the motto of Haines "Alaska's Theater Town." The title shows up in the brochures for the Chilkat Center for the Arts and on and off in various tourist publications. The truth is that no motto has ever really stuck to Haines. We also have tried calling ourselves "The Valley of the Eagles," "The Alaska of Your Dreams," and "Alaska's Best-Kept Secret." At Ted's memorial service, his son Tresham talked about Ted's weekly trips to the town dump. His father, he said, would always come back with more than he'd dropped off. He'd made sets, parade floats, and decorative objects for his home and yard from found objects—treasures, Ted had called them.

The attic of the Greggs' home is filled with costumes, props, and bags and boxes of stuff Ted hauled up over the years just in case he ever needed it. Ted was the one who had authentic, old-fashioned milk bottles for *Our Town*. He played the milkman. Ted also had the cart wheels for Tevye's wagon in *Fiddler on the Roof*. He built the fireplace for *Arsenic and Old Lace* with antique mantel and trim pieces he had salvaged from buildings in Fort Seward. He also built the bar in the saloon for the historical melodrama *Lust for Dust*, about Haines during the Gold Rush. The play, created for tourists, was full of chorus girls and slapstick humor, and much of it rhymed. Jack Dalton was the Bad Guy. In real life Dalton had driven beef on the hoof from Pyramid Harbor to hungry miners up north, charging them a fortune. In the play Dalton said things like "It's time to steer the steer and herd the herd" to his trusty sidekick, Dusty Trails. You get the idea.

A few years ago Tom Morphet took his visiting parents and brother to meet Ted and Mimi. Ted invited them all inside for a family brunch, cooked Swedish pancakes, and afterward got out his tandem bicycle for Tom and his brother to ride. The seats are side by side, and there are double sets of pedals. Ted and Mimi used to ride it in the summer parades, dressed in Gay Nineties costumes. After Tom got the hang of it, Ted went inside and came back with a full-sized bear costume, urging Tom's brother to put it on. He did, and they rode around the parade grounds, with their delighted parents taking pictures. "Who but Ted," Tom said, "would have a bicycle built for two *and* a bear costume?"

Ted decorated pickups, cars, and trailers for every parade in Haines. The floats and costumes he and his family designed and built are still the highlights of our three big annual parades—on the Fourth of July, at the Southeast Alaska State Fair, and, my favorite, at Christmas.

When I was small, Christmas entertainment meant the *Messiah, The Nutcracker,* and *Amahl and the Night Visitors.* Our household included my parents, two sisters, and, for a few years when I was in high school, three grandparents. My grandfather was French, but he and my grandmother had spent much of their lives in England. My father was born in London. So Christmas dinner always ended with a flaming plum pudding and hard sauce. No one under seventy actually ate it, but that's not the point. It was a tradition. My Pennsylvania grandmother, who also lived with us, was a soprano and a pianist. She and my mother, an alto, sang in church choirs.

Our first few Christmases in Haines I was homesick. I missed the eastern holidays, with candles in colonial windows and tiny, delicate white lights. Here, December is dark; the sun rises at about nine-thirty and sets before three, but it hangs so low in the sky that it feels like dusk all day. Often snow and rain obscure the sun completely. That's why everyone uses lots and lots of little and big colored lights. More of them are inside than out, because windy, wet snowstorms rip them off the eaves and short them out. We leave them on all day. The Friday after Thanksgiving may be the biggest national shopping day of the year, but just about every store in Haines is closed. Main Street is quiet. Shops have shorter winter hours, and many are closed until the summer tourist season. The holidays are more about having fun than buying things. And it simply wouldn't be Christmas without the parade, and we couldn't call it a parade without the Snow Dragon. I have never actually seen the dragon, because I'm *in* it, along with seven other members of the Lynn Canal Community Players. When I met the Greggs, they recruited me for various bit parts in *Lust for Dust.* I've also acted in other shows, have served on the club's board of trustees, and directed *Carousel* when I was pregnant with my fourth child, Joanna Jeanne, or J.J. I got the idea for her nickname from the Greggs; their youngest daughter, Kathy Ann, is known as K.A.

This year, as usual, I'm right behind the dragon's head with a fifty-pound fire extinguisher that Fireman Al has filled with flour and strapped to my chest. Every time I squeeze the handle, the dragon spews a floury cloud of "smoke." The twenty-three-foot-long dragon is made of heavy plastic oil drums, cleaned and cut in half, with holes for our necks, all tied together and draped with yards of white and green cloth finished with a foot of tinsel fringe all the way to the ground. Foam fins cover our heads, completing the serpentine effect but making us legally blind. Tom is behind me, cracking jokes and holding the car battery that powers the dragon's red eyes and flashing lights.

A long time ago Ted's son Tresham helped build the Snow Dragon for one of the Lynn Canal Community Players shows, *The Twelve Dancing Princesses*. Ted made a swan-shaped sleigh for the Snow Queen that year too. But while he was towing it back home behind his pickup from that very snowy parade, it skidded into a ditch and was totaled. Today Ted's oldest daughter, Annette Smith, acts as our guide and handler. She looks great in her Sergeant Pepper costume. The parade begins as soon as it's dark, about three. Annette leads us out of the Elks Lodge onto snow-packed Main Street. Santa and his fire truck get their lights and sirens going; the Snowburners snowmobile club starts their engines. A pickup truck of Christians with JESUS SAVES spelled out in lights above them sings carols, and in the dragon's tail the last person turns on the boom box with the traditional parade soundtrack: Alvin and the Chipmunks' Christmas album edited with roars every few tunes.

The dragon bobs and weaves, with all of us passing instructions down the line: "Watch the ice," "Slowly left," "Swing right," "Hop a little." Remember, we can barely see anything. Someone—it must be Tom—suggests that we go into the Fogcutter, so we part the crowd on the sidewalk, take a spin around the bar, and head back out the door. The dragon belches smoke and roars while my children, dressed as Robin Hood's merry band, run alongside tossing lit firecrackers, waving sparklers, and pausing occasionally to launch a bottle rocket. When my mother saw a video of the parade she said the whole thing was vaguely reminiscent of the Tet Offensive.

The chamber of commerce would like something more traditional than the dragon, and last year tried to add an old-fashioned sleigh full of carolers. It seemed like a fine idea. There are summer horse-and-buggy tours now, and a few draft horses winter over. But the fireworks spooked them, and the snowmobiles drowned out the singing.

EACH YEAR DURING the holidays my parents would take us kids into New York to see a Broadway play. When we travel back to see my family now, I always try to include a visit to the theater. Years ago, Chip and I took the children to see *Cats*. It was good, but not nearly as memorable as the musicals they'd seen, and been in, in Haines. It was nowhere near as much fun as the show we saw in Haines a few months later. For *The Sound of Music* there were fifty people in the cast, crew, and orchestra, although that's stretching the last term: Five instrumentalists held together by a strong piano player provided the music. Everyone else had built the set, gathered props, or sewed costumes. Outfitting an Austrian villa with furniture from Haines homes is not easy. First, you have to find someone who actually has a nice Louis Quatorze love seat (or anything close), then convince him to part with it for a few weeks. Ted also used a lot of gold spray paint to dress old set pieces up.

Just before opening night Maria, the leading lady, got laryngitis.

Over coffee at Mountain Market, everyone talked about what would happen if she couldn't go on. No one else in town could possibly sing the part. Since she's the Presbyterian minister's wife, we hoped she had an in with God, but we knew she'd been to the clinic. And someone said they'd even seen her going into the new Chilkat Valley Acupuncture and Oriental Medicine office, above the Alaskan Liquor Store on Main Street.

Did it work? Of course it did. As the curtain parted, we heard Maria loud and clear. *The hills are alive . . .*

The stage was full of our friends and neighbors wearing nun costumes. There was Mrs. Maple, my son's teacher; Annie, the volunteer undertaker; Marie, who has a whole yard full of giant malamutes she sells to Japanese people for a lot of money; and Sylvia and Teresa, who teach out at the Klukwan School. Father Jim got a round of applause when he appeared in his own red vestments during the wedding scene. Having real people play themselves is an old Haines tradition. In *Our Town,* the police chief played the police chief. That play also gave me my own opportunity to play a role awfully close to myself: the Stage Manager. Instead of a suit, I wore a long skirt to tell the story of life and death in Grover's Corners. My family also played a family in *The Best Christmas Pageant Ever.* In that show the real fire department put out the pretend fire.

After helping with sets, props, and programs, I watched *The Sound of Music* knowing all the cast members and rooting for them as you would for a home team. Everyone in the audience did the same thing. We put up with an off-key French horn player, because he's old and we all knew he was doing the best he could. We smiled at the youngest children, who looked like little angels and delivered their lines so you could hear them in the back row. The ballroom scene got the biggest applause because everyone was wearing evening gowns and rented tuxedos from Juneau. They were so finely dressed up we hardly recognized them. When it was over, we presented flowers and locally made jewelry to the guest director, an aging grand dame from South Africa who was a friend of the Greggs'. She told us that Haines was "weird and wonderful, a place out of time." Which we took as a compliment.

I'm still humming "My Favorite Things," and so are my children. Chip's been playing the John Coltrane version on the stereo. No one remembers any of the music from *Cats*. This summer when we hike up Mount Riley, I'm sure at least one of us will break into "the hills are alive with the sound of music." It's our song now; everyone knows all the words. That's why local shows mean more than big Broadway productions, and local customs, shared with friends and family, take the place of other ones from other places. Happiness can be as simple as a familiar tune and someone to sing it with.

AT TED'S MEMORIAL service in the theater the singing kindergarten teacher belted out "Danny Boy" and "Unforgettable." Debra Schnabel played the piano. At the reception afterward on the parade grounds, the sun shone as warm and brightly as it had that first spring day when I'd met Ted. The wind blew paper plates and napkins off the tables. We ate salmon, salads, and cake that the Gregg family had prepared—a meal for a hundred or so. Two of Ted and Mimi's grandsons toasted Ted, and Mimi, too, who smiled and took a theatrical bow. Then we raised our glasses, drank to Ted's spirit, and sang "Auld Lang Syne" together. Mimi had made sure we all had a copy of the words.

"PARTIES," TED GREGG often said, "make the world go round." And he would have known. Ted was one of the few men in this town who actually had dinner parties, as opposed to feeds—as in a game feed or fish feed. Other men ate; Ted dined. As far as I know, he is the only man in Haines who ever wore a silk smoking jacket and cravat. He had many costumes for daily activities, often punctuated by the right hat. At the beach, he wore flowered trunks and a wide Panama hat. When it was stormy, he put on a yellow sou'wester. He had a plaid tam-o'-shanter and a black beret. Sometimes he even wore a dress tartan kilt. Ted really did make his world a stage.

Ted made what he helped create in Haines the standard, instead of comparing it to what he'd left behind when he came here from Connecticut after the war. Ted taught me that while it's good to hold on to some traditions, it's just as important to make new ones — ones that both reflect and spotlight this place and our lives in it. I still listen to Handel's *Messiah* in December and think about New England. But the Snow Dragon means Christmas to me now. And it isn't until I hear Alvin and the Chipmunks' version of "Frosty the Snowman" from inside the dragon costume that I know Christmastime has arrived.

In spring, when the new sun makes everything look good as it falls over Pyramid Island, the river, the sea, and the green mountainsides, I often think about Ted. I watch the crows flying back to their tree on the island and the shadow from a cloud moving across a far slope. A bike tour heads down the road. There's a cruise ship at the dock on the other side of town. In the distance, I can hear planes full of tourists taking off at the airport to see Glacier Bay or Glacier Point. Skiffs are trolling for king salmon out at Letnikof Cove. In twenty years, we've never had another April quite as warm and sunny as that very first one when I met Ted on his front lawn. I remember how he compared Haines to Madeira. I now know that Haines weather is really nothing like that on the balmy island off Portugal. But in a way, he was telling the truth. Lots of people have willed Haines to be a paradise, and because we do, it is. Ted wanted Haines to be like Madeira, and he made it so. And when I was in his company, playing the part of a young mother or an old friend, it was.

DULY NOTED

Pet owners can go through a lengthy grieving period when a beloved animal friend dies. Haines hospice volunteer Beth MacCready is finding that out firsthand after the death of old age of Bonsai, her constant companion for thirteen years. "I was holding him in my arms when he died," she said, but "there's still this sense of disbelief. It's like someone came in and moved all the furniture around." Bonsai lived through two German shepherd attacks and made the news in 1993 when, using standard human CPR techniques, Dave Nanney revived the seemingly dead West Highland terrier, who was choking.

Mother Nature had help recently bringing spring to Haines. Tired of waiting for a thaw and anxious to open for the season, Troy Fotta and Yngve Ollson cleared all the snow out of the woods at the Port Chilkoot Camper Park. It took them two days and many dump-truck loads.

Parents Les and Jan Katzeek and Terry Heinz stayed behind to clean up after a fourth-grade picnic at Battery Point in the rain this week and were given an unexpected treat for their trouble. They were lucky enough to spy a pod of about ten killer whales cruising toward Portage Cove.

Fishing and good weather don't often coincide, but they did recently. Charter boat captain Craig Loomis showed off a tan that looks more Baja than Berner's Bay while he was in town this week. The lifelong Haines resident said he's never seen anything like the eighty-degree weather we've been having. "But hey, I'm loving it," said Craig, who recently received a $750 tip from a happy client. "Can you believe it?" he asked.

I Am Not Resigned

THE SUMMER WE WERE building our cabin, there were a lot of bears around. Although my dog, Carl, was with me, I carried bear-repellent pepper spray in my pocket all the time. The three carpenters working with me were even more cautious; they had rifles. We never did run into any bears. I did suffer from one minor bear-spray attack, though. On a wet afternoon, I wiped my nose with the back of a glove, and in seconds it felt like I'd been punched in the face. My eyes watered, my lips went numb, and the tender rims of my nostrils stung something fierce. The builders noticed and quit working.

"Pepper spray," I squeaked. "Must have leaked in my jacket." The biggest guy acknowledged that the stuff could really sting. Then he launched into a long story about bartending in Hawaii when he was married to his first wife, who left him to join the marines— or maybe it was for an ex-marine—and he had to use bear spray to subdue drunken Samoans when they got out of hand at the bar.

"They'd run down to the beach and stick their head under water to get rid of it. Funniest thing I ever saw," he said. I grabbed his water bottle and poured it on my face. Then I sucked up some water and blew it out my nose. Three times. Carl wagged his tail. He's not much of a protector. He'd rather be sleeping on the sofa.

I used to try to keep my dog off of the furniture, stacking lamps and books on the couch before going to bed. In the morning, I'd catch him wedged into an armchair. When he's in Christian's room, he'll take the bottom bunk and wriggle as close to the wall as he can get, then stretch out, like a person. He weighs 110 pounds and thinks I can't see him. My favorite picture of Carl was taken outside; he's in a lawn chair. And Carl will always get in the truck because the seat is as soft as a couch—and it takes him places. Try getting him to ride in the back, like any self-respecting Alaskan dog, and you end up driving away with Carl chasing behind until you stop, open the door, and let him in.

Water dogs outnumber huskies at least three to one around here. Carl is a black Labrador retriever. He's never been duck hunting, but throw a rock into a pond or the ocean and he'll go after it like a pearl diver. He looks like a seal. The last thing you see before he completely disappears is the tip of his tail. He always surfaces, breathless, with a rock. Not necessarily the one you threw, but still, it was pulled off the mucky bottom with his teeth. Carl does have one hobby he shares with the furry huskies most people associate with the north: He's a runner. Not a take-off-in-the-woods-and-don't-come-back-for-three-days Bad Dog kind of runner. Carl would never run alone, or even with another dog. Carl runs with me, almost every day.

Ten years ago, I was sitting in a doctor's office in Juneau, looking at the framed documents on the wall while he lectured me about getting more exercise. I was tired, eight months pregnant with my fourth child in nine years, and not in a very good mood. I skipped over all of the medical school diplomas and settled on a Portland marathon finisher's certificate. It said 3:43. I memorized it, vowing silently to start training for a marathon as soon as I had the baby, go to Portland to run it, and do it faster than my doctor had.

My dad was a marathon runner, and Chip is, too. Which may be why I didn't think it could be all that hard. When I told Chip about my plan he wrote me up a training schedule, advised me on running shoes and gear, and, most important, came home every day at lunch to stay with the kids while Carl and I went running. Next to reclining on the couch and diving for rocks, running is Carl's favorite hobby. I asked him to run with me when a former police chief warned me that a woman running alone on remote roads might not be safe, even in Haines. The chief said there was a man living in his car, out by the derelict sawmill, who didn't have proper ID to get through the Canadian border. He also didn't have enough money to pay for a ferry ticket south. But he did have a long police record, much of it for sexual assault. "You didn't hear it from me," the chief said. "He's rehabilitated in the eyes of the law, so I can't do anything about it. Wouldn't be legal. But I thought you should know." I ran the Portland Marathon with Chip a year after J.J. was born and beat my doctor's time by twenty minutes. When I called to tell him, he was thrilled. We're all friends now, and he cheerfully takes full credit for my postpartum activity.

Today Carl and I are taking advantage of the extra hours of spring daylight to stretch our run out past the sawmill to Lutak. I'm training for another marathon and need the twenty-plus miles right now. Lutak is a neighborhood of houses clustered on the northern shore of Lutak Inlet, next to the Chilkoot River and Chilkoot Lake, ten miles from Main Street in Haines. There's no city power or telephone. Generators and solar panels run households that range from cabins with outhouses to modern waterfront homes. A gravel road separates the main settlement from a wide, sandy beach and expansive tidal flats. Fish running up the river attract shorebirds, sea lions, whales, and more of the ever-present seals. Everyone loves to watch the seals.

Carl and I usually go all the way out to the lake, but this time we stop at the bridge, where a small crowd has gathered. One woman points out three dead seals on the beach. She says she saw the killers: three Native men and one white man in a green pickup truck. After they shot the seals, they paddled out in a canoe to retrieve them. When they couldn't find them, she says, they put the boat in the truck and drove away. She was so mad she called the paper.

Tom headlined the story SEALS SHOT, ABANDONED AT LUTAK. He used the woman's photograph of a dead seal, belly up, on the flats at low tide. In the background is another dead seal, and the caption explains that a third carcass was just out of sight. "I think it's gross. Just to shoot them and leave them there," Tom quoted her as saying. He also reminded readers that it's not illegal to shoot seals. Alaskan Natives are allowed to hunt them as long as the meat isn't wasted. Lutak residents argued, with pictures to prove it, that the seals had been left to rot.

The next week the paper printed a letter to the editor from one of the seal hunters. He had just moved to Haines but was originally from Gambell, on St. Lawrence Island in the Bering Sea. He didn't argue with the sequence of events. What puzzled him was our reaction. He wrote that in Gambell when a seal is shot and not recovered, a person who finds it before sunset is obligated to return it to the hunter. If the seal isn't found until the next day, tradition dictates that the finder is "lucky enough to keep it." He blamed the people living at Lutak for wasting the seal meat. He wanted to know why no one had asked around town about who owned the new green truck. He pointed out that someone could have put a "Listener Personal" on the radio. Since no one tried to find him, he asked, why didn't they at least butcher the seals? The lost seals could have fed his family for several weeks.

As had others, I assumed the seal killing was a senseless act of violence, disturbing the peace of a rural neighborhood. It never occurred to me that someone should eat the seals, any more than I would think to eat a dog. It also turned out to be more complicated than that. Haines is about 15 percent Tlingit, unlike the mostly Native Gambell, which means most of us couldn't have claimed the seal meat even if we had wanted to.

The hunter views seals as healthier than shrink-wrapped beef and their killing as part of a time-honored tradition. He needs wild game to live, both economically and spiritually. Some of the critics of the seal hunter also live a simple subsistence life. They rely on big gardens, goats, and chickens to feed their families. They rightly object to the sensibility of some hunters to shoot anything that moves, often with no respect for people's homes or safety. Several years ago the old dirt road to Lutak was upgraded to two full lanes, chip-coated, and lined. The people who live out there have seen a lot of changes. Tourists now crowd the road, riverbank, and lakefront most of the summer. Residents are increasingly concerned about finding ways in a growing town to preserve the natural beauty without compromising local customs. We all are worried about how to make a living by sharing the beauty and peace while at the same time protecting it. After hearing the hunter's explanation, the residents acknowledged that they might have overreacted.

ON A CLEAR MORNING a few weeks later, as Carl and I walked on the beach by our house, Carl brought me the forelimbs and shoulder girdle of a seal skeleton. It was clean except for the neatly cut flippers hanging from it like big gloves on a scarecrow. I recognized the carefully cleaned seal remains as a sign that there are enough seals living in Haines to hunt; the U.S. Department of Fish and Wildlife wouldn't allow it if seals weren't so plentiful. I also knew that my Native neighbors are hunting them, even this close to town, without bothering anyone. This time, I considered myself lucky to have stumbled onto a well-used dead seal. It's been a long time since I really changed my mind about something, and I'd forgotten how good it feels: like sunshine after a dark winter.

BUT ALL THAT was a long time ago. Now Carl and I are both going gray: his face and my head. I tell him I don't mind, if he doesn't. Chip likes my gray hair, too; he says he'd feel funny if I still looked twenty-five when he was going bald. Aging is not a big worry for Chip and me. We are in our forties, and with any luck we still have miles to go before we sleep. But at almost twelve, Carl doesn't. His full name is Good Dog Carl—the kids named him after the series of children's books about a rottweiler. They loved those picture stories. When Chip came home with a black puppy, although he was a Labrador, they immediately thought it must be "Good Dog Carl," and so he became, and still is.

Carl was easily housebroken. He never chewed anything he wasn't supposed to, never jumped up and knocked anyone over, never ran away, and even as a puppy seemed to have an old soul. From the beginning, he understood what I was saying. Carl used to run in front of me; now he trots faithfully behind me, his tail wagging like a metronome. When I first noticed a lump on his shoulder, I took him to the vet, who visits seasonally from Juneau. She said it didn't look good. It might be cancer. If she cut into it, the disease might spread. At his age, she said, it would be best to let nature take its course.

CARL IS BARKING and running back and forth, in his stiff way. I see him out the window and go down to the beach to find out what's the matter. A harbor seal is stuck in the sand a long way from the water. She must have fallen asleep in the sun and been left high and dry when the twenty-foot tide went out. She is built like an overinflated torpedo-shaped balloon. Her belly rests on the ground, but her flipper sticks out sideways above it. The only way she can push across the sand is to roll over almost ninety degrees so one flipper can grip the sand, then roll back and use the other flipper the same way. She's going nowhere fast.

I shut Carl inside and call the Fish and Game officer, who sensibly says to wait until the tide comes up, when she'll swim away. But I'm worried. My dog isn't the only one who frequents this beach. A big malamute that lives nearby might stumble upon the seal and instinctively kill her.

It's Thursday, and the paper is at the printer in Juneau, so Steve, who's at home next door, says he'll help me. He walks over with a blanket to drag the frightened animal back into the water. We stand over the seal and she blinks her big wet eyes at us. "She's crying," I tell Steve.

"No, she's not," he says, and tells me that seals need to keep their eyes wet to see. Then he drops the blanket on top of her, and together we roll her into it. She suddenly whips back and forth, shaking the blanket loose and baring salmon-shredding teeth very close to my hands. At least she doesn't seem sick, just frightened. Still, we have to help her get back to the safety of sea, whether she likes it or not. Steve steps behind her and she moves forward, rolling herself, slowly, across the sand with her flippers. Fright and anger have motivated her to make the awkward push. I walk to the other side, and she zigs, and then zags, to avoid us. Like two sheepdogs, we herd her slowly toward the sea, until she slips into the waves. Before leaving, she pops up her sleek head for one last long look. I suppose I could say she was thanking us, but that wouldn't be true. Looking into those deep brown eyes, I didn't feel a soulful connection—certainly not like the one I have when I look into Carl's eyes. There was no mutual acknowledgment of love or even respect from the seal. I wanted to feel it, but she wouldn't let me. "Leave me alone," her wild eyes said. "Go away."

It *was*, though, a look I'd seen before. Actually, J.J. saw the moose first—and screamed. Her sister froze, terrified. Stoli had seen only one other moose this close, a few months before, on our way home from the cabin. Then, Chip and I were closing up the house and let the kids go on down the trail ahead of us. Sarah told us later that the huge bull moose lowered his antlers and charged them. Sarah's a high school all-American swimmer. Her nickname is Xena. She broke a tree branch and wielded it like a sword, yelling for Eliza and the little kids to get up a tree. The moose kept coming, shaking the ground with each step. He was so close Eliza said she could smell his breath when Sarah yelled and threw her stick at him. The moose veered hard into the forest and disappeared.

Now another big moose was standing on the edge of our beach. At first, she looked at us like a curious horse, but J.J.'s scream and Carl's barking frightened her, and she pivoted with a grunt and galloped through the wild roses toward the house. The little girls panicked and raced that way, too. Chip and I ran behind, yelling for them to stop. The last thing we wanted was for the moose to get mad and hurt them. She didn't. Instead, barely snapping a branch, she vanished into the brush.

Moose don't always take off so fast. Last spring, a cow moose had her calf across the road from our house. They wandered into the backyard of a vacation home where a little girl was on a swing. When she screamed and her dog barked, the confused calf ran toward the child instead of away from her. The mother moose charged at the swing set to protect her young. The little girl's mother also ran from the garden into the tangle, to rescue her child. Screams, barks, and the bellowing moose brought the next-door neighbor outside onto his porch, but before he could get close enough to help, the frightened moose chased her calf from the yard and the terrified mother scooped up her toddler and ran to the shelter of a playhouse.

The moose broke the little girl's arm and left her mother badly bruised. They were flown to the hospital in Juneau. After the child's arm was set and the mother's injuries declared miraculously superficial, they decided to spend two weeks convalescing back home in the Lower Forty-eight, far away from any wild animals. A few days later the cow and her calf showed up outside Betty Holgate's kitchen window. She called to let me know that they seemed un- harmed and appeared content, nibbling the fresh green shoots by her stream. "I told her she had a lovely baby, and she seemed to like the compliment," Betty said. The cow even tipped her ears toward Betty as she spoke.

I told Betty we'd been watching a bear and her cubs across the river with a spotting scope. She'd seen them, too. And lately I've been seeing more bears from the car and while out riding my bike. There are lots of them, fairly close to town. Bear viewing has been good and bear hunting even better. Or worse, depending on your point of view. Because spring was late this year, a lot of bears were killed in a short time. Over forty, including twelve big grizzly, or brown, bears. Smaller black bears are baited with doughnut grease from the bakery. A popular place to kill brown bears is a man-made salmon-spawning channel hunters can drive right up to. A little girl's first brown-bear hunt was even featured in the *Eagle Eye Journal*. The child was photographed with her dead bruin. Then there's the story of the hunt gone bad.

It began when three hunters, a father, a son, and a friend, spot- ted a large brown bear on the banks of the Chilkat River, about fourteen miles north of our house. One of them shot it, wounding it in the shoulder. They fired again, hoping to kill it, but missed, and the injured bear swam across the river. The hunters got in a ca- noe, crossed the river, and then followed the bloody trail for nearly three miles on foot through thick brush. Bears are dangerous ani- mals. As with moose, you never want to get between a mother and her youngster, and you really don't want to meet a wounded bear. The hunters had both a safety and a moral obligation to finish the job. It would have been cruel to let the animal suffer a slow death.

They couldn't see the bear, but they noticed that it was bleeding less and resting more. They figured it must be dying. So they were completely surprised when the angry bear came charging back down the trail at them. It was thirty feet away and running fast when a bullet caught it in the chin. The stunned bear didn't slow down. Another hunter fired, this time hitting the bear in the paw, but the recoil from the rifle knocked him off balance, and he fell into the brush. That hunter's father shot the bear in the back as it grabbed his son's leg with its teeth. The father shot the bear again, but the bear wouldn't die and it wouldn't run away. The third hunter shot the bear in the side, and finally in the head. The bear never quit. His dead jaws had to be pried off the son's leg. The men walked back to the boat. The wounded hunter was flown to Juneau, where he spent the night in the hospital, got about fifty stitches, but otherwise was fine. Actually, he's something of hero, what with surviving a bear attack.

Bear biologists don't know how many bears there are in Haines, because they're hard to count. But one bear expert with the Alaska Department of Fish and Game assured me that there were enough for every hunter to kill two every year. He said the greatest threat to bears — and all wild animals, for that matter — is not managed hunts but the destruction of habitat. He asked me if the bears that used to eat dandelions every spring on the bank where my house is come around as often. They don't. I told him about the cow moose and her calf. He said she'd keep having babies in the neighborhood because it's her territory, regardless of how many new homes are built, but it *is* causing her stress. Just by living here, he said, my family is doing more harm to wildlife than hunters are. I may be well meaning, but the animals don't know that.

For my birthday last year some of my also well-meaning friends gave me a beautiful mother duck with eight babies to put in Rutzebeck Lake, which is really a pond next to our cabin. We had planned a big cookout, so of course it rained for the first time all month. Everyone said it was unfortunate, but after we all crowded into the cabin they agreed it wasn't so bad after all. When the ducks arrived in a dog kennel, I knew the weather was a good omen. It was a perfect day for ducks. We opened the kennel door and the mother duck, which I immediately named Ingaborg because she's a Blue Swedish, led her ducklings into the water. There is nothing quite like the sight of a proud mother duck with her ducklings in tow. When the party was over, everyone walked down the trail in rubber boots and rain gear, waving good-bye to the ducks. We spent the night listening to the rain on the metal roof. In the morning, Chip left early for work. After the children and I woke up and ate, we checked on the ducks. Carl led us to the landing where the kennel had been. The ground was full of muddy bear prints. The dog kennel the ducks came in was smashed and sinking, twenty feet out in the pond. There were only six baby ducks left.

That evening a bull moose stepped into the lower end of the pond, and Ingaborg took off full speed toward it with her family paddling behind like little hydrofoils. We thought they were goners, but in the end it was the moose that retreated, not my ducks. But by the middle of the week, we were down to four ducklings and a wounded mother. Ingaborg survived the bear attack and the moose charge only to be eaten by an eagle. The last time we saw her alive she was listing to port and sculling toward the weeds. That afternoon Christian found a pile of down and Ingaborg's carcass picked clean. At the sight of us raking up the remains of his mother, a fifth duckling toppled over in shock, dead. Another duckling was bobbing her head and making odd little circles on the pond, so the girls and I hopped into the canoe and scooped her up with a snow shovel. The two ducklings still on the pond wouldn't let us rescue them. We carried the sick baby duck into the cabin, sat her by the fire, and spoon-fed her Cheerios and milk while Carl stood guard.

By the end of the summer, we had one feisty brown duck left. Chip named him Braveheart. Like his namesake, he lost the battle but won the war. Domestic ducks can live almost anywhere in the world, while eagles, moose, and bears can't. I suppose I could have protected my ducks with a barn, chicken wire, and a shotgun. I was tempted to, especially when everyone was crying at the relentless slaughter. But then Alaska would become just like everywhere else. It may be our backyard, but wild creatures still have the right of way.

THE VET IS IN town for her fall appointments. While she examines Carl, I tell her about the sad fate of my ducks, and she laughs. When I tell her about the seal rescue, she says I'm lucky it didn't bite me. She says it's sometimes best to let Mother Nature take her course; other times, she needs some help. We talk about bears, and she says she agrees with Jay Hammond, our former governor and a big-game hunting guide. He said he quit shooting bears when he realized that the prey was nobler than the hunter. I tell her that although Carl is getting slower, he's still good company. He does sleep so hard sometimes that I have to put my hand on his side to be sure he's breathing. Other times he's almost perky —especially around food. She feeds him about six dog biscuits during the exam. We talk about Carl's cancer, and she draws some blood and says she'll call me when she gets the results.

Two days later she tells me Carl will live a month, maybe two, "tops." She says that a natural death from this type of cancer can be gruesome—he'll suddenly hemorrhage and bleed to death. There will be buckets of blood. "It's not pretty," she says. "You wouldn't want to be there, and you definitely don't want your kids to see it." I ask if she'll come to the house on her way out to the ferry. Chip and I tell the family that Carl has to be put to sleep and why. He's old and has had a good life, a better one than many people. I am calm and thoughtful. Chip is wise and kind. Good Dog Carl will live up to his name to the end, and give us all a good lesson about a good life and a good death. We spend the next few days being extra nice to him. He sleeps on Christian's bed, rides in the front seat, and watches a movie from the couch while we sit on the floor. On his last morning, I cook Carl a steak and we feed him pieces of it before taking him for one last slow walk on the beach.

The vet arrives at ten. We've decided ahead of time to do it on the back porch. The kids opt to stay in the house. There are no tears. This is going really well. Better even than I had hoped. The vet gives Carl a sedative before the big shot, so he won't feel it. Carl rests easily on an old quilt with his head in my lap. While we wait for him to fall asleep, we try to be normal. The vet and Chip learn that they share common friends. They may have even lived in the same house in Wyoming at different times when they were in college. When Carl closes his eyes, the vet injects an overdose of phenobarbital right into his heart.

I am still stroking his warm ear when the vet says, "He's gone." For a second, I can't breathe. I have spent more hours over the last ten years with Carl than with my family. He never went to work or school or slept over at a friend's house. Christian was in diapers when we got Carl; he's in junior high now. Eliza was in grade school; now she's in college. It seems as though Carl has been with me my whole life. That big black dog is in every family scene I can recall. I've stepped around him a thousand times while cooking, run hundreds of miles at his side, and kept my feet warm for eleven winters on his belly as he slept under my desk. I change my mind. I want him back. This is not a good lesson. It is a really, really bad lesson. I feel like a moose kicked me in the chest.

I have written so many obituaries and been to so many funerals that I thought I understood. I thought there was some order in the universe that made each death happen for a reason. I know that from dust we come and to dust we will return and there's not a damn thing we can do about it. I honestly do. And I knew Carl was dying—I planned his death, right down to where we would bury him. Despite all of that, losing this good old dog has undone me. "I know," I think, "but I am not resigned." I can't get the lines from Edna St. Vincent Millay's "Dirge Without Music" out of my head. "I am not resigned to the shutting away of loving hearts in the hard ground. / So it is, and so it will be, for so it has been time out of mind." Yes, I do know. "But I do not approve. And I am not resigned."

It's as if my wise old dog knew I needed this lesson, knew in his big bones that I didn't really get it. It has taken this dog's death to connect me to all the people whose obituaries I've written, and to their grieving friends and families. I have wished that, after every single obituary, I'd known the person better, that I'd asked them one more question while they were living, said thank you one more time, smiled another hello in the grocery store, or invited them over for dinner. Now, one awful burial service comes right back at me. A young man had died in a car wreck. At the cemetery, his sister threw herself on the casket before they lowered it into the ground and yelled, "No" long and loud. At the time, I thought someone should have stopped her, gently pulled her back. She was making a scene. Didn't she know this is how it is with life? We die. Now suddenly I understand. Sure she knew, but she did not approve. Before I can think any further about that, I see my children following me through the windows and look away. I know they are all crying, too, and I don't want to make it worse. I don't want to talk to them right now. I'm afraid of what I might say.

Chip pays the vet and thanks her. "We should be able to do this for people," she says. "It's so much better than a painful, messy death." Maybe, I think, but maybe not. The chant inside my head gets louder. "I know. But I do not approve. And I am not resigned."

When she leaves, we wrap Carl up in the quilt and carry him to the grave that Chip dug yesterday. He starts to fill it in, then stops. He's crying now. Seeing us both so helpless, Christian runs outside and takes the shovel. In a minute, his sisters arrive with more shovels from the shed. They are still in their pajamas. We don't say a word as we pile sand and gravel over Carl.

I don't think my family realizes that my reaction to events can change their perception of them. I don't think they know how much power I have to make a moment good or bad. But I do. So instead of falling on my knees and wailing for Good Dog Carl and all the souls departed from this little town, I turn to the one thing that is both great and good. I stand by the grave and clearly read a few words from the Book of Common Prayer, thanking God for giving us Good Dog Carl, a companion and friend. When I finish, I look up at my family, all crumpled with grief, all trying so hard to take care of one another, and I feel a rush of love. Chip holds out his hand and I take it and we all walk back in the house. Christian speaks first. He asks if I'll cook some bacon for breakfast. Then J.J. says she wants waffles with strawberries.

I say yes to both.

I am still not resigned, and I still do not approve. But I do know that this is what it means to be human, to be a mother and a wife and an obituary writer in Haines, Alaska. This is my life, and I am grateful.